Women and the Egyptian Revolution

Since the fall of the former Egyptian president Ḥusnī Mubarak, female activists have faced the problem of how to transform the spirit of the uprising into long-lasting reform of the political and social landscape. In *Women and the Egyptian Revolution*, Nermin Allam tells the story of the 2011 uprising from the perspective of the women who participated, based on extensive interviews with female protestors and activists. The book offers an oral history of women's engagement in this important historical juncture; it situates women's experience within the socioeconomic flows, political trajectories, and historical contours of Egypt. Allam develops a critical vocabulary that captures women's activism and agency by looking both backwards to Egypt's gender history and forwards to the outcomes and future possibilities for women's rights. An important contribution to the under-researched topic of women's engagement in political struggles in the Middle East and North Africa, this book will have a wide-ranging impact on its field and beyond.

NERMIN ALLAM is Assistant Professor of Political Science at Rutgers University, New Jersey, and was formerly the Social Sciences and Humanities Research Council of Canada Postdoctoral Fellow at the Department of Politics at Princeton University. She holds a D.Phil. in Comparative Politics and International Relations from the University of Alberta, Canada.

Women and the Egyptian Revolution

Engagement and Activism during the 2011 Arab Uprisings

NERMIN ALLAM

Rutgers University, New Jersey

CAMBRIDGE
UNIVERSITY PRESS

CAMBRIDGE
UNIVERSITY PRESS

University Printing House, Cambridge CB2 8BS, United Kingdom

One Liberty Plaza, 20th Floor, New York, NY 10006, USA

477 Williamstown Road, Port Melbourne, VIC 3207, Australia

4843/24, 2nd Floor, Ansari Road, Daryaganj, Delhi – 110002, India

79 Anson Road, #06-04/06, Singapore 079906

Cambridge University Press is part of the University of Cambridge.

It furthers the University's mission by disseminating knowledge in the pursuit of education, learning, and research at the highest international levels of excellence.

www.cambridge.org
Information on this title: www.cambridge.org/9781108434430
DOI: 10.1017/9781108378468

First published 2018

Printed in the United Kingdom by Clays, St Ives plc

A catalogue record for this publication is available from the British Library.

ISBN 978-1-108-42190-4 Hardback
ISBN 978-1-108-43443-0 Paperback

Mom, you are my rock.

Contents

Acknowledgments

These acknowledgments cannot do justice to the deep gratitude I have for my family, mentors, and friends without whom this journey would have been impossible. I thank Dr. Yasmeen Abu-Laban for many years of valuable mentorship, sincere advice, and enlightened conversation. There are simply no words to express my gratitude for her enduring support. She has given me a model to strive for. This book could not have been possible without her.

I am also greatly indebted to Dr. Amaney Jamal, whose expertise and unequivocal support were invaluable to this academic exercise. I am also deeply grateful for my time as a Social Sciences and Humanities Research Council of Canada Postdoctoral Fellow at Princeton University. The fellowship gave me access to a wonderful community of scholars and intellectuals. My thanks go to Dr. Amaney Jamal, Dr. Mark R. Beissinger, and Dr. Nolan McCarty. Elizabeth Nugent, Killian Clarke, Dan Tavana, and Peace Medie are amazing colleagues.

The Department of Political Science at the University of Alberta, my home during postgraduate studies, will always have a special place in my heart. My people there, the faculty, staff, and colleagues, were and continue to be lifelong friends and mentors. Many thanks to Dr. Janine Brodie, Dr. Andy Knight, Dr. Lois Harder, Dr. Judith Garber, Dr. Robert Aitken, Dr. Mojtaba Mahdavi, Dr. Malinda Smith, Dr. Cressida Heyes, Dr. Roger Epp, and Dr. Ian Urquhart. I am beyond grateful to Siavash Saffari for sharing his knowledge and experience, and to Sevan Beukian, Nathan Andrews, Ghada Asaad, Nisha Nath, Mariam Georgis, Hajar Amidian, Nicole Lugosi, and Anya Kuteleva for their precious friendship.

Dr. Bessma Momani offered many thoughtful comments and insightful suggestions and the book has benefited tremendously from her feedback, as it has from the feedback of the two reviewers for Cambridge University Press. Many thanks to Dr. Jacqueline French for her meticulous editing of the text. After numerous reads and several edits, the errors that linger are my own. Thanks are also due to Dr. Lisa Wedeen, Dr. Nathan Brown, Dr. Wendy Pearlman, Dr. Manal Jamal, Dr. Jill Schwedler, and Dr. Marc Lynch, who were generous enough to read sections of this book and related works. I must also thank Dr. Sarah Parkinson who through her lively conversation, sincere advice, and precious friendship continues to inspire me.

I have been fortunate to receive generous financial support from the University of Alberta, Social Sciences and Humanities Research Council of Canada (SSHRC), and the American Political Science Association (APSA) that ensured I was able to fully concentrate on my research. I am also thankful to the International Development Research Council (IDRC) for offering me a Doctoral Research Grant that supported my fieldwork in Egypt.

Thanks to my participants and interviewees for sharing their time and heartfelt stories. They gave life to the theories behind this project. Without their generosity and support, this research would never have come to fruition. Their passion is contagious and the work they are doing has indeed inspired me.

I am also deeply grateful for my time as a Research Fellow at the American University in Cairo (AUC). The vibrant intellectual community at the AUC provided invaluable feedback and insight. I am grateful to Dr. Martina Rieker, Dr. Mona Amer, Dr. Ghada Barsoum, and Dr. Nadine Sika for the enlightened conversations. It has been a privilege knowing my professor, Dr. Bahgat Korany, who has shared his knowledge, wisdom, and experience. I cannot overstate the extent to which he has shaped the ways in which I see the politics of Egypt and how I write about it.

Thanks go to my Aunt Paula and Uncle Ahmed: they were truly my family and kept me motivated through all the ups and downs. Also to my childhood friends, Dina Aboughazala and Mai Abdel Rahman, whose love, support, and understanding – when I failed to call, write, or visit – have carried me through. Although we span three continents, their support throughout my study and research has been unequivocal.

Laila, my beautiful niece – *aka* Cairo-based daughter – has always been on my mind and in my heart, despite the missed birthdays, school concerts, and not always being there for her. Thanks go to my biggest cheer-leader, my sister, Nihal Allam, for telling me I was bright enough to do well on this path and for carrying on doing that until

I finally started to believe it. I am grateful to Ahmed, a friend and soulmate, who for the past five years has given me unwavering support and shown a fascinated interest in my research. His humor, support, and encouragement have helped me beyond words.

My eternal thanks go to my mother for her guidance and unconditional support, and for the confidence she instilled in me. She has always listened and been there for me. She is my muse and I will be forever indebted. My beloved father's pride in my accomplishments and work has been a source of great joy and motivation for me. I thank him for his unconditional care and support.

My precious daughters, Sanna and Janna, are now ten and nine, but someday they will be old enough to start – and hopefully then want – to read my book. I hope they will take it down from some high shelf, dust it off, and then tell me what they think of it. For now and then, I want them to remember that this book would not have been possible without them: this was *our* journey. At times, when things got tough, looking at them reminded me that "this too shall pass," and it indeed did. I thank them for grounding me in many ways.

And, all praise is due to Allah, the Merciful.

A Note on Transliteration and Translation

The essence of this book is relaying the experiences of women in their own words and emphasizing their voices in telling their stories. In keeping with the spirit of the book, the research incorporated extensive interviews and consulted wide scholarship, many of which are published in Arabic. In transliterating Arabic texts, I strived for accuracy and simplicity. The transliteration method used in this book is based primarily on the system adopted by the *International Journal of Middle East Studies*. However, I often dropped diacritical marks that indicate long vowels and emphatic consonants to avoid burdening the reader. For names and places I used local common transliterations.

Most of the interviews were conducted in Arabic and translated into English. I strived to translate the text in a way that maintains the precise meaning while also capturing the lingual emphasis and cadence of the original text. This was not always an easy exercise. I wondered how to capture the irony, conveyed through diction, in a seemingly funny joke. I quickly discovered that much of the story would be lost when attempting to neatly translate a messy, fragmented text. The translation provided thus captures some of these subtleties and ambiguities. I, however, acknowledge that language is the property of its culture and that some elements, words, and ideas simply cannot be replicated when translated into another language.

Introduction: A Dramaturgy of Women, Egypt, and the 2011 Egyptian Uprising

Women will secure their rights only through actively defending and demanding democracy, human rights, and good governance. Through promoting and advocating these fundamental demands for the whole society, women will find a space for their specific rights as well. It is true that our societies are largely patriarchal, but following the Arab Spring these patriarchal systems are en route to decline as the society has begun to understand and appreciate the role of women in the public space, and as women have begun to assert their voices and lead the process of regime change and democratic transition. (Tawakkol Karman)[1]

Powerfully eloquent, Tawakkol Karman described in great pride and with an almost baroque sensuality the sense of empowerment, equality, and agency that characterized women's engagement in the episodes of protests that swept the Middle East and North Africa in 2010–2011. These episodes of contentions have led to the toppling of despotic regimes of long standing in Tunisia, Egypt, Yemen, and Libya. In Yemen, as well as across the Middle East and North African (MENA) region, Karman became known as the "mother of the revolution" (Khamis 2011). In a nod to her influential and inspirational role in the political upheavals across the region, she was awarded the Nobel Peace Prize in 2011.

Beyond national and international commemoration, Karman also became a symbol for thousands of women who participated in the mass protests in defense of dignity, freedom, liberty, and democracy in a number of Arab countries. In Egypt, women's engagement in this new moment of unity, solidarity, and cohesion mirrored the egalitarian movements that came out in support of liberating their nations. Little was said about women's specific rights in the early days of the

---

[1] Author's interview, Tawakkol Karman – the Yemeni activist and 2011 Nobel laureate, Canada: Edmonton, November, 2012. Original in Arabic, my translation.

uprising. It was believed that women would enjoy their full rights only when every citizen, regardless of gender, was guaranteed these rights.

In the years separating the statement that heads this chapter from the current political reality, a lot happened that fundamentally challenged this aura of equality, the aura that had been the defining ideational infrastructure of these uprisings. To all intents and purposes, the unity and solidarity that prevailed among protestors were similar to the critical anthropologist Victor Turner's "liminal moments" (1969, 1974). They, too, were difficult to sustain and soon came to an end following the fall of Ḥusnī Mubarak's regime in Egypt.

Since the end of Mubarak's presidency, female activists – among other political activists – in the country have faced the hurdle of confronting all contentious politics. That is, how to transform the egalitarian spirit of a brief uprising into a long-lasting reform of the political and social landscape (Amanat 2012; Anderson 2011; Brown 2013; Hampson and Momani 2015; Lynch and Dodge 2015; Masoud 2015). In light of the emerging backlash against the uprising,[2] it is easy to look back on women's engagement in this episode of contention with disappointment. I argue instead that when studying women's engagement in the 2011 Egyptian uprising, we need to take into account the overall picture in this rapidly changing region. This requires analyzing women's engagement with an eye to the political, economic, and social challenges and uncertainties that mark Middle Eastern and North African societies (Charrad and Zarrugh 2014; Johansson-Nogues 2013; Moghadam 2011, 2014; Morsy 2014).

The book focuses specifically and primarily on women's engagement in this liminal phase in the 2011 Egyptian uprising that led to the ousting of President Mubarak. The overarching objective igniting this study is to understand how gender issues featured in women's collective action frame in the 2011 Egyptian uprising and the impact of this framing on their experience and activism. The study thus offers an oral history of women's engagement in this initial episode of contention. By closely analyzing women's engagement in the uprising, women are

---

[2] Political scientists and Middle Eastern experts Marc Lynch and Toby Dodge (2015) eloquently describe the current backlash against the uprisings across the Arab world as the rise of an "Arab Thermidor." Thermidor was the month in which the French politician Maximilien Robespierre was overthrown and beheaded. The term is generally used to indiciate the beginning of the backlash following the revolution.

brought to the center of analysis and their agency is reclaimed. Writing *herstory*, feminist scholars contend, is important as women tend to be neglected and undervalued in history (Agah, Mehr, and Parsi 2007; Åhäll and Linda 2012; Amrouche 1988; Elsadda 1998, 1999, 2001, 2004, 2006). A detailed analysis of women's framing strategies will also result in a "thick description" (Geertz 1973) of women's engagement. It will contribute to restoring women's voices and portraying them as active agents. This, in turn, promises to complicate and expand debates on women's participation in national struggles beyond reductionist accounts that view them as misguided or passive.

Cognizant that across the history of Egypt, as well as in many developing and developed countries, genuine advances in women's rights were achieved only after pressures from organized groups of women (Fraser and Gordon 1994; Joseph 2000; Seidman 1999), I place women at the center of my analysis. Specifically, I examine the significance and limitations of women's collective action frame in the 2011 uprising.

Studies on women's collective action frame examine the strategic interpretations of issues offered by frames that are intended to mobilize women. Neil J. Smelser (1971) argues that while grievances are significant elements in originating collective action, they will not lead to participation until they are perceived. Societies are far from perfect and do not meet all of their members' needs; however, there are differences in the degree to which society's different groups perceive them as problematic and seek to change them.

Smelser's perspective corresponds to David A. Snow and Robert Benford's viewpoint that participants in collective actions are not "structurally guaranteed" but rather cluster around master collective action frames (Benford 1993, 1997; Snow and Benford 1988, 1992; Snow, Soule, and Kriesi 2004; Snow, Worden, and Benford 1986). At the most basic, a frame identifies a problem – that is social or political in nature – the parties responsible for causing it, and the possible solutions they offer (Johnston and Noakes 2005: 2; see also Gamson 1975; Snow and Benford 1988, 1992). Frames of collective action, in this sense, redefine a status quo that was perceived as "unfortunate but perhaps tolerable" to "unjust and immoral" and thus mobilize participants to join in repertoires of contention (Tarrow 1998: 91).

This synthetic model is apt to understand the experiences of women in its entirety. As I shall demonstrate in the book, the political process paradigm contributes to elucidating the opportunities and constraints surrounding female activism in Egypt. Framing analysis explicates how opportunities and constraints were perceived by female participants, and how they influenced the women's framing. Together, the two theories highlight female protestors' experience while being sensitive to the contexts surrounding women's activism in Egypt.

The book's dynamic framework is situated within the interdisciplinary field of contentious politics, specifically, under the rubric of the political process approach. Scholars working within the tradition of political process examine the structural, organizational, and behavioral facets of movements (Crozat, Meyer, and Tarrow 1997; McAdam 1982; Porta and Tarrow 2012; Snow and Benford 2005; Snow and Trom 2002; Snow et al. 1986; Soule 1997; Tilly 1995; Tarrow 1998). They, unlike earlier generations of social movement theorists, consider the mechanisms and processes that link the movements' different elements and actors (Crozat et al. 1997; McAdam 1985; Porta and Tarrow 2012; Snow and Benford 2005; Snow and Trom 2002; Snow et al. 1986; Soule 1997; Tilly 1995; Tarrow 1998). In the last decade, the political process model has gained ground in the field of contentious politics and in the social sciences generally. This move, scholars note, is part of a broader shift in the field of comparative politics toward the systemic study of processes and mechanisms (Della Porta 2014; Della Porta and Mosca 2005; McAdam, Tarrow, and Tilly 2001; Tarrow 2012; Tilly 1995). My book builds upon and contributes to this dynamic opening in the field.

To illuminate women's experience and their collective action frame, the research adopted an emergent approach to theorizing; that is, theorizing about women's engagement took the form of a conversation between theory and women's lived experiences. Data was gathered from personal interviews with the following five sets of actors: female protestors who participated in the 18-day uprising, female activists, leaders of nongovernmental organizations (NGOs), state officials, and public figures who are actively engaged in the area of women's rights in Egypt. Data was also gathered from public transcripts as well as secondary literature published in English and Arabic on the topic. I analyzed data using critical discourse analysis (Richardson 2007; see also Blommaert and Bulcaen 2000). This entailed a close and multilayered reading of particular words of participants (i.e. choice of words or diction) and a focus on not only what is being said, but what is occluded from discussion in the attempt to examine the place of gender in women's collective action frames.

In so doing, the research tackled one of the empirical paradoxes of democratization identified by scholars in relation to gender equalities and regime transitions. It also provided an oral history of women's experience in the uprising; the focus was on not only documenting their accounts but also situating their experience within the contentious and conventional politics of Egypt. The research thus offers an emergent knowledge that is actively formed from the standpoint of female protestors and that is situated within the particular social and historical context of Egypt.

The January 25 Episode of Contention

I view the January 25 uprising as an episode of contention within Egypt's contentious politics. The notion "episodes of contention" is conceived by Sidney Tarrow (1993) to explain the phases of heightened conflict across the social system. These phases, social movement theorists explain, are characterized by: rapid diffusion of collective action frames; innovations in collective action; and cumulative effect regardless of the cycle's immediate outcome (Tarrow 1998: 142–144; see also McAdam, Tarrow, and Tilly 2001; 2007: 10).

In the 2011 episode of contention, protestors were the first to engage in innovative collective actions, salient among which is virtual dissidence, as they sensed an opportunity to advance their position through novel means.[3] Like many other protest cycles, however, the uprising did not ostensibly bring major transformation in the traditional

---

[3] In *Blesses and Curses: Virtual Dissidence as a Contentious Performance* (Allam 2014a), I introduce the term *virtual dissidence* to account for the constraints imposed by the macro structure and the array of innovative responses ignited by activists' determination in the uprising. I conceptualize virtual dissidence as a political performance in the repertoire of contention between authoritative regimes and the latter's contenders. The significance of understanding virtual dissidence as emerging from repertoire is that it frames a meso level explanation of collective action and political change. Repertoires of contention tell a story about how contentious claim-making is situated in prior societal experience and interaction with the regime. At the same time, however, repertoires are closely linked with innovation in political action, when understood in the musical and theatrical sense of the word espoused by Charles Tilly, as resembling that of *commedia dell'arte* or jazz.

power structures of Egyptian society or its social schisms – including those that are gender-based. Nonetheless, the uprising left its mark on the protestors' agency and activism. In line with earlier social movement literature, Tarrow observes that episodes of contention, "even defeated or suppressed," leave "some kind of residue" behind them and their effect, "successful or failed," is cumulative in the long term (1998: 146; see also McAdam et al. 2001; Tilly 2008). This is because actions, Pam Oliver writes, "can affect the likelihood of other actions by creating occasions for actions, by altering material conditions, by changing a group's social organization, by altering beliefs, or by adding knowledge"(1989: 2).

The social movement approach to contention is thus premised on a view of political change as a relational and dynamic process. This process can be often constrained by ideational and structural residuals from the former regime, by the structure of contention, and the elites' response to it (McAdam 1995, 1999; Tarrow 1998; Tilly 1995, 1997). In the words of Antonio Gramsci, they operate within "the trenches and fortification" of existing society (1971, cited in Tarrow 2012: 2). Episodes of contention, however, have "indirect and long-term effects" that emerge when the cycle and "its initial excitement" is over (Tarrow 1998: 164; see also McAdam et al. 2001; Tilly 2008). Conceptualizing the 2011 uprising as an episode of contention, thus, entails viewing it as a process instead of an event. It denotes that the period of the eighteen days leading to the ousting of Ḥusnī Mubarak – which is the locus of this study – is part of a cycle of resistance, not the end point of it. This approach is significant for my research; utilizing it, I offer a dynamic explanation of women's engagement in the uprising. In articulating this explanation, I move beyond the time of the uprising or the "moments of madness" – borrowing Aristide Zolberg's term (1972) – and consider how the landscape of gender during and before contention had an influence on women's experience.

Viewing the uprising as part of a cycle of resistance and not the end point of it encourages a more optimistic approach to studying the recent uprisings and their mixed outcomes.[4] Like Tawakkol Karman,

---

[4] Several writers and revolutionary figures express the same concern. *Hal Akhṭa't Al-Thawra Al-Maṣrya?* [Did the Egyptian Revolution Go Wrong?] by activist writer Alaa Al-Aswany (2012), *Thawrat Miṣr* [Egypt's Revolution] by the Egyptian prominent Marxist Samir Amin (2012), and *Paradox of Arab Refo-lutions* by the social movement and Middle Eastern scholar Asef Bayat

I believe, that the Arab uprisings "are the starting point for change," not the "end point."[5] Political economist and social scientist Bessma Momani takes a similarly optimistic stance in her recent book, *Arab Dawn: Arab Youth and the Demographic Dividend They Will Bring*, holding that change is on its way in the Middle East. Building upon extensive grounded research on the region, Momani emphasizes the transformative power of youth in the Arab region.[6] She highlights the demographic shift in the Arab countries, where today one in five Arabs is between the ages of 15 and 24. This demographic shift is significant, Momani explains, given that young people are key agents for development and democratic change. The shift is particularly significant for the Arab region, given the cosmopolitan character of its young generation, she emphasizes. Momani's approach is important for understanding the limits and challenges facing Arab youth in their quest for democratic change. In contrast to a detached and analytically oriented approach to Middle East studies, Momani's research places the diversity of youth experience and the different institutions that frame their experiences at the center of our analysis. By focusing on participants' perspectives and providing them with opportunities to articulate their thoughts, researchers are able to gain understanding and acquire new insights into the prospect for democratic change in the Middle East and North Africa.

While this optimistic perspective animates my research, I also admit the incisiveness of Astride Zolberg's description of the

(2011c) exemplify this observation. In *Hal Akhṭa't Al-Thawra Al-Maṣrya?* Alaa Al-Aswany refers to the January 25 uprising as the unfinished revolution. Samir Amin also commences his analysis by theorizing "the movement" that took place in January 2011 as something "less than a revolution but more than a protest" (2012: 15). In the same vein, the term "Refo-lutions," Bayat suggests, describes the recent uprisings in the Arab world. Bayat (2011c) describes the Arab Spring as a combination of revolutions and reforms, but not a full revolution. According to him, since the uprisings did not result in a completely new system, they cannot be called revolutions; they should be called "Refo-lutions."

[5] Author's interview with Tawakkol Karman, November 2012.
[6] While I use the term "Arab" youth, I acknowledge that the region and its youth are ethnically diverse in ways that are not captured by this term. Consider, for instance, Assyrians, Armenians, Mandeans, and Berbers, to name a few. The term Arab youth and/or Arab region is, also, mainstream expression and – arguably – the most dominant self-identification term used by inhabitants and observers inside and outside the region.

salient institutional outcomes of cycles – or more often the resulting institutional setbacks. These outcomes are evident in historical and modern episodes of contentions including that of the 2011 uprising. Moments of "madness" or "political enthusiasm," Zolberg writes, "are followed by bourgeois repression or by charismatic authoritarianism, sometimes by horror but always by the restoration of boredom" (1972: 205).

Unlike repression and authoritarianism, boredom, I hold in line with earlier literature, is a less common outcome in social movements (Tarrow 1998; see also McAdam et al. 2001; Tilly 2008;). Scholars within the tradition of resource mobilization, for instance, describe the birth of "cognitive liberation" among the older members of the civil rights and anti-war movements (McAdam 1999; Piven and Cloward 1972, 1979). In fact, Zolberg (1972) concludes his articles by acknowledging the effects of protest cycles in inducing subtle social changes and disturbing the status quo. He notes that movements sometimes "drastically shorten the distance" between the present and the future, they are thus, he adds, "successful miracles" (1972: 206).

This is because, as Tarrow explains in his writing on the outcomes in episodes of contention:

Through skills learned in struggle, the extension of their beliefs to new sectors of activity, and the survival of friendship networks formed in the movement, activism begets future activism, more polarized attitudes toward politics, and greater readiness to join other movements. (1998: 165)

The focus in this book is, however, not on elucidating the outcomes of the 2011 uprising. The discussion of the cycles' mediated and indirect effects gives way to my primary objective: understanding the experience of women in the uprising with a view to reclaiming their agency. My occasional reference to the participants' current activism is not to be understood as an attempt to trivialize the scope and severity of gender inequalities in the post-uprising period. My objective is to encourage the reader to approach women's experience with an eye to locating their agency, not their plight. I, thus, position my interviewees as active subjects, not victims, and, espousing Gayatri Chakravorty Spivak's contention, assign them a position of "enunciation" (1988: 129). This positioning, Spivak holds, offers a detailed picture, rather than a simplified rhetoric of women's activism and political participation.

Situating the Egyptian uprising within contentious politics literature and viewing it as an episode of contention yield several advantages for my study. The literature's broad and relational definition of politics is apt to interrogate women's engagement in the uprising and to accommodate the diversity of their experiences. In line with social movement scholarship, I analyze women's experience with an eye to revealing the limits and potentials of their participation. I follow Tilly's (1978) connotation and thus avoid interpreting "gains" and "losses," "narrowly" or "materially." Furthermore, by situating the study within the contentious politics literature, I have utilized the rich theoretical tools provided by this literature and extend its analytical approach to new cases.[7]

In my research, I examine the absence of gender in women's collective action frame, since in the absence of a detailed analysis the omission of gender from women's frame can be misunderstood as a sign of their passivity, and/or false consciousness. To avoid the risk of "Orientalising Egyptian women all over again," borrowing Saba Mahmood's word of warning (2005: 119), my theoretical framework is a synthesis between collective action frame theory and political opportunities. This "synthetic model" has been commonly utilized in the study of contentious politics and social movements because of its dynamic framework (Tarrow 2012).

The premises of this model are that the members of social movements are not independent from the polity they are challenging and that they operate on the boundaries of constituted politics, culture, and institutions (Tarrow 2012: 1). They are "strangers at the gates," writes Tarrow; they demand changes but also accommodate inherited understandings and ways of doing things (2012: 13). Activists, as such, choose their repertoires and frame their participation in light of their relations to a broader map of routine and contentious polices (Tarrow 2012: 13).

This synthetic model is apt to understand the experiences of women in their entirety. As I shall demonstrate in the upcoming chapters, the political process paradigm contributes to elucidating the opportunities

[7] In fact, the features of the Egyptian uprising challenge the wisdom of the earlier generations of revolutionary studies. Earlier theories define revolutions as mostly European violent state versus people (see Foran 1993; Gustave Le Bon 1897) or class conflicts (see Paige 1975; Skocpol 1979).

and constraints surrounding female activism in Egypt. Framing analysis explicates how opportunities and constraints were perceived by female participants, and how they influenced the women's framing. Together, the two theories highlight female protestors' experience while being sensitive to the contexts surrounding women's activism in Egypt.

Whose Rights?

My understanding of women's rights and agency is informed by insights from postcolonial feminism. The theory of post-colonial feminism considers the influence of race, ethnicity, and class in its gender analysis. Feminists within this tradition take a critical stance toward meta-narratives, specifically, the notion of "the women" as a universal subject of feminism, which they hold is essentialist. The image, according to this important body of scholarship, demarcates the cultural differences between the West and the other and thus serves Orientalist discourses (Abu-Lughod 2001; Ahmed 2012; Jiwani 2005a, 2005b, 2006; Mohanty, Riley, and Minnie Bruce 2008; Saliba, Allen, and Howard 2002: 52). This image and the discourse surrounding it, as I continued to observe during my research and throughout my interviews, fail to reflect and capture the diverse experiences of women and their different priorities.

In line with postcolonial feminists' literature, I hold that women's rights are marked by social and cultural fluidity and tremendous diversity. In Egypt, they are situated within and shaped by colonial and nationalist legacies as well as by present religious, class, geographical, and racial dynamics. As Judith Tucker rightly argues, "women's lives – their access to power and economic resources as well as their social and legal standing – surely vary from one community or class to another" (1993: vii). In Egypt, the very term "women's rights" glosses over different conceptions and perceptions of claims that often generate debates among different groups, including women's groups. Most of the claims and the priorities range from the alleviation of poverty, violence against women and illiteracy, to raising legal awareness, spreading feminist consciousness, and increasing women's access to education, work, health care, and political participation (Al-Ali 2000: 16). The status and priority of these claims and demands constantly shift and reshuffle given the experiences of different women in different communities as well as the ideological and religious leanings of different groups. The attention and resources dedicated to these issues are often the function of their place on the national agenda as well as the international interest activists successed in garnering.

At the heart of the discussion of women's rights and gender equality in Egypt is how to challange forms of cultural patriarchy, religious extremism, and neoliberal exploitation of women. The debate over what is and should be women's rights has been largely dominated by two major paradigms: secular and Islamic feminism. The paradigms evolved in certain historical contexts and shifting combinations of religious, class, ethnic, and national dynamics (Badran 2005). Secular feminism builds upon multiple discourses including secular nationalist, Islamic modernist, humanitarian/human rights, and democratic ones (see Badran 2005: 6; see also Al-Ali 2000; Badran 1991). Islamic feminism is religiously grounded discourse; it takes the Qur'an as its central text and affirms that Islam has elevated the status of woman (see Badran 2005; see also Abu-Lughod 2013; Ahmed 1992).[8] Notwithstanding the ideological differences between the two camps, secular feminism anchors its approach within the discourse of religion and emphasizes its rootedness in Islamic teaching. Feminists and women's rights advocates often anchor their claims in Islamic teachings to ascribe indigeneity to their discourse and to negate being labeled as Western agents of colonialism or imperialism.

In several interviews, female protestors would start with what I term *a non-feminist disclaimer*. That is, they would stress that their activism was "nationalist"[9] and/or "socialist"[10] inspired in contrast to being "feminist" inspired. Although my letter of initial contact described my project as "examining women's engagement in the uprising with the objective of offering an oral history of women's participation in the 2011 uprising," a number of my interviewees started the interview with a non-feminist disclaimer.[11] One participant found it important

---

[8] The term *Islamic feminism* or *Islamic feminist* is, however, contested among some female Muslim scholars who are part of and support that paradigm. Consider how Heba Raouf Azzat and Omaima Abu Bakar, Islamic scholars and activists, problematize the concept of Islamic feminisms in their writings and often distance themselves from it in their discussions.

[9] Interviewee 23. Author's interview, Cairo, Egypt, July 2013.

[10] Interviewee 28. Author's interview, Cairo, Egypt, July 2013.

[11] Interviewee 3. Author's interview, Cairo, Egypt, July 2012. Interviewee 4. Author's interview, Cairo, Egypt, July 2012. Interviewee 6. Author's

to convey that she is "not feminist"[12] and that she found the term alienating and limiting to the array of activism that she carries out. Key among the activities she took part in was a campaign against sexual harassment at Tahrir Square. Another female interviewee was skeptical about "whether she could be of any help to my research" as she "was not involved in any women's rights organization."[13] In fact, she has been involved in a poverty-reduction initiative *with special focus on women and young girls* and working on a book in which she documents the music and songs performed by housewives in upper Egypt.

I found the recurrence of this anti-feminist disclaimer surprising for two reasons. First, many of my interviewees were involved in initiatives and campaigns that were clearly focused on women, yet they distanced themselves from framing these initiatives as women-centered. Instead, they framed these initiatives as social, for the betterment of the whole of society and not just women. In social movement literature, scholars have examined this framing strategy in great detail. According to them, social movement participants frame their activism within a broader "master frame" to gain wider support and further legitimacy for their actions (Snow and Benford 1988; see also Tarrow 1993; Tilly 2008).

Second, I was confused about why they would perceive my research as fit for strictly the feminist canon given the absence of the "F word"[14] from my research description. Later in the interview, I would ask my participants how they felt the label "feminist activist" or "women's rights activist" was perceived in Egyptian society. Of my 118 participants, 84 felt that feminist activists were broadly stereotyped and feminist ideologies carried a negative connotation among Egyptians. Some offered a more nuanced response, suggesting that it depended on the recipients' level of education and socioeconomic class.

These exchanges illustrate particularly well the effect of colonial history, identity politics, and simplistic cultural readings of religion on the framing of women's rights and feminist activists. They are emblematic

interview, Cairo, Egypt, July 2012. Interviewees 23, 28. Interviewee 18. Author's interview, Cairo, Egypt, July 2013.

[12] Interviewee 28.
[13] Interviewee 23.
[14] Interviewee 10. Author's interview, Cairo, Egypt, July 2012.

of the ambiguities and cross currents surrounding the meaning and interpretation of women's rights in Egypt.

Raison d'Être of the Study

Why female protestors did not explicitly voice women's rights and gender equality demands in the 2011 Egyptian uprising is the main question that drives this study. Besides this overarching question, the following questions are also investigated: What was the collective action frame adopted by women during the Egyptian uprising in 2011? How did women's experience in the uprising influence their engagement and participation in the uprising? How did the political process, particularly the politics of state-sponsored feminism, shape women's framing strategies?

In answering these questions, I undertook an in-depth study of women's collective action frame in the period January 25 – February 11, 2011 and elucidated its significance and limitations. The start date of the research signals the eruption of the uprising in Egypt following the success of the Tunisian revolution. The end date marks the resignation of Ḥusnī Mubarak, the former Egyptian president.

While the research's main focus is the period of the 18-day uprising, I will occasionally build on historical events, reflect on current ones, and suggest possible future trends. I choose to focus primarily on this initial episode of contention to capture and anatomize this key moment in the history of Egypt, and evaluate its gender dynamics. Apart from a number of studies, these dynamics did not receive enough attention and documentation in the literature discussing the recent uprisings in the region. A detailed analysis of these early interactions is, I suggest, important to partially explain the decline in the status of women's rights during periods of democratic transition.

To capture these dynamics, I document women's engagement from the standpoint of female protestors. Women's participation is studied and analyzed using insights from contentious politics literature. In particular, I utilize the concept of framing to elucidate the significance of women's collective action frame and its limitations. The book thus advances social movement theory by applying the political process model to non-Western cases and expanding the contours of its political opportunities and framing thesis to integrate gender structures and frames (see Giacaman and Johnson 1989; Beinin and Vairel 2011).

While the literature on social movements offers many valuable insights and interesting lines of inquiry, studying women's engagement in the 2011 Egyptian uprising brought to light the present omissions and shortcomings of the literature. The analysis uncovers the ways in which collective action frames are not merely a deliberate formulation in response to the legitimacy and resonance of the dominant framing of political struggles. While accounting for these factors provides collective action frames with credibility and salience, activists continue to take cues from the surrounding environment during political struggles. This study thus complements social movement scholarship by foregrounding the important role of gender structures in movement processes and the ways in which issues of interpretation and meaning-making are central to the story of all social movements (Gould 2009: 11).

The book also makes a significant contribution to the field of political science more broadly. By offering an analysis of the opportunities and challenges to women's political activism and engagement in contentious episodes, I reveal the ways in which female activists come to their understandings of politics and political participation. Specifically, I uncover the factors that make political action conceivable at all, or that make some forms of activism thinkable while others are, or become, wholly unimaginable (Gould 2009: 3–9). This analysis is important as it helps to explain how political imaginaries – or what Deborah Gould (2009: 3) eloquently terms "political horizons" – get established, consolidated, stabilized, and reproduced over time, and with what sorts of effects on political action. Answering these questions is important for the field of political science, as it promises to uncover the processes through which power is exercised and reproduced in our forms and frames of activism and the ways in which a prevailing or hegemonic political discourse might be challenged and transformed.

The proposed framework also explains – in part – how the absence of gender from women's frame at the time of the uprising limited their rights in the period of democratic transition. The research thus adds to our stock of knowledge on the gendered processes of regime change and the divergent outcomes of women's mobilization in national struggles. The proposed framework, however, does not cover all relevant factors. It highlights only how the revolutionary moment might have contributed to the current gender order in Egypt. Despite its limitation, the model can be explored across additional cases and in combination with other factors.

Finally, the concluding recommendations may as well prove useful to the women's movement in Egypt and the Middle East and North Africa region as a whole. In the concluding chapter, I highlight the importance of building networks and spreading gender awareness at the grassroots level to influence policies and advance women's rights. While I do acknowledge that this approach will not necessarily lead to an immediate increase in women's political representation, it will have a positive cumulative effect on gender relations and political participation in the longer term. The results can thus be used to better inform projects and programs designed to address gender inequality. These lessons are of great importance to international and national policymakers who are interested in a grassroots, bottom-up approach to women's empowerment. Understanding the complexities of women's experience is central to designing and implementing effective policies.

Data and Methods

The methodology employed in this research adopts an "emergent" approach to theorizing, common in feminist and critical scholarship (Collins 1990; Hesse-Biber and Leavy 2007; Letherby 2003). In line with this approach, theorizing about female protestors' experiences in the uprising takes the form of a conversation between theory and women's lived experiences and interpretations. The data for this project was gathered from semi-structured personal interviews and public transcripts and analyzed using critical discourse analysis.

Semi-structured interviews use open-ended questions to encourage participants to elaborate on their answers (Mayan 2009:71; Morse and Richards 2002). This method of data collection is important for this study as it allows the researcher the flexibility to examine interviewees' responses. It also gives participants the opportunity to respond in their own words, rather than forcing them to choose from fixed responses. Denzin and Lincoln (2000) sum up the importance of semi-structured interviews, describing them as meaningful and culturally salient to the participant, unanticipated by the researcher, and having a rich and explanatory nature. The organic nature of the data contributes to the emergent approach characterizing this research.

To this end, I conducted 103 in-depth interviews in English and Arabic with five sets of actors between June 2012 and December 2014 in Egypt; I went on another round of fieldwork in the region for my concluding chapter on hope and disappointment in 2016/2017 and conducted further interviews. In total, between 2012 and 2017, I conducted 118 interviews. The five sets of actors that I have interviewed are, first, female protestors, aged 18 years and above, who participated in the 18-day protests. It is worth noting that while I strove to choose participants from different social and economic backgrounds in order to avoid biases and attain rich data, the nature of the research is qualitative, and therefore uncovering potential different experiences of women according to socioeconomic status, while often highlighted, is not the main aim of the study.

Second, I carried out interviews with female political activists. This population was approached through the Egyptian Center for Women's Rights, a Cairo-based NGO. Participants were snowballed from this stage. In addition to snowball sampling, a call for participation and recruiting material was also posted in community organization and on listservs. I have carried out interviews with activists from the Kefaya [Enough] and April 6 Youth movements as well as members from Jama't Al-Ikhwan Al-Muslimīn [the Muslim Brotherhood Organization] given their active role and presence in the 2011 uprising.

Third, I carried out interviews with representatives of the following NGOs:

- Al-Mar'a wa Al-Dhakira [Women and History Forum]
- Al-Markaz Al-Maṣrī -l-ḥuqoq Al-Mar'a [The Egyptian Center for Women's Rights]
- Al-Baqiyat Al-ṣaliḥat [Good Deeds Organization]
- Mo'saasat Qaḍaya Al-Mar'a [Centre for Egyptian Women's Legal Assistance]
- Nazra -l-Dirasat Al-Nisawīa [Nazra for Feminist Studies]
- Rabiṭat Al-Mar'a Al-Arabīa [The Alliance for Arab Women]
- Tawasul [Engagement].

Interviews were also carried out with members and leaders from numerous initiatives, salient among which are Operation Anti-Sexual Harassment (OpAntiSH) and HarassMap.

The choice of these NGOs and initiatives is purposive, given their grassroots approach to women's rights as well as their participation in the uprising. Furthermore, to increase the richness of my data and avoid biases, the NGOs included do not share the same ideological bedrock; they considerably differ in their aims and focus.

Interviews were also carried out with a number of senior officials at different international and regional organizations in light of their engagement with gender equality and women's rights in Egypt. Among the participants who were willing to be identified are the following: Dr. Maya Morsy, former regional gender practice team leader at the United Nations Development Program/Middle East Office (UNDP) and current president of Egypt's National Council for Women; Dr. Nahla Abdel Tawab, regional director of the Population Council in the Middle East; and Shaheda El-Baz, director of the Arab and African Research Center at the American University in Cairo (AUC). Fourth, I interviewed state officials who are engaged in the agenda of women's rights in Egypt. Specifically, I interviewed former consultants and current directors at the National Council for Women's Rights and the National Center for Social and Criminological Research.

Finally, I interviewed public female figures, namely: Abla El-Kahlawī, Tawakkol Karman, and Amina Shafiq. El-Kahlawī is among the most famous female *ulamā* (Islamic scholars) in the Arab world. She held the position of dean of Islamic and Arabic Studies at al-Azhar University, Women's College in Egypt (Allam 2013). Tawakkol Karman is the co-recipient of the 2011 Nobel Peace Prize, for her leading role in the struggle for democracy and human rights in Yemen. Amina Shafiq is the first and only female secretary-general of the Egyptian Press Syndicate (1989–1993) as well as a symbol of 1960s leftism in Egypt. These figures are chosen because of their historical involvement in women's rights issues and their diverse backgrounds.

I followed the normal ethical protocol requiring the use of pseudonyms in place of real names of interviewees, unless participants indicated that they wanted their real name to be mentioned. In several cases, however, even when participants were well-known public figures and indicated that they wanted their real name to be mentioned, I continued to use pseudonyms to protect their identity considering the ongoing crackdown on political activists in Egypt. I was able to cross-check data and appreciate the complexity of women's engagement in political struggle given the richness of data and the diversity of participants.

In order to elucidate women's experience in the uprising from their own perspective, the interview guide included questions on the following themes/domains: women's grievances; mobilization strategies; and roles during the uprising. I also examined the role of women's organizations during the uprising, the implication of state feminism on the women's rights agenda and how discussions over gender inequalities and women's rights were perceived at the time of the uprising.

My textbook knowledge of research methods and design had to be adapted to fit the reality on the ground. Following the interviews, I would go through my notes and read the interview transcripts. This timely review of data was important in order to locate gaps in knowledge and identify new themes that are worth further investigation. Following this review, I often included new questions, reframed existing ones, and added new contacts to my list of interviewees.

Besides interviews, I regularly attended panels, discussions, workshops, and conferences held at universities, libraries, and cultural centers in Egypt. Also, my conversations and discussions with scholars and researchers at the Cynthia Nelson Institute for Gender and Women's Studies and the AUC forum at the American University in Cairo – where I served as a research fellow in the fall of 2014 – were very insightful. The purpose of this endeavor was to verify that the picture/explanation that emerged from the previously collected data was accurate.

In addition to interview data, data from public documents was compiled to further understand women's engagement in the uprising. By analyzing these documents, I gained further insights into how women's participation was framed and perceived in the national and international media as well as in Egypt's popular culture.[15] To this end, I examined the following documents:

a. Key Egyptian and North American newspapers, namely *Al-Ahram*, *Al-Wafd*, and *The New York Times*. I analyzed their coverage of the uprising using MAXQDA; a software program for qualitative analysis.

b. Scholarly work in English and Arabic examining the uprising in the form of books, journal articles, and the like. Some of this scholarly work was accessed through the University of Alberta Library website. Other scholarship was accessible only through the library at the American University in Cairo, the Social Sciences Library,

---

[15] A survey of the revolutionary pamphlets and songs sheds light on how women's participation was framed in Egypt's popular culture.

Faculty of Economics and Political Science library and Media Studies library at Cairo University, in Egypt.

c. Revolutionary pamphlets and pictures of women's graffiti at the time of the uprising. These materials were accessed through the Women and Memory Forum (WMF) library. The WMF is a national nongovernmental organization in Egypt; its focus is on researching and documenting the role of women in Arab and Middle Eastern societies.

d. Three key Facebook groups dubbed as influential in mobilizing protestors, namely: "We are all Khaled Saīd," "The Day of Rage," and "January 25th" groups.

Public transcripts and interview data were treated within the prism of critical discourse analysis (Richardson 2007; see also Blommaert and Bulcaen 2000). This entailed a close reading of participants' responses with a view to what was being said and the context of the discussion in the attempt to examine the place of gender in women's collective action frames.

Specifically, I organized data into three frameworks/themes. The three frameworks/themes are: women's collective action frame; political opportunities; and women's experience at the time of the uprising. The first theme, that is women's collective action frame, helped in answering how gender issues featured in their collective action frame. The second theme ascertained the key political opportunities and constraints that shaped women's engagement in the uprising. The final theme emphasized the context within which women carried out their activism at the time of the uprising.

Combining in-depth semi-structured interviews with media and public transcripts yields qualitatively rich data. The data offered a nuanced analysis of the political opportunities and framing strategies that influenced women's engagement in the uprising.

Scope and Limitations

This study focuses specifically on women's engagement in the Egyptian uprising. While I am aware that women did participate in other Arab Spring uprisings, and often faced similar challenges, this study does not address such participation in great detail. The subject of women's participation in the Arab Spring, however, certainly warrants further research and study.

Specifically, I find two questions to be of great significance for expanding the application of my argument beyond this book to future research. The first question is related to obtaining more observations "across space" (King, Keohane, and Verba 1994: 219). The second – and to some extent interrelated – question is related to "conceptual traveling" (Sartori 1970): that is, to what extent can my model *travel* beyond the case of Egypt – the case study in my book – and across different cases of mobilization such as the January Jasmine revolution in Tunisia and the Libyan Arab Spring of 2011, to cite a few?

While answering these questions is beyond the scope of my book, my analysis offers a plausible framework to understand women's engagement and the status of their rights during and after the Arab Spring.

Second, it is difficult to evaluate the effect of my identity as an Egyptian female studying in North America – thus an outsider often perceived as among those benefiting from the emerging "academic tourism"[16] in the region – on my interviewees and their responses.

For example, in one of the interviews with a director at a national institution for women's rights, the director denied that sexual harassment was a problem in Egypt. She insisted that the number of incidents were insignificant and blamed women who dressed liberally, or who were, like me, "young and present in the public space." I am not sure how to situate her answer, but I could not but feel during the interview that notwithstanding my Egyptian origin, my status as a researcher who is studying in Canada placed me as an outsider. Thus, she, the director, might have felt that it was her duty to conceal and deny the phenomenon in the presence of a "perceived outsider" like myself.

---

[16] Academic tourism is a concept that emerged during a discussion at the workshop "The Ethics of Political Science Research and Teaching in MENA," held on June 9–11, 2015, at King Mohammed V University in Rabat. The workshop was jointly funded by the American Political Science Association MENA Program and Carnegie Corporation of New York and co-hosted by the London School of Economics Middle East Centre. Along with a number of scholars, I organized the workshop to hold a discussion between researchers and scholars facing shared challenges, in terms of human subject protection, increased state surveillance, and working in conflict areas and with vulnerable people. Among the key themes that came out during the discussion are the ways in which many researchers from outside the region, that is academic tourists, have better access and funding opportunities than locally based scholars. This result is a problematic power relation where researchers based in the MENA region often must settle for support roles in research projects that come in from abroad.

Finally, while the political situation in Egypt has been continuously evolving and changing over the past six years – following the 2011 uprising, the latest political developments in the country have been even more dramatic. Following the election of President Abdel Fattah el-Sisi in June 2014, the former defense minister who toppled the former president, Muhammed Mursī, amid popular protests against the Muslim Brotherhood, the ruling regime has been repeatedly warning citizens against a "conspiracy" to bring down Egypt. I observed while at my fieldwork the narrowing of the political landscape and the rise of hyper-nationalism among citizens. Civil society organizations and political oppositions were working amid a hostile environment in which state security forces were cracking down on the NGOs' activities and public opinion was desperately supporting a police state in the hope of stability.

Eid Mohamed and Bessma Momani (2014) eloquently capture this febrile momentum in Egypt in their article "The Muslim Brotherhood: Between Democracy, Ideology and Distrust." While the article's main focus is exposing the myth of political Islam in Egypt, its conclusion captures the complex and contradictory political sentiments in Egyptian society, following the ousting of Muhammed Mursī from the presidency. The authors describe how critics of the current state are often labeled "buzz-killer," or even worse "terrorist-sympathizers" (Mohamed and Momani 2014: 210–211). They rightly point to the difficulty of carrying out rational conversation about the current state of affairs in Egypt, and during my fieldwork I observed how emotions were running high and cynicism and distrust among revolutionaries and youth were at record levels.

I also recognized with disappointment the sense of despair growing among intellectuals and activists in Egypt. By the time I was leaving Egypt, many political activists had already fled the country and others were planning to move. This stood in stark contrast to the spirit that characterized my earlier round of fieldwork in 2012. Back then, I carried out a preliminary round of fieldwork in Egypt; this was undertaken in the period following the ousting of the former president, Ḥusnī Mubarak. At that time, hopes for change and progress were high among my interviewees. During my more recent round of fieldwork, in 2014, the court had dropped all charges against Ḥusnī Mubarak and his former interior minister, Habib el-Adly in connection with the killing of protesters during the 2011 uprising (Dearden 2014).

The disappointment and disillusionment that engulfed me after witnessing the protesters, devastated by this verdict, shouting and screaming in anger while riot police stood in preparation for disruption has brought about a period of soul-searching in me, for which there is no apparent end in sight. The experience has left me asking fundamental questions about the nature of uprisings and the role of civil resistance in social and political change. These questions are at the heart of my book.

Organization of the Book

This book is organized into an Introduction, six chapters, and a Conclusion.

In the Introduction, I present a general overview of the study and an exposition of its objectives and rational. Chapter 1, "Women in Egypt's National Imaginary," highlights the centrality of women to historical and modern projects of nationalism in Egypt. I briefly survey nationalist and feminist contributions to studying women's experience in political struggles before examining the framing of women's participation in the 1919 revolution and the 1952 Free Officers' revolution, in Egypt.

Chapter 2, "Media and the Framing of Women's Engagement in the 2011 Egyptian Uprising,"[17] interrogates the visibility and representation of women in national and international media coverage of the 2011 Egyptian uprising. Two central questions animate this chapter. First, in comparison to men, how did the media in Egypt frame women's engagement in the uprising of 2011? Second, did the image of female participants challenge or perpetuate traditional gender and – specifically in the case of the *New York Times'* coverage – orientalist stereotypes? I draw upon 174 news stories published on the websites of two widely circulated national newspapers: *Al-Ahram* and *Al-Wafd* and 224 international stories published by the *New York Times*. The stories offer a detailed coverage of the popular uprising between January 25 and February 12, 2011. I carried out a textual analysis of news, editorials,

---

[17] A version of Chapter 2 was published in the *Sociology of Islam Journal* under the title "Activism and Exception in Covering Egypt's Uprising: A Critical Reading of the *New York Times'* Representation of Female Protestors" (Allam 2014b).

and commentaries, and read the text through the lens of postcolonial feminist critique, utilizing discourse analysis. My analysis suggests that traditional motifs of passiveness coexisted alongside new ones of feminine agency in the coverage. By evoking the myth of female passiveness and framing women's activism within a feminine framework, the coverage, I suggest, assuaged the effect of their activism in deconstructing gender stereotypes. The analysis also explicates the variation and multiplicity involved in the practice of "othering" and avoids erasing the participation of women as subject of patriarchy or Orientalism in shaping the discourse.

Chapters 3 to 5 are the epicenter of my analysis; together they contribute to understanding how women framed their participation in light of their relation to a broader map of contentious and routine politics.

Chapter 3, "Trenching Dissent: Women's Collective Action Frame in the Uprising," highlights the significance and meaning of the collective action frame adopted by women during the 18-day uprising. I interrogate women's collective action frame and examine how the omission of gender influenced their participation in the uprising. The most misunderstood aspect of women's experience in the uprising is the absence of gender from their collective action frame. In the absence of detailed analysis, the omission of gender can be misunderstood as a sign of the women's passivity, and/or false consciousness. To avoid the risk of "Orientalising Egyptian women all over again," borrowing Saba Mahmood's word of warning (2005: 119), I utilize frame analysis to understand their engagement in the uprising. Building upon frame analysis, I argue that the omission of gender from women's collective action frame is not a sign of passivity, but part of the process of frame alignment.

In Chapter 4, I expand the contours of framing theory to consider the influence of women's experience during contention on their collective action frame. Participants, I hold, are involved in ongoing framing alignment and articulation. They not only tap into the wider cultural predisposition in framing their participation but also continue to take cues from the surrounding environment during times of political struggles. Building upon my participants' accounts, I argue that women's subjective experience of solidarity and equality during the 2011 protests contributed to the absence of gender from their collective action framing. During this phase the unity and solidarity among participants were ostensibly real and felt by female protestors. I use the case of the absence of sexual harassment to demonstrate the prevalence of the sense of "communitas" and to highlight the conjunctural limitation of this "liminal" phase (Turner 1974). Given the widespread equality and solidarity during the 18-day uprising, women actively framed their participation utilizing the citizen frame. This frame was viewed by women as sufficient to incorporate gender equality rights and to sit within the post-uprising agenda. The analysis presented in this chapter aims to capture the experience of female protestors in its entirety. It presents "an archeology of women's recollections," in which I highlight overt indeterminacies, ambiguities, ruptures, and shifts in women's experience.

Chapter 5, "'Intu Bito' Sūzān' (You are Suzanne's Clique): Gender and Political Opportunities in the 2011 Uprising," extends and further elaborates the arguments presented in Chapters 3 and 4. In this chapter, I examine how the character of opportunities influences women's framing strategies. Espousing a political process approach, I argue that groups differ in how they experience and perceive political opportunities in collective action. This is because opportunities mainly reflect the values of their early architects and the groups' prior relations with the regime. They, however, can evolve and support new challengers depending on the structure of contention and the group's prior interaction with the regime. I thus argue that the uprising did not necessarily open up an opportunity for women to demand gender equalities. This is, in part, due to the policies of state-sponsored feminism; these policies, feminist critics observe, damaged the discourse of gender equality and shifted the location of women's struggles in Egypt (Badran 1988; Baron 2005; Hatem 1994; Sholkamy 2012a).

In the final chapter, "What Holds Next? The Politics of Hope and Disappointment,"[18] I conclude by offering suggestions for future research in the region, a region that is increasingly marked by politics of disappointment. In mapping the field in which politics unfolded in the Middle East and North African region after the Arab Spring,

---

[18] An abridged version of the concluding chapter was published at the London School of Economics Middle East Centre blog under the title "What Holds Next? The Politics of Disappointment." The full article can be found at: http://blogs.lse.ac.uk/mec/2015/08/11/what-holds-next-the-politics-of-disappointment/

researchers, I contend, should analyze the conditions under which the politics of disappointment prevail. Most importantly, this analysis should be carried out with an eye to how actions and activism continue nonetheless to take place. In the Conclusion, I review the findings of the book and its contributions to the discipline.

1 | Women and Egypt's National Struggles

Roses and basil were on that day
the only weapons on which they relied.
The hours of struggle seemed so long
that embryos might have become grey-haired.
But then the women became feeble,
for the fair sex has no physical strength.
They were defeated and fled,
dispersed, to their palaces.
What a glorious army indeed!
What a victory, to have defeated women!

(Hafiz Ibrahim, 1929, quoted in Baron 2005: 115)

Hafiz Ibrahim's poem "Muzaharat Al-Nisa'" [The Ladies' Demonstration] is one of the most important written memorials to the 1919 Egyptian uprising. It has been central to constructing the nation's collective memory of it. Collective memory is the site of identification and conflict for a nation. It not only constructs the past but also organizes the experience of the present and the future. Jacques Derrida (1973) describes this simultaneity with his famous strategic concept of deconstruction. Deconstruction and construction, Derrida argues, are mutually exclusive. Something new in thinking can only be evoked by supplementing something already given; new meanings do not erase established ones but write over them, and thus are always bound to them. The representation of women in Ibrahim's poem, as such, in part describes and inscribes broader views and debates on women's political participation in Egypt. The poem is an example of the different ways in which nationalist regimes have constructed the image of nationalist women and manipulated the discourse of women's rights in Egypt.

In this chapter, I focus on the framing of women's engagement in Egypt's national struggles. I argue that the experience of Egyptian women in the 1919 nationalist uprising and the 1952 Free Officers' revolution crystallizes the tension between nationalist and women's rights discourses in Egypt. Women's experience, I contend, is remembered only selectively, at key moments and when it serves some symbolic purpose. Notwithstanding the resisted path of change following political struggles, I explore how women's mobilization has contributed to democratizing and gendering the public and political sphere in Egypt.

In the attempt to develop this particular argument, I, first, critically survey the literature on women's participation in nationalist movements to situate the experience of women in Egypt's uprising of 1919, and the 1952 Free Officers' revolution. Second, I examine how women's engagement at these key political junctures has been commemorated and remembered in a number of relevant literary and artistic productions. I analyze women's experiences in the past, with my eyes on the present. My objective is to identify continuities and ruptures in the framing of women's national activism in Egypt.

This chapter, thus, presents a nuanced view of women's engagement in political struggles at the time of revolutions and their status in the new regimes. It builds upon and contributes to the literature on women and the process of nation-building. This is done while problematizing the tendency in mainstream literature to theorize a single, common relationship between the nationalist movement and women's rights. Despite the rich debate and the theoretical insights that have been provoked by the literature, for the most part, nationalist-motivated political movements are still more often "objects of fear and scorn than of systematic study" (Vickers 2006). This obscures the complexity of the issue and overlooks the positive influence of revolutions on women's post-revolution movements. As such, the analysis presented in this chapter functions in de-essentializing the category of women, while suggesting areas for continuities or junctures in the assumed relationship between women and political struggles. In so doing, I bridge the experience of Egyptian women to the experience of women in other parts of the world and situate it within the broader body of feminist research.

Women's Engagement in Political Struggles

Women's engagement in national revolutions has been the subject of study in nationalist and feminist literatures. Their contributions range from an examination of theoretical dilemmas to case studies in a variety of contemporary and historical settings. The case studies document women's meaningful, though often hidden, experiences during the revolutions and analyze their experiences through "maternalist" and/or "warrior women" frameworks (Edmonds-Cady 2009; Hatem 2000; Noonan 1995; Tètreault 1994).

The maternalist framework exemplifies the theoretical and practical practice of posing motherhood as a basis for political action and political action as a motherly obligation for women (Edmonds-Cady 2009; Noonan 1995). That is to say, women's participation in political struggles is framed as a mothering response to the danger imposed by the regime on her children. The maternalist framing focuses on women's feminine roles in political struggles but also acknowledges women's non-traditional roles that bend gender expectations. It, however, places women's activism squarely in the context of the nationalist struggle and does not ascribe feminist meanings to them.

In contrast, the term "women warrior" or "women fighter" is used to describe women's militant participation in armed political struggles. Warrior women are female participants who fought side by side with men at the forefront of several armed struggles (Tétreault 1994). For instance, in the Vietnam war and Eritrean liberation struggle during the 1960s and 1970s, the image of a khaki-clad woman warrior – indistinguishable from men in some cases – brandishing a rifle became symbolic of the nationalist movement (Bernal 2001: 131).

Women have often moved across these frames in past struggles. For instance, case studies of Palestinian women's resistance to Israeli colonialism highlight the different functions performed by women during the first and second Intifadas. As a "mother of all boys," militants, politicians, and grassroots organizers, Palestinian women took up diverse roles throughout the history of the conflict (Allen 2003: 655–657; Jad 1990). The same holds true for women in Africa, the Middle East, Asia, and Latin America who supported combatants and/or were the combatant themselves (for a collection of case studies see Joseph 2000; Joseph and Najmabadi 2003; see also; Stephen 1997; Tètreault 1994; Volo 2004; West and Blumberg 1988; Zaatari 2006).

It is worth noting that women's mode of participation not only is the product of their personal choice and/or the nature of the struggle but is often dictated by the culture and environment within which they carry out their activism. To participate in protests, the "heirs of Zaynab" in Iran and Palestinian women in the "Intifada Hijab"[1] had to adhere to a certain role. Their role was to wear their veils as a sign of opposition to imperialism (Afshar 1985). Women participating outside this role – that is demonstrating without covering their heads – were considered anti-revolutionary and insufficiently nationalist (Allen 2003: 657; Azari 1984: 268; Hammami 1990: 26).

Women's participation as such was encouraged by nationalist and Islamist alike in the Middle East and North Africa and beyond. Yet with the end of political struggles, the new regimes often ignored women's demands. Several studies in Latin America document how the new states brought a reassertion of traditional gender expectations (Jaquette 1973) and the waning of women's mobilizations and representation in formal political power (Waylen 1994). The same tendency has been observed in the Middle East and North Africa following regime change and political struggles.

The Gender "Pitfalls of National Consciousness"

The failure of new regimes to improve gender equality after revolutions has been the foci of several feminist and nationalist studies. The studies question whether women's post-revolutionary experiences lived up to their expectations or imaginings during the nationalist struggle. In this regard, scholars have drawn attention to the ways in which the process of nation-building after the revolutions is premised on particular gender identities and meanings (Abu-Laban 2008; Boehmer 2005; Dhruvarajan and Vickers 2002; Joseph 2000; Vickers 2006, 2008; Yuval-Davis 1997).

Similar to Franz Fanon's efforts to reveal the ethnic "pitfalls of national consciousness" (1963: 148–205), several feminist contributions unveil the *gender pitfalls of national consciousness*. Within this tradition, scholars have analyzed the ways in which nationalist projects essentially "gendered nations" (Yuval Davis 1997) and "masculinized citizenship" (Zubaida 1989) following national liberation struggles. They have, thus, questioned the influence of a number of

---

[1] The same was true in the first Palestinian Intifada, when a campaign was waged in Gaza to impose hijab. In what analysts interpreted as "Intifada Hijab" (Ababneh 2014; Allen 2003: 657; Hammami 1990: 26), hijab came to signify women's commitment to the nationalist movement.

factors in shaping the political openings and ideologies available to women's movements in transitional periods (Viterna and Fallon 2008; Waylen 1994). Among the key factors highlighted in the literature are the nature of political struggles (Jayawardena 1986; Terman 2010; Yeganeh 1993), and the legacy of women's previous mobilizations (Kumba 2001; Noonan 1995; Viterna 2006; Viterna and Fallon 2008).

Broadly speaking, this body of work acts as a *caveat emptor* for women who wish to participate in revolutions. Examining the process of nation-building and the construction of citizenship following major revolutions, scholars conclude by criticizing national struggles and typically argue that women were used during them only to be relegated to home and hearth after (Hatem 2000; Joseph 2000; Tètreault 1994; Vickers 2008; Yuval Davis 1997).

Scholars stress this sentiment to a different degree. While the majority of early feminists displayed an absolute cynicism (Woolf 1938; Petteman 1996),[2] their non-Western counterparts have often contextualized their skepticism toward women's participation in liberation movements (Berkovitch and Moghadam 1999; Jayawardena 1986; Terman 2010). Valentine Moghadam and Kumari Jayawardena have argued in the past, that in Asia and the Middle East "feminism and nationalism were complementary, compatible and solidaristic," but they conclude, "(t)his has changed" (Moghadam 1994: 3; see also Jayawardena 1986). This is because, anti-modern nationalism[3] in contrast to modern nationalism is on the rise (1994: 6–7). They believe that the former expands women's rights, while the latter constrains them.

Contrary to Moghadam and Jayawardena's view, a number of studies argue that religious movements have the potential of liberating women as well (Parashar 2010; Terman 2010). Writing on the Iranian revolution, Rochelle Terman (2010) argues that the Islamic revolution has liberated women by mobilizing them in the public

---

[2] Australian Jan Jindy Pettman is skeptical about the possibility of positive relations between women's rights and nationalism. She recognizes that the relationship can be negotiated in different ways over time and place, but accuses nationalist movements of mobilizing women's support and labor, while simultaneously seeking to reinforce women's female roles and femininity (1996: 61).

[3] Scholars associate anti-modern nationalism with the rise of religious fundamentalists.

sphere. Terman (2010: 290) claims that the revolution aimed at creating a female subject that is "simultaneously pious and politically active." This particular form of subjectivity, however, "exceeds and defies the categories and dichotomies" of earlier social norms (Terman 2010: 290). This unique subjectivity gives rise to a productive tension in that women are using this new identity to act in ways that are both beyond and contrary to what the Islamist regime initially anticipated (Terman 2010: 290; see also Al-Qasimi 2010; Zahedi 2007).

In addition to the nature of the movement, women's post-transition movements benefit from women's pre-transition activism and influence their gains under the new regime. Women whose pre-transition activism was political or distant from traditional understandings of the feminine were better able to organize and pressure the regime for women's rights (Kampwirth 2002; Shayne 2004).

The strategies and frames used prior to transitions can also constrain the materialization of gender equity. In Latin America, female protestors appropriated the authoritarian regime's discourse of the pious woman and selfless mother in framing their political participation and struggle for democratic reform. This framing, however, constrained women's activism in the period following the uprising. The new political actors used women's feminine framing to justify women's exclusion from the public space and to encourage female activists to return to the private sphere (Chinchilla 1994; Fisher 1993).

Scholars therefore conclude – with varying certainty – that the women's movement failed to secure their full rights after transition because the movement failed to convert the pre-transition frames into strong feminist discourses following regime change and democratic transition. This view does not go uncontested. Some argue that feminine movements often evolve into "feminist" ideologies (Molyneux 1985; Stephen 1997; Viterna and Fallon 2008). While subscribing to the rationale underpinning this argument, Jocelyn Viterna and Kathleen M. Fallon (2008: 672) critique the paucity of studies written about which movements evolve, which languish, and whether this broadening of movement goals results in gendered changes within the state apparatus. Egyptian women's involvement in the 1919 revolution can be seen as an example of these *feminine turning feminist* movements.

Women and the 1919 Revolution

In contrast to the Urabi Revolt of 1881/1882,[4] which has been characterized as a "manly event" (Russell 2004: 87), the Egyptian 1919 revolution, against British colonialism, was led by female participants. Women's national activism prior to 1919 ranged from signing petitions to launching boycott campaigns; yet it was the "ladies' demonstration" of March 1919 that came to be one of the most prominent symbols of women's national activism (Baron 2005; Bier 2011; Botman 1991; El Saadawi 1997; Hatem 1994, 2000; Mariscotti 2008; Rizk 2000). Following the exile of male nationalist leaders in March 1919 by the colonial forces, women led protests and rallied for the release of male nationalist leaders and for Egypt's independence.

Much of the literature documenting women's engagement in this revolution utilizes a class lens in analyzing the different and often contradictory experiences of female participants. Class, many argue, assigned different roles, dictated different counter-colonial responses, and brought different gains for women who participated in the revolution (Baron 2005; Bier 2011; Botman 1991; El Saadawi 1997; Hatem 1994, 2000).

Elite women, including Safiya Zaghloul and Huda Sha'rawi, led the masses, lower-class women participated in street protests with men, and rural-class women in the countryside provided food and assistance to male activists. Nawal El Saadawi, Egyptian feminist and a physician by training, observes that "little has been said about the masses of poor women who rushed into the national struggle without counting the cost, and who lost their lives, whereas the lesser contributions of aristocratic women leaders have been noisily acclaimed and brought to the forefront" (El Saadawi 1997: 258).

Class also played a role in the colonists' chosen method of discipline. Many observers argue that it is not coincidental that female national martyrs came from lower classes. Meanwhile, elite protestors were only punished by keeping them under the glow of the blazing sun for several hours (Badran 1988; El Saadawi 1997). Ijlal Khalifa's work was central in articulating this argument, too, particularly

---

[4] The Urabi Revolt was carried out by Egyptian army officers, who were dissatisfied with the preferential treatment of the Turkish-speaking Ottoman elite and with the dire economic conditions.

in her book: *Al-Harakah al-Nisa'iyya al-Haditha: Qissat al-Mar'a al-'Arabiyya 'ala Ard Misr* [The Modern Women's Movement: The Story of the Arab Woman in the Land of Egypt] (1973). In it, Khalifa notes how class had an impact on women's experiences in the 1919 uprising. "The daughter of the wealthy or aristocratic class," she writes "is the one who participated in the revolution and the adept political work after it" (cited in Ramdani 2013: 50). The daughter of the middle and lower classes, however, "is the one who died as a martyr by the hand of colonialism, who felt its humiliation and oppression."

The Framing of Women's Engagement in the 1919 Revolution

The literature on the 1919 uprising highlights two important facets of the framing of women's participation. First, women's activism was placed within a maternalist frame in historical texts and national symbols (Ahmed 1992; Badran 1995; Baron 1997, 2005; Russell 2004). Second, women themselves constructed their activism in the revolution through a maternal discourse (Golley 2003; Rizk 2000; Shafiq 1956; Sha'rawi 1987).[5]

The women-led demonstrations of 1919 quickly became part of the national memory, but as Baron (2005: 113) observes, "the collective memory of this 'iconic moment' fractured along gender lines." For instance, Hafiz Ibrahim – the famous Poet of the Nile – in his poem, "The Ladies' Demonstration," discussed earlier, praises women's participation in the revolution; however, his poem concludes by reminding us of women's physical weakness. He thus mocked the British troops' victory because it was a victory over women and not men. Other major work narrating the uprising emphasized women's secondary role in it; they detail how women supported and mobilized their men. The work of the prominent historian Abdel Rahman al-Raf'i is

---

[5] In signing the 1919 petition, prominent women activists chose to sign and identify themselves in relation to their husbands, fathers, or brothers (Ahmed 2010). Even when the post- revolutionary regime did not honor women's rights, many studies highlight women's compliance with the maternalist construction of women's rights (see Hatem 1994, 2000; Bier 2011; Rizk 2000; Osman 2012). For instance, the program of the Feminist Union emphasized the need for women's access to education and social services and, as Hatem (1994: 33) points out, focused on enabling middle-class women to be better mothers and wives.

exemplary in this regard. He praised women for their participation in the national uprising, but then, in a footnote, restricted the role of women to caring for the poor and sick.

Motifs of family and motherhood were invoked as well in commemorating women's leadership in the uprising. For instance, as a nod to Safiya Zaghloul's heroine role in leading protests, she was designated as "Um El-masrayeen" [the mother of Egyptians] and her home, the headquarters of protest mobilization, was christened "Byt Al-Umma" [the house of the nation].

The term "domestication of female public bravery," I propose, describes the ways in which women's participation has been framed and celebrated using domestic vocabulary in Egypt. These gendered representations of symbols within nationalist movements have been an important area of study in feminist scholarship (Cusack 2000; Hatem 2000; McClintock 1993; Yuval Davis 1997). Feminist scholars reveal similarities in the ways in which women served as idealized symbols in revolutionary struggles and how this representation of women shaped their treatment in the new order. The domestication of female public activism serves to contain the effects of women's public activism and maintain gender hierarchies. Recent work, however, critiques this depiction of women's experiences as an extension of their domestic task in the home to the outside, in the service of the nation. (For critique, see Ahmed 2010; Bier 2011; Elsadda 2006; Hatem 2000: 38–39; Osman 2012; Pollard 2005.)

This maternal nationalist framing reached its apogee in Egypt in the interwar years with the creation of the image of Egypt as a national mother (Baron 2005: 135). The fiction, Baron (2005: 135) asserts, generated a sense of solidarity and relatedness among people who were otherwise strangers or divided along class, race, ethnic, and religious lines. The "mothers" and "fathers" provided comfort, creating a sense of collective belonging and suggesting that the welfare of the people was in the right hands (Baron 2005). Yet assertions that the nation was a family, Pollard (2005) explains, were also meant to insure obedience to the male nationalist leaders and to silence dissent.

These gendered representations of symbols within nationalist movements have been an important area of study in feminist scholarship (Cusack 2000; Hatem 1992, 2000; McClintock 1993; Yuval Davis 1997). Feminist scholars reveal similarities in the ways in which women served as idealized symbols in revolutionary struggles and how this representation of women shaped their outcome in the new order.

In *Bananas, Beaches and Bases*, Cynthia Enloe explicates how masculinity and nationalism have always been parallel discourses. Whether through media projections or literary texts, women were often consigned to representational roles, and men were presented as the real performers in popular portrayals of national struggles (Enloe 2000: 44). This, I suggest, holds true in the case of Egypt. The history of women's representation in Egypt's nationalist movements indicates a tension between representations of the nation as a woman and representations of women defending the nation, with the first prevailing in the national imagery (Baron 2005; Botman 1991; Hatem 2000).

This tension is often projected in the visual representation of national symbols in Egypt. For example, in the statue of the Egyptian nationalist leader Mustafā Kāmil, in Cairo, Kāmil is depicted in modern Western clothes standing erect, delivering a speech (Baron 2005: 65). At the pedestal of the statue is a bronze relief that shows a seated young peasant woman, with head covered, of smaller dimensions than Kāmil. This differential representation confirms Tricia Cusack's critique of the process of nation-building. The nation, Cusack (2000) argues, has been traditionally conceptualized as "Janus-faced"; that is: looking both ways, to the past and to the future.

According to Cusack (2000: 67), women are often the object of the "backward look" that is associated with tradition; meanwhile men are seen to embody the forward-thrusting agency of national progress, especially in religious societies. The young veiled peasant woman in Kāmil's statue represents Egypt under British occupation. By this time, the motif of the nation as a woman was popular in Egypt's nationalist memory (Baron and Pursley 2005: 523). In Anne McClintock's (1993) view, such practice, while construing women as the symbolic bearers of the nation, denies women any direct relation to national agency.

Feminism and Women's Rights after the Revolution

The traditional depiction of women's experiences within the maternalist frame and discourse omits feminist meanings and implications that might have developed as a result of women's activism in nationalist struggle. The rise of feminist consciousness and activism in Egypt following the 1919 uprising is exemplary of these long-term outcomes

(Badran 1988; Baron 1997, 2005; Russell 2004). This important body of work seeks to reclaim women's history and experience in Egypt's national struggles. Scholars within this tradition highlight some of the ways in which women fought concurrently as feminists and nationalists (Badran 1988; Baron 1997).

Following the 1919 revolution, middle- and upper-class women formed their first formal political organization, the Wafdist Women's Central Committee (WWCC), electing Huda Sha'rawi as its president (Badran 1988). Notwithstanding the WWCC's ties to the "patriarchal Wafd," commentators are quick to point out that the WWCC functioned as a space to challenge patriarchal politics and men's domination over policies (Badran 1988; Baron 2005; Russell 2004). For instance, women publicly criticized the male Wafdist leaders for neglecting the WWCC views on the Wafd independence proposal, at the end of 1920. It is in this sense that the Egyptian feminist movement has feminized and democratized Egypt's political and public sphere. Beyond Egypt, the democratic effects of the women's movement in Middle Eastern societies have been elucidated in a number of important studies (see, for example, Hatem 2005; Libal 2008; Sadiqi and Ennaji 2006).

Huda Sha'rawi – the first Egyptian feminist and leader of the 1919 revolution – bitterly critiqued the hypocrisy of male nationalist leadership. She wrote: "[I]n moments of danger when women emerge by their side, men utter no protest. Yet women's great acts and endless sacrifices do not change men's views of women" (Sha'rawi 1987: 131). In an attempt to nudge women away from the public and political sphere, key national figures began to openly critique women's independent behavior and insistence on their citizenship rights (Badran 1988; Baron 2005; Sha'rawi 1987).

These attempts proved to be counterproductive as they created deeper resentment among nationalist women who again openly criticized their male counterparts in 1922 over the terms of independence. The terms of independence did not address Egypt's relation to Sudan and failed to oust the British troops from Egypt. Badran (1988: 28) narrates how Huda Sha'rawi telegraphed her disapproval to Saad Zaghloul in an open letter to the newspaper *Al-Akhbar* and demanded that he step down. She, herself, resigned as president of the WWCC, and with a number of other feminist nationalists established the Egyptian Feminist Union, on the fourth anniversary of the first women's public demonstration, in March 16, 1923 (Badran 1988: 28–29).

Women's expectations were crushed and their demands were further ignored with the denial of women's suffrage. This was a big affront to female nationalists who prided themselves on their contributions to the national cause and their access to power. In fact, many commentators view this development as a turning point for feminist nationalists, who felt betrayed after their participation in the nationalist struggle (Ahmed 1992; Badran 1988; Baron 2005; El Saadawi 1997, Sha'rawi 1987). As such, female leaders took their case to the international arena. The Egyptian Feminist Union sent a delegation comprising Huda Sha'rawi, Nabawiyya Musa, and Saiza Nabarawi to a meeting of the International Woman Suffrage Alliance (IWSA) in Rome, in May 1923 (Badran 1988). The nationalist feminists' move to the international arena mimicked that of the male Wafdist leaders' independence strategy. Like the male leaders of the Wafd in 1919, the feminists reached for the Western audience and solidarity (Badran 1988; Baron 2005).

On their return from the IWSA meeting, Huda Sha'rawi and Saiza Nabarawi removed their veils as they stepped into a large crowd of cheering women (Badran 1988). Several feminists place great emphasis on the significance of this move, considering it as demarking "the end of the hareem system – the end of the seclusion of women and the segregation of the sexes – and the beginning of a public, open, organized feminist movement in Egypt" (Badran 1988: 29; see also Hijab 1988: 51; Lanfranchi and King 2012; Sha'rawi 1987; Zuhur 1992: 41). Badran (1988) and Baron (2005) extend this argument, asserting that the significance of this move lay in giving a real face to female leadership, after their voices were first heard in press a half-century before.

Following the victory of the Wafd and Saad Zaghloul, feminist activists were further excluded from the political landscape. They were not allowed to attend the opening ceremony of the new parliament in 1924, a welcome being extended to the wives of ministers and high officials only. In Badran's words, it was "a truncated celebration – a celebration of patriarchal reassertion rather than national triumph" (1988: 29). As a response, the WWCC and the Egyptian Feminist Union (EFU) joined forces and struck against the opening of parliament, proclaiming thirty-two nationalist and feminist demands, including, among other demands, the right to vote (Badran 1988).

Women's experience in the uprising as such contributed to establishing a strong women's movement and a well-developed discourse on women's rights. Their activism, as they confronted the new regime, had a number of important implications. It contributed to politicizing women, connecting them to transnational feminist networks and expanding their activism. For example, Saba Mahmood (2005:153) explains that Zaynab Al-Ghazali was able to acclaim a position of leadership in the Muslim Brotherhood during the 1950s and the 1960s because of her considerable exposure to a well-developed discourse of women's rights that dates back to the turn of the twentieth century. A discourse, Mahmood stresses, "was crucial to her formation as an activist"(2005: 153). Women's participation, notwithstanding the gendered outcomes of the 1919 uprising, had thus carved out new political and public roles for women.

Women and the 1952 Free Officers' Revolution

Unlike the literature on the 1919 national movement, studies on the 1952 Free Officers' revolution dedicate scant space to women's experiences at the time of it. This is because the Free Officers' revolution had been a male business; it was planned and carried out by the free officers in Egypt's army (Sedra 2011). Women's experiences after the revolution, specifically, the centrality of women in the regime's nationalist discourse, have been discussed, however, in great detail. The literature draws attention to how the new regime co-opted women's rights into its nationalist program and suppressed independent feminist movements (see Abdel Halem 2012; Bier 2005, 2011; Hatem 1994, 2000, 2005; Muhamed 1979; Nelson 1996). Most importantly, recent expansions in the literature examine the ways in which state feminism has constructed the "working women" figure as an expression of the regime's modernization project (Bier 2005, 2011; Hatem 1992, 1994; Keddie and Baron 1991; Meriwether and Tucker 1999; Russell 2004). This, in my view, is crucial for understanding the status of women in modern Egypt, since the politics of state-sponsored feminism envisaged by the former Egyptian president Gamal Abdel Nasser in the 1950s and 1960s remained the dominant discourse for women's rights under his predecessors. These policies of state feminism had weakened the women's movement in Egypt and distanced it from its grassroots bases.

The Premises of State-Sponsored Feminism

In the early years of Nasser's rule, the discourse of women's rights was absent from the nationalist agenda. The early nationalist literature, such as Nasser's book *The Philosophy of the Revolution* (1954) does not include any mention of women and their rights. Laura Bier (2011) notes the absence of the wives of prominent Free Officers from public occasions and views this as mirroring the absence of women from the regime's early agenda. For instance, it was not until 1956 that Nasser's wife, Tahia Kazem, made an official public appearance welcoming Tito, the former leader of Yugoslavia and his wife. This, several observers note, stands in stark contrast to the visibility of female members of the royal family, who were well-known public figures in their own right (Baron 1997; Bier 2011; Russell 2004).

The regime's attitude toward gender issues, however, soon shifted, as Gamal Abdel Nasser moved to co-opting women's rights in his nationalist discourse (Abdel Haleem 2012). This co-optation took the form of state-sponsored feminism. Women in Egypt, as in many Middle Eastern and African societies, have historically functioned as the contours of nationalist thoughts and the modernization project (Badran 1988; Baron 2005; Sayigh 2007; Sonbol 2005; Terman 2010). Under the Nasserist modernization project, the state adopted a top-down approach and implemented legal reforms to advance gender equality. The most iconographic expressions of the regime's gender politics are the 1956 Constitution, the 1961 Charter for National Action, and the legislative and administrative decisions enacted by the regime to mobilize women to join the workforce.

While the regime had portrayed these legislatures as a leap for women's rights, these legal steps were scrutinized in a number of feminist studies (Abu-Lughod 1998; Al-Maaitah et al. 2011; Bier 2011; Hatem 1994, 2000; Russell 2004). Laura Bier, in her recent book *Revolutionary Womanhood* (2011), eloquently captures the essence of these discussions and explains the contradictory nature of state-sponsored feminism. She rightly explains that "the concept of rights granted to the universal (purportedly un-gendered) citizens coexisted with gender-specific obligations that women (and men) were expected to meet" (Bier 2011: 34). That is to say that the gender-neutral rights held by women as citizens coexisted with new, gender-specific responsibilities. For instance, Article 19 in the constitution states that the state will facilitate the reconciliation of women's contribution to the workforce and her obligation within the family (Jumhurīat Miṣr 1956: 11).

Furthermore, although the constitution recognized universal suffrage, the procedural law established gender-specific procedures for the registration of voters. Men were automatically registered as voters; in contrast, women had to petition the state to include them in the list of registered voters (Muhammad 1979: 73). As such, while the revolution represented a push for women's rights generally, the revolutionary regime prioritized women's social rights as mothers while hindering their political rights as citizens (Hatem 1994, 2000; Muhamed 1979). In this sense, women's rights ostensibly incorporated the right to education and public participation, and excluded the right to meaningful political and economic participation.[6]

Consistent with the state's feminist discourse is the regime's successful move to suppress independent feminist initiatives. The Free Officers, Mervat Hatem explains, associated women's rights with the aristocratic activities of the Feminist Union and the social agendas of the *ancien régime*, which in turn legitimated and necessitated the former's suppression (2000: 46). A common strategy was the incarceration of prominent women's right advocates, such as Doria Shafik – the head of Ittihad Bint Al-Nil [the Daughters of the Nile Union] – and Inji Aflatun in the 1950s. The conflict was not merely over the agenda of women's rights or to curb potential challengers and immanent threats. In 1957, Doria Shafik was put under house arrest after she carried out a hunger strike against Abdel Nasser. Her name was barred from all Egyptian texts and most of her original documents were destroyed. The issue thus is one of control and consolidation; the aim is to consolidate the regime by establishing full control over social groups and weakening their ability to organize.

While most scholars claim that the 1952 revolution marked the end of independent feminism in Egypt, others like Mervat Hatem (2000) and Laura Bier (2011) stress that the politics of gender did not disappear. They have noted the emergence of a younger generation of professionals and intellectuals who gained access to the newly established institutions. Amina Al-Sayed, Bier (2011) highlights, despite

---

[6] This is not unique to Egypt; several scholars observed the same policies and inconsistencies in the context of Iran (see Terman 2010; Yeganeh 1993).

being part of the system and working within it, did not endorse state polices passively. In fact, she played an active role in contesting the gendered parameters of Nasser's nationalist project.

Women as the Contour of the Nationalist Project

The developments introduced by Nasser'sregime were significant, as they changed the landscape of women's rights in Egypt. Given their significance, feminist scholars have turned to interrogate the model of state-sponsored feminism with special focus to its discursive and ideological functions (Abu-Lughod 1998; Ahmed 1992; Bier 2011; Hatem 1994; Hijab 1988; Keddie and Baron 1991; Nelson 1991; Podeh and Winckler 2004). The figure of *al-mar'a al-'amela* [the working woman] was central in the regime's agenda and official discourse. Through a series of legislations and administrative decisions, the state redefined the category of the working women to encourage their participation in the workforce. The regime constructed the figure as a signifier of gender equality and as evidence of modernity; such claims were refuted by several feminists. In their studies, scholars have interrogated the figure of the working woman by examining its official discourse and policy outcomes. Their analysis emphasized the inconsistency and inadequacy of the approach for altering gender inequalities (Abu-Lughod 1998; Bier 2011; Hatem 1994; Keddie and Baron 1991; Russell 2004).

Despite the state rhetoric and legal commitment to facilitate women's economic participation, the overall number of women in the labor force, studies confirm, remained relatively low (Bier 2011; Hatem 1992, 1994; Muhammad 1979). In explaining the discrepancy between the policies and their gender outcome, scholars have examined the ideological function underpinning the policies. According to them, the figure of the working woman was not a genuine effort by the regime to alter gender inequalities; rather, it was important in constructing the image of a progressive postcolonial society and a modern socialist public sphere (Abu-Lughod 1998; Bier 2011; Hatem 1992, 1994; Russell 2004). The outcomes of the socialist development, specially the participation of unveiled and active women in the public sector, were presented as symbols of the regime's success in transforming Egypt into a modern socialist nation. The mythical representation of women as the nation, Bier (2011: 16) writes, was replaced by the representation of women as symbols of the state and the success of state-driven modernization.

Some scholars go as far as arguing that the model of state-sponsored feminism was a way to effectively govern women and reproduce gender hierarchies. Timothy Mitchell (2000: 136) argues that the formation of an educated Egyptian motherhood was part of the process whereby the "inaccessible" and "invisible" world of women and family would be rendered visible and thus governable by the institutions and modern powers of the state. The backdrop of this critique is the modest outcomes of gender policies. They did not deliver real cultural changes and/or substantial gender equalities. Hatem (1994) explains that the inadequacy of these developments was due to the persistence of gender inequalities in the private realm of the family. The private realm of the family was not the focus, as the promotion of women's rights was secondary to the consolidation of the regime.

Campaigns encouraging women's economic participation were accompanied with extensive discussions over how to balance women's duties at work and at home (Abu-Lughod 1998, 2005; Bier 2011; Hoodfar 1997). Exempted from these discussions, I notice, is men's role. These discussions were directed to women only, rarely including men; in fact, there were no parallel discussions over men's responsibility to perform domestic labor, or balance work and family commitments. Hoodfar (1997: 106–107) views Nasser's encouragement of women's entry into the labor market as the first "official devaluation" of women's domestic labor. The emphasis on women's responsibility to carry out domestic labor and the exemption of men from these duties contributed to maintaining gender hierarchies and safeguarding men's privileged position in Egyptian society.

Concerns over men losing their privileged position were captured in several media productions of this era (see Bier 2011). The complicated and multiple tensions between women's duty to participate outside of the home and their continued centrality inside the home were reflected in the 1960s movies and literature (Bier 2011). This is important given the significance of the Egyptian movie industry, which has a long tradition and a dominant position within the Arab world. Once the Egyptian cinema became nationalized by the Nasser regime, it was perceived as a threat by colonial powers in the neighboring Arab countries. For example, the French colonial power in the Maghreb formed a "special department" on African problems that was "responsible for setting up a production centre in Morocco whose official mission was to oppose the influence of Egyptian cinema" (Salmane, Hartog, and Wilson 1976, quoted in Schochat 1983: 22). As Ella Schochat (1983), the media scholar explains, the Egyptian movie industry was influential in propagating culture and national ideas in society. Given its significance for nation-building in Egypt, the nationalization of the industry by the Nasserist regime meant that "the state had nearly complete control over the different branches of the film industry, which previously had been in private hands" (Schochat 1983: 26).

Anxieties about women's work and independence found expression in popular movies such as *Lel Regal Fakat* [For Men Only] (1964)[7] and *Miraty Modeer 'am* [My Wife Is a General Director] (1966),[8] to name a few. The producers highlighted some of the common concerns in society, such as the risk of men losing their authority as husband and the potential displays of female sexuality in the workplace (Bier 2011). The movies, however, only played on these anxieties without providing a solution to these tensions.[9]

Bier (2011) reveals how such concerns were voiced by male writers and feminist advocates of women's work alike. In her occasional column for *Hawwa'*, Latifa al-Zayyat (1923–1996), an active writer and commentator on gender issues, advised women to leave their femininity at home before descending into the street (Bier 2011). Salama Musa – the secular women's right advocate – adopts a stance similar to that of al-Zayyat. In his book *Al-Mar'a Lyst Lu'bat al-Rajul* [Woman Is Not the Plaything of Man] (Musa 1956: 72–78), Musa lists numerous objects that he felt had no place in the office, such as cologne, chic dresses, high heels, laughing and raised voices. Introducing a class perspective,

---

[7] The movie tells the story of two young female graduates who disguise themselves as men in order to work as oil engineers at an oil refinery – strictly a male domain – in the desert.

[8] The movie reveals the troubles associated with women in senior positions, and the ways in which this creates tensions, especially when their husbands work under them.

[9] It is sad to see the same theme produced in recent movies like *Taymur and Shafiqa* [Taymor we Shafika]. In this 2007 movie, Shafiiqa, a young ambitious Egyptian woman, has to quit her job as minster of environmental affairs to marry Taymur, a domineering male figure, who manipulates the relationship without any discussions or compromises. I think the movie reflects continuities in the cultural and social devaluation of women's work in Egyptian society. It is, arguably, a case in point that the policies of state feminism did not completely alter societial views toward women's rights and gender equality.

he shamed women who can afford these goods and accused them of being part of the corrupt Egyptian bourgeoisie.

In sum, the complicated and multiple tensions that exist between women's duty to participate outside of the home and their continued centrality in national projects were the subject of several nationalist and feminist studies. Analyzing the popular discourse that ran parallel to the policies of state-sponsored feminism, scholars have concluded that the regime did not work toward eradicating gender equalities; its approach aimed to modernize gender relations in the public realm in order to construct the image of a modern society. This aim was critical in mapping out the contours of a socialist, postcolonial public sphere (Bier 2011; Podeh and Winckler 2004; Russell 2004). Women were key to constructing the image of a modern and nationalist society because of their important role as the bearers of identity and cultural norms. Across history, women in the Middle East and beyond were used to demarcate cultural differences and reflect modernity.

Following the Nasserist regime, subsequent regimes adopted the same strategy as a way to polish their international image and strengthen their control over civil society and independent women's movements. The implication of this full control of the agenda of women's rights in conjunction with the cosmetic changes in gender policies and legislation distanced the discourse of women's rights from its grassroots bases and moved it toward the regime in power. These bio-politics of control remained in place under successive regimes; under Sadat's regime as well as that of his predecessor Mubarak. The 1980s, the historian Lucia Sorbera (2013) writes, were years when a new generation of women, highly educated and with international networks, appeared on the scene. This generation of feminists was crushed between two powers: the secular forces represented by the regime and the religious forces represented by the Islamist movement (Sholkamy 2012a; Sorbera 2013). On one side, the regime stopped every independent initiative and appropriated gender issues under its name (Sholkamy 2012a). On the other side, the Islamist opposition has mobilized the lower classes, to which feminism and gender issues are alien in terms of class and culture (Meriwether and Tucker 1999; Nelson 1991; Sholkamy 2012a; Sorbera 2013; Zuhur 1992). In this context, Sorbera (2013) argues, in line with earlier research, that feminism was perceived by the majority of the population as an elitist movement that was incapable of producing grassroots activities.

Conclusion

The analysis reveals the tensions involved in documenting, remembering, and commemorating women's engagement in political struggles. Scholars have highlighted the ways in which men, early in revolutions, tend to encourage, in varying degrees, women's nationalist activism and to vocally support women's rights and their struggle for liberation and equal citizenship rights. However, with the end of political struggles, the figure of the strong, politically active woman is resented. The case-study-based scholarship highlights that male nationalists accept female nationalists' activism where it suits them and under duress. However, as male nationalists came to power, they ignored women's views, deprived women of their citizenship rights, and pushed female activists from the public sphere.

The tension over women's engagement in political struggles is evident as well in the ways in which their heroism is praised and constructed in the collective memory and national commemoration. In this regard, women's political culture has often been excluded from the collective memory or remembered only selectively at key moments, when it served some symbolic purpose. Woman as a symbol, Baron (2005: 117) argues, is thought more important than woman as historical actor. Memory of women's activism tends to pale in comparison to men's and is often constructed using familial and domestic concepts. For instance, the motherist framing has dominated scholarly and public accounts of women's participation. Its relevance is due to its feminine character that does not disturb traditional gender hierarchies (Badran 1988; Baron 1997, 2005; Hatem 1994; Pollard 2005).

Underpinning this argument is the assumption that political and gendered national forces contribute to constructing our collective memory of women's engagement in political struggles. This construction is deliberate, as it services certain overt and covert interests. Carol Marvin and David W. Ingle, in their book *Blood Sacrifice and the Nation: Totem Rituals and the American Flag* (1999: 2–5), explain that the dynamic that embeds heroes and legends in a population's collective memory sheds at least as much light on the commemorators' intentions and needs as on the essence of those commemorated. As national heroines come to represent and reflect the traits of the model female citizen, female nationalists and heroines were constructed in a way that exhibits not only heroic traits and actions but traditional gender roles as well.

In the same way, women's experience following the 1952 Free Officers' revolution crystallizes the tension between nationalist and women's rights discourses. The regime's claims to liberate women brought important rights, but these rights were contingent upon gender-specific obligations that women were expected to meet as proper national subjects and citizens (Bier 2011: 6; Hatem 2000; Nelson 1996). In her study of the role of women in the nation-state, Nira Yuval-Davis (1993) reminds us that the state constructs the citizenship of men and women in terms of their national tasks. The major national task for women in almost all national states is closely related to their biological role in reproduction rather than their ideological role (Yuval-Davis 1993).

In line with this framing, the nationalist discourse in Egypt granted women maternalist citizenship rights[10] while curtailing their political rights. Emancipation of women included rights to education and public participation, but not meaningful political and economic participation. In many ways this reflected the continued belief that the primary role of women was in the family as mothers. So while the revolutions claimed the status of a new women's rights order, the revolutions in Egypt did not completely "modernize" gender relations or instill equality in the private and public domains.

Despite this seemingly disappointing relation between women and political struggles, scholars are quick to point out the liberating consequences of these struggles on women's activism. For instance, scholars cite the growth of feminist movements in Egypt after the 1919 revolution. Notwithstanding the nationalist regime's hostile attitude toward women's rights, women's participation in the nationalist struggle provided a strong base of experienced activists, as well as established national and international networks and collaborations. Meanwhile, the 1952 Free Officers' revolution brought state feminism, which resulted in co-opting the women's movement and suppressing independent feminist organizations. Women's agency, however, can still be

---

[10] The reference here is for the rights extended to women on the basis of their role as wives and mothers. For instance, the Egyptian state granted women maternity leave to guarantee their economic equality with men. However, the same effort is not exerted to facilitate their political participation and hence promote gender equality in the political realm.

located within the state feminist arrangements and its gendered agenda (Bier 2011; Mahmood 2005; Podeh and Winckler 2004). As the prominent feminist scholar Judith Butler attests, the possibility of agency can be located within the structures of power (1990: 15). In the case of Egypt, the increased numbers of female professionals brought progressive changes for women and opened up venues for their public participation.

2 | Activism and Exception: Media and the Framing of Women's Engagement in the 2011 Egyptian Uprising*

In her seminal work *The Symbolic Annihilation of Women by the Mass Media,* Gaye Tuchman (1978) attributes the absence and misrepresentation of women in media to a form of "symbolic annihilation." Media content, Tuchman and several scholars contend, reflects and reinforces power hierarchies including gender-based and/or racial-based schisms (Armstrong and Nelson 2005; Busby 1975; Friedan 1965; Friedman 1977; Janus 1977; Ross 2011; Tuchman, Daniels, and Benét 1978). In this chapter I survey the representation of women in media coverage of the 2011 uprising as an exemplar of what Gramsci called "the trenches and fortification" of existing order (Gramsci 1971 cited in Tarrow 2012: 2). This is particularly important given the role of media in constructing the national memory. This survey reveals the continuity in the framing of women's activism in Egypt's political struggles. In Chapter 1, I focused on the historical framing of women's engagement in Egypt's political struggles, specifically in the 1919 nationalist revolution and the 1952 Free Officers' revolution. In this chapter, I analyze women's experiences in the present, with an eye on the past. My objective is to identify continuities and ruptures in the framing of women's activism in Egypt.

Two central questions animate this chapter. First, in comparison to men, how did the media frame women's engagement in the uprising of 2011? And second, did the image of female participants challenge or perpetuate traditional stereotypes? The chapter draws upon data from 174 news stories published on the websites of two widely circulated national newspapers – *Al-Ahram* and *Al-Wafd* – and 224 news stories

---

* An abridged version of this chapter was published under the title "Activism and Exception in Covering Egypt's Uprising: A Critical Reading of the New York Times Representation of Female Protestors," *Sociology of Islam* (2014b): 310–327.

published on the website of the *New York Times* during the 2011 Egyptian uprising.

According to the Oxford Business Group report (2011), *Al-Ahram* had a daily circulation of 1 million, with a substantial part sold abroad, mainly in Arab states. *Al-Ahram* also has subscribers in most of the world's countries and is often available in the newspaper selections in libraries worldwide. The newspaper provides wide coverage of world affairs, but its coverage of Egyptian affairs is closely aligned to the official discourse and the government's views. It has often been accused of being heavily influenced and censored by the Egyptian government. *Al-Wafd*, meanwhile, is the oldest opposition journal in Egypt and is one of the highest circulated papers among those dailies owned by a political party in the country (Allam 2014). During the Egyptian revolution in 2011, Osama Heikal was the editor-in-chief of *Al-Wafd*; Heikal was Egypt's information minister from July to November 2011.

The stories offer a detailed coverage of the popular uprising between January 25 and February 12, 2011. I carried out a textual analysis of news and commentaries, and read the text through a feminist lens, utilizing discourse analysis. Texts, I maintain, are forms of social actions; their shapes and forms are not random or arbitrary but, rather, determined by social structures and prevalent discourses (Foucault 1980; Van Dijk 1991, 1993, 1997). Media coverage as such disseminates dominant ways of seeing and interpreting events while simultaneously foreclosing other accounts (Foucault 1972, 1980; Van Dijk 1991, 1997).

This analytical venture is significant as it offers a glimpse into the context and the environment within which women carried out their activism. The survey also draws attention to how women's activism is predominately portrayed in broader society and presented to the international audience. While for the purpose of this book, the representation of women by the national media is more important to ascertain the general trends and dominant views in Egypt regarding women's activism, I surveyed the image of women in the *New York Times* (*NYT*), an internationally renowned newspaper as well. The *NYT* is a widely read newspaper with an international scope. It is largely considered as the paper of record used by historians and analysts in their studies and research. The newspaper is also known for its extensive coverage and interest in Middle Eastern affairs. My selection of the newspaper is not based on its political stance and/or leaning; the selection is solely based on its wide dissemination and broad readership. The image of female protestors presented in the newspaper is thus influential in shaping the popular discourse and perception of Middle Eastern women, as it is widely circulated to audience and readers in Western societies. Surveying the presentation of female protestors in a Western newspaper is significant as well, given the importance of the international dimension in the 2011 uprising. Not only did the uprising garner extensive international coverage and interest, but protestors were also keen to direct their messages to the national and international audience (see Hamdy and Gomaa 2012; Matar 2012). I do acknowledge that the assumptions and the functions underpinning the image of women are different in the two media spheres, and in this chapter I treat them as such. I utilize the national and Western coverage to delineate the broader local context and international nexus of women's activism.

My objective is not teasing out convergence and divergence between the national and Western coverage. This, in my view, would risk reducing the many complexities surrounding the representation of women in these different spheres. I also do not treat the coverage as a source for identifying women's collective action frame. Instead, media coverage is utilized in this chapter to shed some light on the dominant context within which women carried out their activism and framed their experience. As such, the national coverage will be treated separately from the Western one. I will also highlight their underpinning assumptions and the dominant motifs that marked the image of women in them.

During my interviews with female protestors, they often critiqued the media framing and representation of their engagements. Participants often felt that the media did not capture their experiences in their entirety. The theme of media representation, or more astutely, the media misrepresentation, came out as well during our discussion of the status and the perception of the women's movement at large in Egypt. The chapter surveys some of the images of female participants in some national and international newspapers and juxtaposes them with the interviewees' statements and how they perceived their engagement and participation.

The analysis presented contributes to the overall aim of the book. The overarching objective of this chapter is to deconstruct some of the hegemonic discourses and frames surrounding women's engagement in the 2011 Egyptian uprising. The critical reading presented in the chapter exposes and resists gendered frames applied in documenting the experience of women in social movements. By offering a media survey of the representation of female participants, I contribute to highlighting the power structures and configurations that female participants have to work within.

My point is to provoke critical attention to some of the dominant frames that women negated in framing their experience, and to reveal some of the ways in which covert gender stereotypes are embedded in the media representation of women's activism in political struggles. A focus on the image of women in the coverage of the uprising serves these objectives and extends the feminist insight to new cases, namely the Egyptian uprising. This analytical exercise is also significant given the implications of media on the social schisms in society and its centrality in demarcating cultural difference as well. In this regard, the image of women that I elaborate corresponds to Egypt's social context and the representational history of women in Western media. This is not to be understood as an attempt to evaluate the papers' coverage, or to gauge their objectivity. Such analysis would require a comparative and/or longitudinal study, which I do not claim to undertake in this study.

What this chapter does offer, though, is a close examination of the media projection of women's contribution at a key political juncture in Egypt's modern history. Media content, Annabelle Sreberny and Karen Ross (1996) in line with much early research on media effects hold, "frame[s] our understanding of public life, set[s] the agenda of policy issues and influence[s] the political process" (103). This framing, Robert Entman (1993) notes, essentially involves selection and salience. Communicators, he explains, make conscious or unconscious framing judgments by selecting some aspects of a perceived reality and making them more salient in a communicated text. An analysis of media framing of women's activism, as such, illuminates the ways in which gender stereotypes are embedded within and make themselves manifest in text.

Women's Visibility and Representation in National Newspapers

Women in Middle Eastern societies, as studies in the subfield of gender and political communication document, are often portrayed in passive roles and secondary to men (Abd al-Majīd 2007; Allam 2004; Sakr 2004, 2007; Sreberny-Mohammadi 1993). The gendered representation of women, however, appears less prevalent in the media coverage of national struggles. It is in times of political struggle that women tend to become more active in the public sphere, traditionally occupied by men (Al-Malki, Kaufer, and Ishizaki 2012; Giacaman and Johnson 1989; Kaufer and Al-Malki 2009; Skalli 2006, 2011).

During the 2011 uprising, female participants often felt that the media played a central role in producing stereotypes and misrepresentations of their engagement in the struggle. The image presented, as several of my interviewees forcefully described, did not capture how they viewed their engagement and participation.[1] Participants felt that this misrepresentation and underrepresentation chipped away at their image as agent-ic strong women demanding reform and change for themselves and their country.[2] The object of their frustration was the mute image of the female protestor, where she is present in images, her voice absent from the discussion and from the actual narrations and coverage.[3] Their frustration was further intensified in the period after the uprising as talk shows and printed coverage focused on a number of key female figures and ignored the rank and file of the movement.[4] Even when these female activists were present in the coverage or invited to share their views, they were granted limited space compared to their male counterparts.[5] In my survey of the media representation of female activists, these themes, among others, did come out as well.

Women's engagement in the uprising was highlighted and acknowledged to a varying degree in the news stories; women were mentioned in 59 percent of *Al-Wafd* coverage compared to 29 percent of *Al-Ahram* coverage. On the whole though, *Al-Wafd* covered the uprising more extensively than did *Al-Ahram*, making up 131 stories of the

[1] Interviewees 7, 9. Author's interview, Cairo, Egypt, July 2012.
[2] Ibid.
[3] Ibid.
[4] Interviewee 9.
[5] Interviewees 7, 9.

sample. This is not surprising, given *Al-Ahram*'s close affiliation to the regime; in fact, the newspaper was one of the tools used by the former regime to belittle the intensity of demonstrations.

Women, however, were less visible as sources of information compared to men, and in 78 percent of the cases where women were quoted, the articles were written or co-written by a female author.[6] Given the history of women's under- and misrepresentation in the Egyptian media, these findings suggest the growth of media interest in including women in their coverage at the time of the uprising. In its 2010 media report, the Global Media Monitoring Project (GMMP 2010) found that only 27 percent of media content in Egypt centered on women, and 61 percent of this content reinforced gender stereotypes.[7] The GMMP report also noted that women had rarely functioned as experts in news stories in contrast to men who dominated the "expert" categories.

Deploying a critical cultural approach, several scholars have elaborated on how these tendencies contribute to framing women as passive in overt and subtle ways (Al-Malki, Kaufer, and Ishizaki 2012: 243). Analyzing gender and racial stereotypes in media, Evelyn Alsultany (2012) asserts the importance of examining the ideologies which underlie images and story lines. According to Alsultany (2012: 14), interrogating an image in relation to its narrative context "reveals how it participates in a larger field of meaning." In the next section, I analyze the image of women not merely the visibility of women in the coverage. I am not interested in measuring shifts or changes; rather, I find the presence of gender stereotypes intriguing given the active

---

[6] According to the 2010 Global Media Monitoring Project report (GMMP 2010), this trend has persisted in Egypt over the past ten years. In fact, the same tendency, scholars observed, can be ascertained in Western media as well. Studies have shown that female editors use women as their sources more frequently than their male colleagues (Tuchman et al. 1978; Zoch and Turk 1998). Naomi Sakr (2004: 8), an expert in media studies of the Middle East, observes that women's visibility and audibility improves in media content that is produced by women even when female producers are not primarily advocating a feminist agenda.

[7] The underrepresentation of poor rural women, compared to upper-class urban women, has been emphasized in several studies as well (Abu-Lughod 2005, 2014; Allam 2004; Qāsim and Dasūqī 2000; Sakr 2004, 2007). While these observations are intriguing, their significance and interpretation are not examined in this study. A detailed coverage of these nuances requires a separate study in fact.

participation of women in the uprising and considering the significance of this key historical juncture in Egypt's modern history.

Visibility and Representation: Coloring the Coverage

Notwithstanding the visibility of women in news stories, this, I hold, is not a sufficient indicator for their overall presence and audibility. What really matters is the image and representation of women in the coverage. In this regard, I critique the occasional reference of Egyptian women among the disadvantaged and powerless in the uprising coverage (Al-Bady, Salah, and Sharaby 2011; O. Ibrahim 2011; Metawea 2011). Rosemarry Ridd, in "Powers of the Powerless" (1987), explains the grounds for locating women among the weak and powerless groups by the media at time of conflicts. Ridd (1987) observes that the Western media tends to interpret women's actions as reproductions of men's struggles or as temporarily meeting a serious crisis situation where even women – and often children – are needed. She suggests that such differential framing may be interpreted as carrying a message that, although conflicts are men's domain, women are allowed to actively support the struggle, and even join in, if the situation is deemed desperate enough.

Under such circumstances, deviations from traditional framing may take place, though some basic traditional portrayals are maintained (Lachover 2009; Ridd 1987). In the Egyptian uprising, female participants, for instance, were occasionally introduced by their relation to a male family member, as the "daughter of"; "wife of," and so forth (Al-Bady et al. 2011; Al-Mansi 2011; A. Ibrahim 2011; O. Ibrahim 2011; Saiid 2011). Although such representations may reflect cultural norms in Egyptian society, they arguably contribute to reinforcing women's image as dependent, particularly if the coverage places great and/or sole emphasis on them. For instance, female participants in one of *Al-Wafd*'s headlines were referenced as "The Judges and their Wives at the Day of Rage" (Al-Mansi 2011). This is significant given the role of headlines in shaping readers' views. Headlines are often the only item read by readers (Fallah 2005; Russell 2004; Van Dijk 1991). Headlines can bias readers' opinions, Van Dijk (1991) explicates, because they represent what – in the editor's view – is the most important information.

Emphasizing the woman's status as a judge's wife and overlooking her motivations, aspirations, and even profession shifts the central focus away from her. Research in social psychology suggests that such information plays an important function in impression formation and influences judgments (see Wyer and Carlston 1979; Wyer and Strull 1994). The literal and figurative presence of a male figure accompanying women in the uprising contributes to undermining the image of an independent active woman expressing political agency (Al-Bady et al. 2011; Al-Mansi 2011; A. Ibrahim 2011; O. Ibrahim 2011; Saiid 2011). This is further evinced by the absence of women from the expert category in the uprising coverage and the framing of their activism using motifs of femininity and nurturing.

Two common frames, I hold, were utilized by the media in portraying women's engagement in the uprising: the feminine frame and the maternal one. The feminine frame is characterized by a focus on the activists' appearance and status, while the maternal frame portrays women's engagement in the uprising as an extension of the traditional domestic duties associated with motherhood and the practice of caring. In the following section, the two frames will be discussed in greater detail. Despite the different connotations embedded in each frame, they often served the same function. Both framed women's participation as personal stories that "appeal to the heart and the eye" (Lachover 2009: 122).

The Feminine Frame

The uprising coverage occasionally emphasized the participation of women in demonstrations despite what is perceived as an added difficulty: the fact that they are women and often *beautiful* (Arafa 2011; A. Ibrahim 2011; Saiid 2011). Among the possible gender-specific risks that threaten females in Egypt's public space – let alone a crowded demonstration – is sexual harassment. In this regard, many news stories were fixated on reporting the absence of sexual harassment against female protestors during the 18-day uprising (Al-Mahdy 2011; Al-Shamy 2011a; Shabān 2011).

In one of the stories entitled "Yum Al-Ghaḍab Yakshf Aṣalat Al-Shaʿb Al-Maṣry" [The Day of Rage Unleashes the True Ethics of Egyptians], published by *Al-Wafd*, the male reporter estimated the number of protestors to be 45,000, 5,000 of whom, according to the reporter, were females and "despite being mostly *beautiful*, were not harassed" (Shabān 2011, emphasis added). The media's excessive attention to females' physical appearance is commonly critiqued in the subfield of gender and political communication. Maria Braden (1996) notes the way in which a woman's political activism is often trivialized by the media by focusing on her physical appearance. By insisting on such details, the reporter deliberately or subconsciously belittled the female protestors' engagement in the uprising. Furthermore, stressing that they "were not harassed," although they were "beautiful," frames the act of sexual harassment as an inevitable result of being female, beautiful, and present in a public space. It also implicitly, I hold, presents female protestors as possible victims.

Appropriating Einat Lachover's analysis, stories about female protestors were thus used "to add color" to the news and appeal to the heart and eyes (2009: 120–122). They occasionally served as a distraction and a break from the reports of clashes, government statements, and other pieces of hard news. For instance, one of *Al-Wafd* 's news stories concluded with a discussion over a women's Facebook group entitled "I Want to Marry a Tunisian Protestor" (Arafa 2011). The Facebook group, according to the news story, was designed as a nod to the bravery of Tunisian protestors who toppled the Tunisian regime. The group aimed at mobilizing Egyptian females and males to follow the footsteps of their Tunisian counterparts. The article cited the Egyptian men's critiques of this page and their advice to Egyptian women "to participate in the uprising for the sake of the nation and to focus on the larger national cause instead of merely seeking to get married" (Arafa 2011). The reporter made a passing reference to the men's version of the Facebook group; he described it, however, as a counter response to the women's group.

So while the article briefly highlighted women's engagement, the reporter's decision to extensively cover the women's group, and to detail men's critiques of it, is notable and problematic. Echoing Evring Goffman's (1974) original definition of framing, Robert Entman (1993) argues that communicators in media make conscious or unconscious framing judgments. Through the presence or absence of keywords, phrases, stereotypes, sources, and sentences, they provide thematically reinforcing clusters of interpretations and judgments (Entman 1993: 52). In this sense, while I do acknowledge the significance of including female protestors in the coverage, the approach is inadequate for capturing women's experience in full and deconstructing the legacy of traditional gender stereotypes.

The aforementioned framing, intentionally or unintentionally, contributed to assuaging the effect of women's activism in challenging these traditional misrepresentations. It implicitly framed some women's motivations as self-centred and shallow in comparison to men's claimed selfless and nationalistic sentiment. The coverage of their engagement in this particular article reinforces my earlier observation. That is, in several cases, the coverage of female activists and protestors in Egypt functioned in breaking the dry coverage of the uprising and in this particular incident provided comic relief at the expense of women's less acknowledged heroism.

Wedding stories at Tahrir Square were also an eye-catching and popular topic in media coverage of the uprising; however, they were reported from the perspective of the nationalist-groom (Al-Shamy 2011b; Eman and Nasef 2011; "Zawaj Jadid fi Al-Midan" [New Wedding Ceremonies at Al-Tahrir] 2011). The depiction of the groom in the media coverage of the Egyptian uprising carried great resemblance to Lachover's critique of the "soldier-bridegroom" frame (2009: 124); a frame evoked by the mass media in Israel to portray the wedding ceremonies amid the 1967 war. The uprising coverage, similarly, emphasized the husband's determination to carry on with the wedding plans despite the unrest, and without exception, his plan to continue protesting soon after the ceremony (Al-Shamy 2011b; Eman and Nasef 2011; "New Wedding Ceremonies at Al-Tahrir" [Zawaj Jadid fi Al-Midan] 2011). By contrast, the bride occupied the margins of the news stories and was rarely framed in an active role.

The Maternal Frame

An equally salient frame in the news stories is the maternal frame. The stories occasionally lauded the mother/wife contribution to the nation by raising sons, encouraging and mobilizing her male relatives, and carrying out traditional domestic duties associated with motherhood and the practice of caring (Al-Bady et al. 2011; Abdel Maksood 2011; Koraa, Farouk, and Ibrahim 2011; "Ibni fi Al-Midan" [My Son Is in the Square] 2011; "Bel Tawfir: Tudir Al-Mar'a Al Miṣrya Shw'un Baytaha" [With Prudence: Egyptian Women Can Manage the Family Budget] 2011). I do not view the above-mentioned roles of women as passive ones. Women's exercise of agency is not conditioned by the location of her activism. This practice, which I term the *spatial conditionality of agency*, occasionally reproduces the arbitrary public/private divide. In my view, mothers who chose to stay in their homes during the uprising looking after their young ones, as well as those who prepared food for the protestors, are not less agentic or nationalist than those who protested at the front rows.

What I am critical of, though, is the wailing-mother/wife frame that was occasionally invoked by media (Al-Bady et al. 2011; Abdel-Maksood 2011; Koraa et al. 2011). This frame was used to elaborate and characterize the motivation of some female protestors. In this regard, women's statements and personal experience were included more often than their opinion or expert commentary. They were occasionally quoted as victims and non-experts, while men were commonly portrayed as politicians and experts (Abdel-Maksood 2011; Al-Bady et al. 2011; Koraa et al. 2011). In so doing, the media depicted women's participation as personal, particular, and for a self-centered cause. Meanwhile, men's engagement was presented as universal and motivated by political, nationalist sentiments rather than personal ones. The image of women, as such, arguably functioned in attracting the attention of the audience and did not completely move beyond traditional stereotypes.

To conclude, my analysis of media contents in the two widely circulated national newspapers suggests that traditional motifs of passiveness coexisted alongside new ones of feminine agency in their coverage of women's participation. By evoking the myth of female passiveness and framing women's activism in relation to tropes associated with femininity, the coverage, I suggest, assuaged the effect of women's activism in deconstructing traditional gender stereotypes. In the following section, I turn to highlighting the dominant frames that marked the representation of women in the uprising coverage by a key Western newspaper, that is the *New York Times*.

Female Protestors in the *New York Times*: New Images and Old Stereotypes

Attention to the place of women in the colonial portrayal of Arab and Muslim societies has provoked prominent feminist and postcolonial studies; these studies have revealed the patriarchal gaze and the Orientalist premise of colonialism[8] (Said 1978; see also Alloula

---

[8] Several scholars have criticized Edward Said's analysis of Orientalism for not thoroughly probing the relationship between imperialism and gender (see, e.g., Abu-Lughod 2002; Miller 1990; Yegenoglu 1998). Notwithstanding

1987; Esposito 1998; Esposito and Mogahed 2007; Graham-Brown 1988; Vivian 1999). In *Algeria Unveiled*, Franz Fanon describes the French colonial project to unveil Algerian women as a project to control the colonialist horizons and destroy Algerian culture (1965: 42). Meyda Yegenoglu extends this critique in her foundational book, *Colonial Fantasies: Towards a Feminist Reading of Orientalism* (1998). She argues that images of sexuality in Orientalist discourses are not simply tropes in the representation of non-Western women but are, rather, crucial in demarcating cultural differences between Western and Middle Eastern societies.

After all, Orientalism is not just about representations or stereotypes, as postcolonial feminist Lila Abu-Lughod (2001: 105) reminds us. Rather, it is about how these representations are linked to the project of ongoing Western domination. According to this line of thinking, the fetishization of the burqa, in the media, foreign policy, and some feminist texts, contributed in projecting Afghani women as an "object of imperialist rescue" (e.g., Ahmed 2012; Jiwani 2005a, 2005b; Mohanty, Riley, and Minnie Bruce 2008; Saliba et al. 2002: 52; Shirazi 2003). It, thus, further justified the US war on terror in the aftermath of September 11 and beyond.

This critical line of feminist inquiry cannot be attributed solely to the influence of Said's Orientalism (Burke and Prochaska 2008). In explicating the genealogy of Orientalism, Gyan Paraksh (1995: 205) situates Said's work within a larger discursive shift in literary studies, history, and anthropology. The shift, he explains, was animated by poststructuralism, feminism, and neo-Marxism. An influential poststructuralist text in this regard has been Gayatri Chakravorty Spivak's essay "Can the Subaltern Speak?" (1988). Analyzing the colonialist "othering" of Indian women, Spivak has exposed the ways in which Western feminism, even as it takes an interest in women in the "Third World," can reproduce the axioms of imperialism through reinforcing stereotypical imperialist assumptions (Spivak 1985; see also Morris 2010; Young 2004).

such criticism, Said's Foucauldian theorization of Orientalism has inspired a considerable number of studies in the subfield of postcolonial feminism (see, e.g., Abu-Lughod 2002; Ahmed 1992; Amos and Parmar 1984; Lewis 1996; Mabro 1991; Saliba, Allen, and Howard 2002a; Hoodfar 1997; Mohanty 1984; Spivak 1988; Smeeta 2007; Tucker 1998).

A recent manifestation of this relation is evident in the ways in which the war on terror discourse was articulated and circulated. In securing moral justification for the military intervention in Afghanistan, Western governments have relied on the services of several liberal feminists and native informants/Orientalist spokespersons (Abu-Lughod 2002; Ahmed 2012; Dabashi 2006; Mohanty, Riley, and Bruce 2008; Posetti 2007). However, in the post-September 11 geopolitical context, these cultural politics have evolved displaying more complexity and ambiguity, especially when compared to the traditional dichotomy of "us versus them."

Western governments, critics maintain, have been able to sustain support for the politics of the war on terror beyond 9/11 through distancing themselves from the clash of civilization rhetoric and seemingly embracing a language of diversity and anti-essentialism (Allison 2013; Alsultany 2012, 2013; Bayoumi 2010; Fallah and Nagel 2005). While these representations often challenge stereotypes, several experts have exposed the ways in which they contribute to a form of "multicultural or post-race illusion" (Alsultany 2012: 21; see Allison 2013). A close analysis of these ostensibly positive representations reveals their Orientalist undertone. It explicates their function in solidifying a liberal and cosmopolitan image of the United States. In essence, they are thus by-products of latent Orientalism expressed in its manifest form.[9]

Threading these perspectives into my analysis of the coverage provides a useful tool for understanding the discursive construction of Egyptian women in the *NYT* reporting. To reiterate, I am not interested in measuring shifts or changes but instead utilize media stories to highlight some of the ways in which the broader audience framed their participation. These frameworks could not totally distance their discourse from the representational history of the "other" in the West and its tendency to dehumanize as well as demonize the "other."

---

[9] Said has distinguished latent Orientalism, which remains unchanging and unified, from its manifest expression in words, actions, and policy decisions. Manifest Orientalism, Said explains, changes across time and among writers; it is thus able to reflect variation and historical change (Allison 2013; Said 1978; Young 2004). Homi Bhabha, however, criticizes this typology. According to him, the typology may contribute to splitting the very object of Orientalist discourse as knowledge.

Furthermore, analyzing the Western media coverage is significant as participants emphasized during the interviews the important role of the international media and how they negotiated a very fine line and complex framing. In framing their claims, they were cognizant of the need to secure international support and to appeal to the Western audience. However, they were also aware of the need to situate and root their claims and movement within the local and national context to shield themselves from potential criticism and "accusations of foreign allegiances."[10] "You do not want to be seen by bystanders as an agent of any perceived Western agenda,"[11] one of my interviewees explained. She added, "[b]ut also you want to communicate your message to Western powers in a vocabulary that will resonate." The issue is thus how activists mitigate and reconcile the need to frame their demands in a vocabulary that resonates with different spheres of influence – local and international.

Many of my interviewees acknowledged the positive effect of media coverage in disseminating the message and demands of protestors. However, the very same participants often also criticized the coverage for "trying so hard to box the uprising and its demands within ready-made metaphors and Western ideals."[12] Female participants explained the complex and contradictory dynamics that influenced and shaped the ways in which they framed their engagement and role. They struggled to present themselves as nationalist agents but were also mindful not to appear as irrational populists. They recall how they carried out acts of resistance whenever and wherever possible and acted forcefully and independently, distancing themselves from being labeled feminists or agents of the West.

In the context of the Middle Eastern "other," Bessma Momani (2015) emphasizes the ways in which Western media coverage of the Middle East contributes to dehumanizing Middle Eastern society and people. She rightly points to the dominance of the image of the balaclava-clad radical Arab teen in Western media coverage of the region. Less emphasized in the coverage is the positive change among the Arab youth; images of educated young Arabs, and/or young female Arab entrepreneurs are often relegated in the coverage. Western audiences

---

[10] Interviewee 38. Author's interview, Cairo, Egypt, February 2014.
[11] Interviewee 4.
[12] Interviewee 33. Author's interview, Cairo, Egypt, February 2014.

exposed to this unbalanced coverage, Momani argues, lose sight of the actual human beings affected by conflict and focus on numbers, ideologies, and governments instead (Momani 2015).

This representation, critical Middle Eastern scholars emphasize, is purposeful (Said 1978; see also Alloula 1987; Esposito 1998; Esposito and Mogahed 2007; Graham-Brown 1988; Vivian 1999). Across history and in recent times, non-Western women were represented in ways that serve US foreign policy and interest in the region. My understanding of foreign policy reflects Katherine Allison's critiques of Orientalism/Occidentalism and recognizes that elite foreign and domestic policy practices are explicable in relation to the creation of state identity (Allison 2013: 667; Falah 2005; Hennebry and Momani 2013; Van Dijk 1991).

Locating the Subaltern

The image of the anguished, despairing woman in the coverage of conflicts in the Middle East, the cultural theorist Ghazi Falah notes, has become almost a "stylization" in mainstream Western media (Falah 2005: 307; Wilkins 1995). It was an image frequently present in the *NYT* coverage of the Egyptian uprising too, particularly in news stories reporting the spread of crimes and looting. Women were frequently quoted to reveal the distress caused by this state of lawlessness (e.g., *NYT*, January 31, 2011: A.1, A.6, A.7, and A.19). Men, on the contrary, were depicted protecting their neighborhoods and taking the matter into their own hands (e.g., *NYT*, January 29, 2011: A.1; January 30, 2011: A.1; January 31, 2011: A.6, A.7, A.8; February 1, 2011: A.27, February 3, 2011: A.27; February 4, 2011: A.1). This differential representation of women derives from and reinscribes the myth of female passiveness. The myth, according to feminist critics, has traditionally shaped Western media representation of women in conflict, and especially its coverage of contentious politics in the Middle East.

Building upon Rana Kabbani's postcolonial critique, I argue that the myth of female passiveness, or inertness, transposes from the gender codes of Western societies to their international outlook in foreign policy. In her classical text, *Imperial Fictions*, Kabbani (1986: 85) claims that gender stereotypes in Orientalism describe more accurately the West and its oppressive social codes. Kabbani's argument is relevant in understanding the representation of Western nationals who were visiting or residing in Egypt at the time of the uprising. Like their Egyptian counterparts, the women were frequently quoted as anguished, distressed, and "anxious to get out," as they found themselves in a "freaky" and "frightening" situation (*NYT*, January 31, 2011: A.7). The men accompanying them, however, were portrayed as calm, often taking up the responsibility of securing flight for their families.

By maintaining a certain prescribed notion of femininity – read passivity – in describing Western and non-Western female characters, the *NYT*, I suggest, remained faithful to its role as a "circuit of culture," utilizing the late cultural theorist Stuart Hall's (1997) terminology. Articulating his view on the role of media, Hall (1997) contends that in every society, the media function as a circuit of culture. Its representations, he explicates, reflect societal and cultural norms and instruct us on how to act with respect to our identities.

In a similar manner, Gaye Tuchman's research on gender stereotypes in media echoes Hall's theorization of its role. Tuchman (1978) has frequently criticized the media representation of women and exposed its role in producing social guidelines for gender and enforcing gender hierarchies in societies. In light of these and other similar critiques, the representation of Western and Arab women as inert can be viewed, in part, as reflecting Western norms of femininity; it is important in regulating the gendered and racial boundaries of acceptability and deviance (Al-Saji 2009; Ortega and Alcoff 2009). It thus conforms to Abu-Lughod's (2001) observation of the centrality of women in the long-standing cultural polices that link and span the Middle East and the West.

It is also important to note that the coverage has often featured positive portrayals, by highlighting the actions of Egyptian female protestors, Fayeqa Hussein, "who filled a Styrofoam container with rocks" (*NYT*, February 3, 2011: A.1); or Um Ibrahim Abdel-Moḥsin, "who had ferried rocks to the barricades for two days" (*NYT*, February 5, 2011: A.7). What remains missing, though, is the women's personal narrative and/or account. Spivak's connotation is useful in postulating the negative implications resulting from overlooking women's accounts – particularly those of ordinary poor ones, such as the aforementioned protestors. According to Spivak, the existence of records of the "subject-consciousness of women" is insufficient. It is important, she explains, that subaltern women are assigned a position of "enunciation" (1988: 129).

Analyzing examples of colonialist othering of Indian women, Spivak identifies the absence of women's accounts with the planned "epistemic violence" of the imperialist project (1988: 204).[13] The result is an aporia in knowledge – a blind-spot where understanding and knowledge is blocked (Spivak 1988: 289; see also Spivak 1985; Morris 2010). Underlying my attention to women's accounts is a concern over who controls the production of knowledge. This is significant as, in line with Spivak's argument, the narratives of subaltern women, who are often marginalized, offer a detailed picture rather than simplified rhetoric.

Chandra Talpade Mohanty (1984) reads intentionality in this symbolic absence of "Third World" women in the Western academic cycles and its feminist research; the studies, while making reference to women from developing societies, have often overlooked their voice. A similar pattern could be discerned in the uprising coverage. In a number of news stories, the image of the silent apolitical wife was juxtaposed with her politically active husband (e.g., *NYT*, February 1, 2011: A.1; February 8, 2011: A.27; February 11, 2011: A.27). Furthermore, the activists' wives were referenced only upon the imprisonment of their husbands and their accounts have been communicated to the media through a male family friend, or a fellow male activist (e.g., *NYT*, January 30, 2011: A.1; February 8, 2011: A.10). For instance, following the disappearance of Wael Ghonim – a key figure in the uprising – Ghonim's friend Habib Hadad communicated the message of Ghonim's wife to the media. This was not, I suspect, due to the difficult situation that his wife found herself in or to guarantee her security, since Hadad was quoted again following Ghonim's release describing how Ghonim's wife was "happy and emotional" (*NYT*, February 8, 2011: A.10). This pattern, assessed in accordance with Mohanty's insight, contributes to the construction of "Third World differences" (Mohanty 1984: 334). According to postcolonial theories, the difference between "us" and "them" is the binary construct at the core of what constitutes the West.

---

[13] The violence involves, Spivak explains, establishing the native as the self-consolidating other, and persists when, in postcolonial discourses, the subaltern is silenced by both colonial and indigenous patriarchal power (1988: 204).

Consequently, through reconstructing the "other," there is the possibility of reconstructing the "self" as well. That is, a complete refashioning of the image of the Arab and Muslim women in Western media will inevitably result in revising the image of the West. Appropriating this view on the coverage suggests that the myth of female victimhood and/or passiveness was in part sustained in order to preserve the historical self-image of the West as the savior of inert women in the Middle East. This is particularly relevant considering how the media and governments in Western societies and beyond were taken aback by the onset of the uprising, which they had not foreseen, and the expeditious unfolding of events. The media struggled in assessing the uprising and its prospects for bringing about change; that being so, it did not drastically revise its discourse and old frames in representing protestors from the MENA region.

The Construction of Exception and the Assuagement of Female Activism

While the *NYT* coverage often evoked traditional stereotypes in framing women's participation in the uprising, it frequently portrayed them as imbued with agency as well. On the face of it, such depiction might seem indicative of a disruption of Orientalist representations of gender in the Middle East. However, it often failed in moving completely beyond the hegemonic modes of essentialism, as reflected by the passive female in Middle Eastern societies.

Among the mechanisms frequently used in covering women's participation was the framing of protestors within what I term the *exceptional activist* figure. The figure denotes the *NYT* framing of female activists as exceptional in some way and thus not conforming to traditional depictions or following classical representations. Female activists were frequently constructed in the coverage as exceptional by highlighting their privileged socioeconomic status (e.g., *NYT*, January 30, 2011: A.1; February 9, 2011: A.14), Western roots (e.g., *NYT*, February 6, 2011: A.12; February 10, 2011: A.1), and/or Western lifestyle (e.g., *NYT*, February 3, 2011: A.27). The significance of the exceptional activist figure, I suggest, lies in its ability to assuage the effect of women's activism in challenging Orientalist tropes of female victimhood and passiveness in the Middle East.

For instance, by highlighting the dual Western–Egyptian citizenship of some activists, the reporters, intentionally or unintentionally, contributed to promoting a limited representation of women's activism. It suggests that they are more emancipated by their dual citizenship. While I acknowledge that the inclusion of these activists in the coverage reflects a positive development, the approach is inadequate for fully capturing women's experiences and for deconstructing the legacy of old misrepresentations.

A possible source of its limitations is the emphasis on the Western element in introducing a more complex representation of Egyptian women. At the extreme end of any critique, it can be denounced as an attempt to rearrange rather than reject the vocabulary of Western supremacy. Female protestors with a Western background (or who perhaps had lived in or had associations with Western societies) were directly quoted in the report, and the coverage detailed their experiences and included their views (e.g., *NYT*, February 6, 2011: A.12; February 10, 2011: A.1). Several women who did not display such affinities or associations were also quoted; however, the reporters were inconsistent in presenting their views.

My intention is not to criticize the reference to some activists' dual citizenship; rather, I wish to draw attention to the media's consistency in granting them an opportunity to articulate their views in contrast to their Egyptian counterparts. This does not necessarily mean that imperialist impulses underpinned the reporters' approach. In fact, their Western background was often emphasized in order to validate the women's criticism of US foreign policies.

My concern regarding this tendency is about its unintended consequence, such as indirectly reinforcing the centrality of the West. To justify glossing complexities in the name of gaining quick support for a just cause is, in my view, insufficient in eliminating old misconceptions. The approach may in fact risk privileging and celebrating Western elements over non-Western ones. These risks can be ascertained in the language and structure of argument in the following example.

In a news story discussing the prospects of democracy in Egypt, the reporter described one of his two female interviewees as "Sherine a university professor." The other woman was introduced as a friend of the reporter who enjoys "Western tastes that include an occasional glass of whiskey" (*NYT*, February 3, 2011: A.27). Highlighting her Western taste for alcohol rather than her occupation or name is an unsettling manifestation of Western universalism. While the two women had expressed their guarded optimism about the future of democracy in Egypt under a possible Muslim Brotherhood rule, their views were introduced differently in the coverage. The reporter, sympathetic to Sherine's view, supplemented her opinion with historical evidence and supporting arguments. In validating Sherine's view, he quoted his Westernized friend expressing a similar view to that of Sherine's. To reiterate, I do not necessarily read intentionality in the reporter's approach; rather, I advocate for a more nuanced and complex approach in representing and supporting non-orthodox views when expressed by non-Western women.

The denouncement of Western anxiety over Islamists gaining power and of US foreign policy in the Middle East, discussed in the aforementioned example, were often the subject of scrutiny in news stories as well (e.g.; *NYT*, February 3, 2011: A.27; February 5, 2011: A.1; February 6, 2011: WK.8, A.10; February 7, 2011: A.23). The ostensibly progressive representation of Islam and women was also evident in the positive depiction of veiled activists (e.g., *NYT*, January 30, 2011: A.1; February 1, 2011: A.1; February 3, 2011: A.1; February 6, 2011: WK.8; February 8, 2011: A.27). This reconciliation of the veil and agency in media and governmental discourses, Rosa Vasilaki (2011) argues, is located within a complex refashioning of the concept of agency. Subsequently, the representation of Muslim women has moved from the discursive framework of victimization to one of empowerment. The shift, Katherine Allison (2013) suggests, is not neutral. The emergence of what Allison terms "agential Muslim women" in the US discourse on terrorism has functioned in solidifying the US self-image. The image domestically "confirms liberal pluralism" and internationally "projects an American/universal cosmopolitanism" (2013: 669). Similar dynamics, I demonstrate, can be ascertained in the uprising coverage. The coverage recognized and celebrated the agency of veiled protestors.

In one of the news stories, the reporter saluted the courage of two veiled protestors as they stood "surrounded by thugs" looking "timid and frail" as the thugs "jostled and shouted at them" (*NYT*, February 3, 2011: A.27). The women explained that they participated in the demonstrations because they "just want what you have" (*NYT*, February 3, 2011: A.27). The "you" here is in reference to the American reporter. The inclusion of this quotation corresponds to Allison's argument that the successful recognition of the agential Muslim women is often constructed in contrast to the hostility of her society. This serves to confirm "the certainty of the US self" and "its claims to universality" (Alison 2013: 668–669).

The contradicting impulses in the representation of women can be understood in light of Evelyn Alsultany's (2012, 2013) argument on the "complex simple mode of representation." By highlighting the exceptionalism of Egyptian female activists and Western recognition of the agential Muslim women, the *NYT* coverage balanced negative images with positive ones. According to Alsultany, this mode of representation postulates a "new standard alternative to (and seems a great improvement on) the stock ethnic villains of the past" (2013: 162). Sayres Rudy (2007: 33) expands this even further arguing that the US-led war on terror depended upon the denunciation of racism and the adoption of a "progressive view of Islamism." This is because, Alsultany (2013) explains, the production and circulation of positive representations of the other have become more effective than an overt propaganda that demonizes the other, especially in the declaration of war and the passage of racist policies.

By attempting to distance itself from the clash of civilization rhetoric and essentialist views of Muslim and Arab women, the representations produced by the uprising coverage appeared, seemingly, complex. However, as postcolonial theory would confirm, it represents one form of how Orientalism in its manifest form is able to accommodate historical changes and incorporate variations. Furthermore, the coexistence of traditional motifs of passiveness and new ones of agency, from a postcolonial lens, corresponded to the US attempt to juggle its traditional interests and long-standing relations with a regional dictator and the apparent outbreak of democracy that they had long claimed to cherish (Byman 2012: 289; see also Dalacoura 2012; Williams and Popken 2012).

Conclusion

During my interviews with female participants, many criticized the media framing and representation of women's engagement in the uprising. Participants often felt that the media, both national and international, did not capture women's experiences in their entirety. In this chapter, I surveyed some of the images of female participants in selected national and Western newspapers. I juxtapose these images in the following chapters against my interviewees' statements and how they perceived themselves and their engagement and participation.

My analysis of two popular newspapers in Egypt suggests that traditional motifs of passiveness coexisted alongside new ones of feminine agency in their coverage of the uprising. By evoking the myth of female passiveness and framing women's activism within a feminine discourse, the coverage, I suggest, assuaged the effect of women's activism in challenging traditional gender stereotypes. While women's participation was acknowledged to varying degrees in the coverage, the picture became more complex as I analyzed the ways in which the media depicted the participants. For instance, female protestors in the coverage were occasionally accompanied by male relatives. This, I hold, portrayed women as dependent on men and in need of protection. The coverage paid excessive attention to the female activists' physical appearance as well, and in several cases belittled their motivations in subtle ways. Men, on the contrary, functioned as information sources and/or experts in the news stories, and their participation was framed as nationalist, political, and selfless.

In the same manner, the modest visibility and audibility of Egyptian women in the NYT coverage cannot be read as a sign that diversity was achieved. I do not rule out the potential long-term effect of these images in challenging the hegemonic discourse; however, I remain skeptical about its immediate influence in deconstructing it. Through the survey presented here, I therefore aim to open new analytical ventures that are worthy of further investigation.

My objective was not teasing out convergence and divergence between the national and Western coverage either. To reiterate, this in my view would run the risk of reducing many complexities surrounding the representations of women in both spheres. Rather, I view the myriad of women's representations in both spheres as useful in charting the local, national, and international context of their activism. They also represent some of the dominant frames that women had to negate in framing their experience.

The coverage is utilized in this chapter to shed some light on the many dominant contexts within which women carried out their activism and framed their experience. Notwithstanding the temporal and spatial limitations of my study, it also offers an original analysis of some of the implications of the uprising on media representation of the Middle East. Furthermore, a focus on the Egyptian uprising provides original examples of heterogeneity and regularity in Orientalist and gendered discourses and extends feminist postcolonial insights to new cases.

The significance of this analytical exercise is to expose some of the tensions under which women carried out their activism as well as revealing some of the ways in which power is exercised through media discourses. The chapter as such contributes to situating the experience of women within the boundary of polity. The analysis also explicates the variation and multiplicity involved in the practice of othering and avoids erasing the participation of women as subject of patriarchy or Orientalism in shaping the discourse. By scrutinizing the power of media discourses in shaping and influencing gendered and geopolitical schisms, those made subject to these schisms can find ways to challenge and deconstruct these claims, representations, and stereotypes.

3 | Trenching Dissent: Women's Collective Action Frame in the Uprising*

RESPONDENT: ... the fact that many Egyptians do not know that the nationalist leader Makram Ebeid is Coptic is not a sign of our national unity, it is primarily because our history textbooks do not mention his religion; that is why young generations did not know he is Coptic!

INTERVIEWER: Well, why do you think his religion is not mentioned in history textbooks?

RESPONDENT: I do not know. I have just always felt that the national unity talk is sometimes real but also and for sure partly orchestrated, particularly at times of contentions and political struggles.

INTERVIEWER: Hmmm.

RESPONDENT: We think that a strong social fabric needs to be colorless; this myth is deeply ingrained in our collective memory of nationalist struggles, and thus at times of political struggles we all feel a duty to perform within its contours.[1]

The mainstream framing of modern and historical political struggles in Egypt is often constructed around the discourse of national unity. Political struggles are documented as a story of unity and solidarity where religious, class, and gender differences meant few if any signs of distinction among participants. The example of the Coptic nationalist leader Makram Ebeid, a key figure in the country's anti-colonial struggles in the 1920s, is often cited as one example of this national unity. This is because, as the story goes, many Egyptians are not aware of his religion.

However, as the above quote suggests, his religion is deliberately omitted from history and collective memory in Egypt, and this

---

* An abridged version of this chapter was presented under the title "Trenching Dissent: Women's Collective Action Frame in the Uprising" at the American Political Science Association (APSA) MENA Workshop, Tunisia, June 7–14, 2014.
[1] Interviewee 31. Author's interview, Cairo, Egypt, July 2013.

omission contributes to constructing a "colorless social fabric." The success of political struggles is believed to be contingent on staging national unity based on a colorless[2] social fabric in which differences are not endorsed but rather omitted. This myth is especially influential during political struggles in which participants feel a duty to stage this performance of unity and solidarity and thus communicate power to their opponents. My aim in this chapter is to demonstrate that women's framing of their participation in the 2011 uprising must be read against this broader public discourse, a discourse that champions "colorless" framing of collective action.

Erving Goffman, in his classic book *The Presentation of Self in Everyday Life* (1959), examined this performative aspect of social interactions in great detail. In his book, Goffman described the world as a "stage" on which all social interactions are carried out by "staged people." They use the main stage to play roles, perform routines, and confront others while wearing masks. For critical anthropologist Victor Turner, the dramaturgical phase begins when people "exert their wills and unleash their emotions to achieve goals which until that time have remained hidden or may even have been unconscious"(1979: 65). These crises are inherently dramatic as participants deliberately perform and show their actions to others; actions thus assume a "performed-for-an-audience" aspect (Turner 1979: 63).

Appropriating this perspective, Robert D. Benford and Scott A. Hunt depict social movements as "dramas in which protagonists and antagonists compete to affect audiences' interpretations of power relations in a variety of domains" (1992: 38). In these dramas, participants attempt to replace "a dominant belief system that legitimizes the status quo with an alternative mobilizing belief system that supports collective action for change" (Gamson, Fireman, and Rytina 1982: 15). Participants in social movements are thus not merely influenced by the structure. Rather, they cluster around "collective action frames" (Benford 1993, 1997; Snow and Benford 1988, 1992; Snow, Soule, and Kriesi 2004; Snow, Worden, and Benford 1986).

---

[2] At times of political struggle, the social fabric, it can be argued, appears colorful in mien yet colorless in content. That is, participants showcase that they come from different walks of life and thus the social fabric appears colorful, but the discourse among participants is often colorless in the sense that the unity of demands is highly emphasized.

At the most basic level, a frame identifies a problem that is social or political in nature, the parties responsible for causing it, and the possible solutions they offer (Johnston and Noakes 2005: 2; see also Gamson 1975; Snow and Benford 1988, 1992). Frames in the "theatre of contention" redefine a status quo that was perceived as "unfortunate but perhaps tolerable" to "unjust and immoral" (Tarrow 1998: 132) and thus mobilize participants to join repertoires of contention. This symbolic politics of social movements is, however, paradoxical (Snow and Benford 1992; Tarrow 2012).

The major dilemma of constructing collective action frames is to mediate between inherited symbols that are "familiar" but lead to "passivity" and new ones that are "electrifying" but may be too "unfamiliar" to lead to action (Tarrow 1998: 107). In mitigating this tension, collective action frames in social movements are woven from a blend of "inherited and invented fibres" to garner support and legitimacy for collective action (Tarrow 1993: 118; see also Snow and Benford 1988). Frames are thus culturally and politically embedded and are the outcome of social interactions broadly as well as the shifting opportunities and constraints at the time of contention.

This chapter focuses on women's collective action frame in the social drama of the 2011 Egyptian uprising. I approach women's collective action frame as not simply impermeable to external influence but as a response to the inherited cultural materials and historical framings of political struggles. The analysis offered in this chapter highlights some of the factors intrinsic to women's framing that have contributed to ensuring that women's collective action frames resonate with bystanders, allies, members of the public, and the media. The resonance of women's collective action frame, I highlight, was necessary to facilitate and legitimate their participation in collective action; however, it arguably contributed in part to limiting their rights in the post-uprising period.

In carrying out this analysis, I adopt a threefold approach. In the first section, I interrogate women's collective action frame to elucidate its intrinsic features. These features, I demonstrate, have provided women's collective action frames with the necessary credibility and resonance. Building upon frame analysis, in the second section I highlight the mainstream framing of women's political participation in Egypt. Frame analysis considers the effect of history, politics, and culture on the framing of participation in collective action. I build upon frame analysis to situate women's collective action frame during the uprising within the mainstream historical framing of political struggles and women's activism in Egypt. This framing, I argue, temporally concealed differences and inequalities that had traditionally obscured women's participation in politics yet limited their rights in the period after the uprising. From a gender perspective, the absence of women-centered demands implies the absence of *conceptual* spaces for women. In these spaces, feminist organizations, unions, and political parties articulate gender concerns and build networks and consciousness-raising groups that could eventually turn into a women's movement.

By offering a gender analysis of these early interactions, the chapter contributes to explaining the nature and implications of their gender dynamics. It recovers women's voices in the writing of history and opens up new ways of understanding the Egyptian uprising.

Women's Collective Action Frame: The Citizen Frame

Collective action frames emphasize subjective and symbolic aspects of social movements. In an important series of papers, sociologist David Snow and his collaborators build upon Goffman's (1974) concept of framing, arguing that collective action frames construct meaning for action. In Snow and Benford's words, a frame is an "interpretive schemata" that simplifies and condenses "the world out there by selectively punctuating and encoding objects, situations, events, experiences, and sequences of actions within one's present or past environment" (1992: 137). At times of collective action, the frame defines the motivations, grievances, and demands of the movement's members as well as their identity (Gamson 1975; Givan et al. 2010; Snow and Benford 1988, 1992).

The citizen frame is commonly deemed as the collective action frame adopted by different groups including women during the 2011 uprising in Egypt. When asked why they participated in the uprising, all female protestors and activists – interviewed by the researcher during 2012–2014 – framed their participation on the basis of their citizenship. During the 2011 uprising, women voiced basic citizenship demands and did not include gender-specific demands (see Ghonim 2012; Morsi 2014; Taher 2012, to cite a few). These basic citizenship demands coalesced around justice, freedom, and dignity. They demanded the fall of the regime and the prosecution of former president Husnī Mubarak and his family. Another demand called for *Huriyya* (freedom): freedom to participate fully in political life, to vote in free and fair elections, and to express their views and opinions without censorship or fear of persecution.[3] A third demand was *karama* (dignity) and the end of police abuse, torture, and humiliation.

By adopting the citizen frame, several female protestors stress, the movement at large was able to secure wide support[4] and encourage greater mobilization.[5] This is because the frame tapped deep-rooted and widely shared grievances in its *diagnostic* framing of the problems. The diagnostic nature of some frames, James Scott (1992: 224) has argued, explains how a "revolt spreads like 'wildfire' looking like a very organized, coordinated uprising, when in fact, it was not." As thousands came out to protest against the dominant communist party in Czechoslovakia, Vaclav Havel emphasized the significance of their form of sporadic organization, its energy, and spark. In a question underscoring the significance of their organization, he asked:

Where did young people who had never known another system get their longing for truth, their love of freedom, their political imagination, their civic courage and civic responsibility? How did their parents, precisely the generation thought to have been lost, join them? How is it possible that so many people immediately understood what to do and that none of them needed any advice or instructions? (Havel 1990)

In the case of Egypt, this is explained in part by the adoption of the citizen frame by the different groups who participated in the 2011 collective action. The frame created what Tilly (1997: 133) calls "lineaments of durable connection." That is, the citizen frame became the major means through which different and diverse protestors, both men and women, religious and secular, built solidarity, expressed unity, demonstrated their challenges and sought external support (Al-Aswany 2012; El-Nagar and Abo-Dawood 2012; Amin 2012; Korany and El-Mahdai 2012; Louër 2011). Protestors often pointed out how different groups adopted the citizen frame regardless of their affiliation and their religious, political, and social leanings. During

---

[3] Interviewee 61. Author's interview, Cairo, Egypt, October 2014.
[4] Interviewee 1. Author's interview, Cairo, Egypt, July 2012.
[5] Interviewee 12. Author's interview, Cairo, Egypt, July 2012.

the 18-day uprising, members of the Muslim Brotherhood, a protestor rightly emphasized, did not voice any "demands specific to the [Muslim Brotherhood] organization."[6] They did not, for example, demand lifting the ban on their political representation – a ban that has been in place for most of the group's history. Members of the organization joined protestors demanding bread, freedom, and social justice like everyone else, my participant added. Writing on the Muslim Brotherhood's participation in the 2011 Egyptian uprising and their political missteps after the uprising, Eid Mohamed and Bessma Momani (2014: 198) stress that protestors were not protesting in favor of an Islamic government; they were protesting in favor of the people's right to choose.

The frame also created what scholars of social movements term "a movement of movements," as I shall demonstrate in Chapter 5. This is significant, Tilly (1997) contends, for communicating power to opponents. It staged, I suggest, a *lineament of diversity*. This diversity was significant in showcasing the importance of the voiced demands and their popularity across different sects of society, including women,[7] an observation confirmed by several individuals interviewed for this book.

The frame also legitimated and energized women's participation in the uprising. This is because to legitimate collective actions, frames, stress Snow and Benford (1992), need to resonate with the population's cultural predisposition. Snow and Benford (1988) define the symbolic resonance of frames as the degree to which a particular frame resonates with cultural norms and familiar concepts. Social movement scholars have analyzed the concept of frame alignment in order to understand the dynamics that contribute to the survival and resonance of contentious language and frames.

Snow and his associates have devoted great attention to examining the process of "frame alignment." Frame analysis describes the ways in which frames are oriented toward action in particular contexts and fashioned at the intersection between a target population's culture and the movement's own norms, strategies, and goals (Tarrow 1998: 110–111; see also Snow and Benford 1992; Snow et al. 2004). They emphasize the

---

[6] Interviewee 18. Author's interview, Cairo, Egypt, July 2013.
[7] Interviewee 4. Interviewee 44. Author's interview, Cairo, Egypt, February 2014. Interviewee 46. Author's interview, Cairo, Egypt, June 2014. Interviewee 68. Author's interview, Cairo, Egypt, November 2014.

influence of frame alignment on the movement's success. According to them, an unfamiliar frame can alienate people and thus the movement will fail to gain popular support. But also a frame that is nothing more than a reflection of the values of its society will not bring major changes (Tilly and Tarrow 2007: 110; see also Zemlinskaya 2009).

Viewed from this perspective, the absence of gender from women's collective action frame is not a sign of passivity but rather part of the process of "frame alignment." By framing their participation around their "Egyptianness," several participants argue, they were able to negotiate their differences with those opposing their participation from a position of power.[8] "We are all citizens of the same country," a young female protestor explains: "we shared the same responsibilities and duties: the responsibility to defend it [Egypt], and the right to be in the [Tahrir] square."[9]

Some even argued that introducing a gender-explicit frame would have limited women's participation. The absence of gender issues, an activist from Al-Fayoum, a conservative rural town in Egypt, explained was a "blessing in disguise";[10] it implicitly extended women's rights – that is, their right to participate in politics and to occupy the public space.[11] Introducing gender issues even as a demand would risk opening up debates about the proper gender roles and gender risks, "don't you think?"[12] a young female protestor asked me, stressing that this is not necessarily what went through her mind then. The process of frame alignment is not always easy, clear, or uncontested. Scholars note how different groups in a social movement compete among each other, with media agents, and with the state for "cultural supremacy" (Tarrow and Imig 2000: 110).

Frames thus need to be built around strong ties that, Tilly asserts (1997: 133), "do much of the work that would normally fall to organization." Constructing a resonant and modular collective action frame was thus particularly significant for the success of the 2011 uprising given the absence of leadership (Bamyeh 2012; Clarke 2014; Goldstone 2011). The lack of leadership, Momani and Mohamed (2014) explain, was a natural by-product of the nature and direction of the movement.

---

[8] Interviewee 4. Interviewee 5. Interviewee 2. Author's interview, Cairo, Egypt, July 2012.
[9] Interviewee 5.
[10] Interviewee 81. Author's interview, Al-Fayoum, Egypt, November 2014.
[11] Ibid.
[12] Interviewee 4.

The movement's participants, they rightly observe, were more focused on participating in democracy than ideology (Momani and Mohamed 2014: 198). In the absence of ideology, leadership, and organization, a discourse grounded in their rights as citizens and nationals of Egypt offered different participants, including women, a source of framing that easily aligned and resonated with the population's cultural predisposition and communicated a uniform message to the regime in power.

During the interviews, participants often utilized the same language used in describing nationalist and liberation struggles against colonialism, and they similarly described how the uprising was an attempt to "liberate"[13] Egypt.[14] Unlike colonialism, their enemy was not Western and/or foreign forces; the enemy they were fighting against was a "local colonist,"[15] that is, the corrupt regime of Mubarak. Prior to the uprising, the April 6th movement often mockingly referred to Egypt as the Egyptian Occupied Territories ("Corruption Award [Fassad Award]" 2011). Several protestors described in great detail how the struggle was one aimed at "reclaiming Egypt."[16] They proudly shared how their experience in the uprising revived their sense of ownership, belonging, and loyalty. They contrasted the revived sense of attachment they felt during the uprising with the sense of political apathy that prevailed in the period that preceded it. "I stopped following the news"[17] was a very common confession made by a number of my female participants, describing their political apathy before the uprising.

In emphasizing this sense of detachment, a couple of my participants cited the popular song "Yaksh Twla'" [To Hell with It][18] in reference to Egypt. The song, they described, exemplifies the general spirit of political despair among the youth in this time before the uprising. The phrase "To Hell with It" was also commonly posted on Facebook profile pictures and printed on shirts. The song, one participant explains, "[o]ffered a logo,"[19] that is, it captured the anger and resentment that many among the youth were already feeling. This state was fueled by the sense that

---

13 Interviewee 56. Author's interview, Cairo, Egypt, October 2014.
14 This national sentiment exists at a level deeper than any particular government and is part of the foundational sentiment in Egypt.
15 Interviewee 70. Author's interview, Cairo, Egypt, November 2014.
16 Interviewee 9.
17 Ibid. And many others who would explain how they stopped following events on the political landscape, and/or refrained from participating in elections.
18 The song is composed and performed by Yasser Al-Manawehly.
19 Interviewee 49. Author's interview, Cairo, Egypt, June 2014.

the country was lost to the corrupt regime and was held captive by these corrupt forces in power.[20]. Protestors in the 2011 uprising thus attempted to liberate their country, but in this context, the liberation struggle was fought against the internal security forces and the government in power.

The emphasis on national unity[21] in framing political struggles in Egypt is also part of the broader negative view of identity politics and the lack of support for identity-based demands in Egypt. Civil society organizations, whether secular, liberal, or leftist, have been excessively cautious on issues related to identity politics and gender rights in Egypt. For example, the liberal parties and groups have always avoided offending Islamists and conservative segments of Egyptian society, an activist explained, citing their position in the 2001 Queen Boat controversy in Egypt.[22] Egyptian human rights activists did not condemn the crackdown and arrest of fifty-two gay men on the charge of debauchery, and their subjection to anal probes following the police raid on the Queen Boat in Cairo (Mourad 2013). According to Amra Shalakany (2007: 9), "the Egyptian human rights community faced a stark choice: Either defending the Queen 52 and risking being painted as supporters of 'sexual deviance' by the viciously homophobic press, or, alternatively, staying clear of the case and risking alienating colleagues from the international human rights community."

The political apathy of Egyptian human rights groups can be attributed to their fear of being labelled agents of the West and/or anti-Islamic (Awwad 2010; Mourad 2013; Shalakany 2007). The liberals' stance could also be the result of the continued relegation of gender, race, and identity politics from the realm of political struggles. As Sara Mourad (2013) argues, their stance also magnifies the undertheorized nature of liberal politics in the Arab world. It points to a need for a more nuanced understanding of the position of liberals and seculars – not just Islamists – on issues related to gender rights and sexuality (Mourad 2013).

The unease with which women's rights are viewed and treated at times of struggle is part of the broader skepticism surrounding the "murky

---

[20] For a general discussion of political alienation, see Finifter 1967; Nachmias 1974. For a discussion of political alienation as a source for political activism, see Thompson and Horton 1960.

[21] Egypt is not exceptional in this regard; national metaphors and discourses have been central in historical and modern struggles around the world.

[22] Interviewee 42. Author's interview, Cairo, Egypt, February 2014.

terrain of identity politics,"[23] as several of my participants reminded me, and how "the business of identity politics is unpopular in Egypt"[24] – as in many Arab societies, I would add. One of my interviewees claimed that the majority of the population views identity politics as an "American/Western thing, really"[25] and, as other participants added, a "colonial strategy"[26] and/or "a foreign conspiracy"[27] aiming to "divide and conquer."[28] The conventional framing of historical and modern successful political struggles in Egypt was constructed, as already mentioned, around the discourse of national unity, where differences are omitted and the unity of demands and voices is celebrated. In the national imaginary and popular discourse, attaining this national unity has been ingrained as a necessary pre-step for staging a successful political struggle (Badran 1988; Baron and Pursley 2005; Hatem 2000, Pollard 2005).

For example, one of the celebrated symbols of Egypt's struggle against colonialism during the 1920s is the unity between the mosque and the church, described in popular culture and artistic production as the unity between the crescent and the cross, with the crescent symbolizing Muslims and the cross symbolizing Copts in Egypt. Attaining this national unity was viewed as one of the success factors in Egypt's nationalist struggle and as a significant factor in ending colonialism (Al-Faqi 1985; Ebeid 1964; Sedra 2011). Introducing group-based demands, whether by women, religious and/or sexual minorities, would ostensibly put this unified image and consequently the movement at large at risk.[29]

The emphasis on solidarity and the concern to present a unified face to the opposition is among the challenges and constraints of Egyptian

---

[23] Interviewee 4.
[24] Interviewee 33.
[25] Interviewee 5.
[26] Interviewee 55. Author's interview, Cairo, Egypt, October 2014.
[27] Interviewee 62. Author's interview, Cairo, Egypt, October 2014.
[28] Interviewee 30. Author's interview, Cairo, Egypt, July 2013.
[29] Interviewees 1, 4, 5, 12, 28. The debate over identity politics in social
    movements and whether such a focus may often produce movements that
    are divisive, insular, sectarian, and incapable of garnering support, expanding
    membership, increasing resonance, and negotiating with allies is common
    in social movement research (Tarrow 1998: 9; see also Gitlin 1996). This is
    the criticism that Todd Gitlin makes of contemporary American "identity
    politics" in his book *Twilight of Common Dreams* (1996), a weakness that
    in this case he does not find in class politics of the past. In contrast though,
    Benedict Anderson ironically asks, contrasting the many monuments to

society. Women participating in the political struggles in Egypt would more likely reflect them and root themselves within them. In framing their participation, women framed their activism building upon this cultural reservoir to achieve resonance and modularity. This framing proved useful in facilitating their activism, as it concealed gender differences and inequalities that traditionally obscured their activism. This is particularly significant in the case of Egypt, where a gender-explicit approach to equality and women's rights is weak in public debates and often a subject of mockery in media productions.

The Framing of Women's Political Participation in Egypt

A gender-explicit approach to women's activism – in contentious and/or routine politics – has been less popular in Egyptian society. The gender dimension has often been misrepresented by the media and overlooked in popular accounts. This misrepresentation has contributed to further situating the discourse of women's activism within the framework of national unity. Another implication is that female political activists distanced themselves from feminist discourse and from gender-explicit frameworks. By framing their participation around their citizenship, women mitigated tensions surrounding gender, citizenship, and identity that have long shaped and animated the public discourse around women's political activism.

In Egypt, the media is among the most influential shapers of the Egyptian "self/selves." The media, Egyptian novelist Sonallah Ibrahim (1981) stresses, is central to the everyday lives of citizens, shaping both the individual's private identity and the collective national imagination.[30] In her study of the media representation of Alia El-Mahdi, an Egyptian female activist known for her controversial nude protest actions, Sara Mourad (2013) argues that the media framing of

nationalism with the lack of memorials to social class, can one even imagine "a Tomb of the Unknown Marxist" (1991: 10). That is, while in the course of history individuals and groups have been prepared to sacrifice their lives for their visions of good society which they represented, nationalism, John Schwarzmantel (2008) explains – elaborating Anderson's contention – has a monopoly on images and constructions of self-sacrifice and heroism in collective memories.

[30] In Ibrahim's 1981 novel *Al-Lajna* [The Committee], he writes that due to the state's preoccupation with diversification, it also diversified its methods of "persuasion": "these [Arab] regimes used to have a sole method of persuasion,

women's activism transcends contentious media representations of women to reach into the heart of Egyptian and Arab revolutionary citizenship.

Women's rights organizations are often represented by Egyptian media as "elitist organizations"[31] and/or "aristocratic clubs"[32]; its members are often misrepresented as "cappuccino ladies,"[33] "vicious females,"[34] or "masculine women."[35] While there is a myriad of media productions that narrate the bravery of male activists and historical political figures, the stories of female activists and feminists in Egypt have never made it to the mainstream movie and/or television industry.[36]

Several media productions have focused on the life stories of a number of Egyptian female celebrities. In these productions, the characters' nationalist acts are sometimes highlighted – for example, in the media production of the life story of the singer Um Kalthoum and of the actress and belly dancer Taḥia Karyuka, to cite only a few. The life stories of Egyptian female political activists and women's rights advocates, however, "have rarely made it to the screen."[37] Their activism, one of my interviewees noted, can be the subject of "a book, not a movie."[38]

The absence of female heroines with an explicit gender agenda in media production is situated within the broader misrepresentation of women in Egypt's media (Abu-Lughod 2005; Al-Mahadin 2011; Allam 2004; Qasim and Dasuqi 2000; Sakr 2004, 2007). It is also a manifestation of the "failure and the shallowness [Ikhfaq wa Saṭḥyat]"[39] of the top-down approach that the ruling regimes in Egypt have adopted in advancing

which was through imprisonment and torture. Diversification, however, put new methods at their disposal that range from assassination to television and parliaments."

[31] Interviewee 20. Author's interview, Cairo, Egypt, July 2013.

[32] Interviewee 33.

[33] Author's interview, Maya Morsy, former Regional Gender Practice Team Leader at the United Nations Development Program/Middle East Office (2014–2015), and current President of the National Council for Women, Cairo, Egypt, October 2014.

[34] Interviewee 38.

[35] Interviewee 4.

[36] I am unaware of any literature examining the media representation of the women's movement in Egypt, and thus I relied on my participants' insights and my knowledge and exposure to Egyptian media.

[37] Interviewee 16. Author's interview, Cairo, Egypt, July 2012.

[38] Interviewee 23.

[39] Interviewee 40. Author's interview, Cairo, Egypt, February 2014.

women's rights. While the policies of state feminism in Egypt have produced a number of women-friendly policies and legislations, they did not alter the way in which society viewed and treated women, as reflected in the media portrayal of them (Hatem 2005; Sholkamy 2012). In an interview with Nahla Abdel-Tawab, regional director of the Population Council[40] in Egypt, Abdel-Tawab explained how achieving gender equality and women's rights requires not only a formal and technical shift in our policies and processes but also a social and normative shift in Egyptian society. To challenge and change gendered power relations, there need to be change and development in gender relationships and social structures in the family, at work, and at the state level.

Female heroines in political struggles are, however, positively depicted by the media when their activism is framed across nationalist lines. The discourse of women's right to political participation, one protestor stressed, is often celebrated and supported when it is introduced "subtly (Makhfya) ... within the larger discourse of social equality."[41] Women's activism, another protestor confirmed, is most "gracefully" portrayed when it is a "subheading ('nwan Far'y)" under nationalism.[42] The significance of this alignment between gender and social equality frames as well as women's political activism and nationalism is further explicated in the following conversation with a media analyst at the Cairo office of an international broadcasting corporation:[43]

RESPONDENT: The image of the *muscled feminist* is not particularly appealing in Egyptian society.
INTERVIEWER: Hmmm ...

---

[40] The Population Council is an international, nonprofit, non-governmental organization. The council conducts biomedical, social science, and public health research in developing countries. Headquartered in New York, the Population Council has 18 offices in Africa, Asia, and Latin America and carries out research in more than 60 countries. The council's office in Egypt has conducted extensive research on youth and women issues. It has published extensive national surveys of young people in Egypt in 1997, 2003 and in the wake of the 2011 uprising. The Egypt office also manages the International Network to Analyze, Communicate, and Transform the Campaign Against FGM/C (INTACT) to advance research on female genital mutilation (FGM) and facilitate the dissemination and use of research findings.
[41] Interviewee 43. Author's interview, Cairo, Egypt, February 2014.
[42] Interviewee 45. Author's interview, Cairo, Egypt, February 2014.
[43] Interviewee 29. Author's interview, Cairo, Egypt, July 2013.

RESPONDENT: You look quite skeptical.

INTERVIEWER: Not really. Just thinking it through.

RESPONDENT: Consider how the television series *Zaat* is quite a success in Egypt these days. While gender equality and women's activism is one of its underlying themes and objectives, the author intelligently weaved it under the broader frame of social equality and national struggle. They sugar-coated it, you can say.

INTERVIEWER: Well *Zaat* was written in 1992, is this...

RESPONDENT: But it was only produced as a television series in 2013, after the uprising.

INTERVIEWER: Yes, but is this still the case, that women's rights and activism need to be concealed under the master frame of social equality and nationalism to gain support, even after the uprising.

RESPONDENT: Yes, I believe this was the case at the time of the uprising and remains the case after the uprising.

At the time of the interview in 2013, the television series *A Girl Named Zaat* was being aired in Egypt during the month of Ramadan. The Ramadan series is based on the novel *Zaat*, published in Cairo in 1992. In 1993, *Zaat* was nominated as the most important novel of the year. State institutions, however, did not endorse the decision. A decade later, the novel was awarded Egypt's most prestigious literary award, yet Sonallah Ibrahim, the author, declined the "honor" (Haist 2010). Notwithstanding the high number of Ramadan series, *Zaat* scored the highest rating during that month (Awad 2013).

Zaat is the name of the novel's heroine, an allusion to the medieval Arab folk epic of the warrior princess Zaat al-Himma ("the lady of noble intentions"), who performed heroic acts in the Arab-Byzantine wars of the eighth and ninth centuries. The word *Zaat* also means "self" in Arabic. The novel is a modern epic in which Zaat, a typical member of the urban middle class, struggles against the adversities of everyday life. The plot starts in the 1960s, as Zaat is forced by her husband to discontinue her studies and become a housewife and the mother of two daughters and later a son. As the 1970s begin and the cost of living increases, she starts working at a newspaper, in the department of proof-reading and copy-editing – a euphemism for censorship in Egypt's print media (Haist 2010). Through her job, Zaat is exposed to the malaise of political life and becomes politicized. Her personality stands in contrast to her apolitical female colleagues who often critique Zaat's leftist leanings and are preoccupied only with the challenges of everyday life as mothers and wives. In the novel, Zaat is transferred to the archive as a punishment for her ideas and for being a sympathizer of the former leftist president Gamal Abdel Nasser as well as for displaying antipathy toward Egypt's liberal president, Anwar Al Sadat.

Throughout the novel, Zaat performs acts of resistance and demonstrates resilience in her work and at home. She vainly tries to mobilize her neighbors to clean the neighborhood. She decides to practice her rights and responsibilities as a citizen and report a can of olives tagged with a false use-before date to the police and health authorities. Supported by her friend Himma, meaning "the will" in Arabic, she enters a bureaucratic nightmare as she tries to submit an official complaint. For all her efforts, Zaat makes hardly any impression on the worsening living conditions, the decay of public morals, the collapse of state institutions and agencies, and society's drift toward religious fanaticism and political conservatism (Haist 2010; Johnson-Davies 2006).

Mainstream interpretations of *Zaat* do not assign a gender fault line to the novel. Critiques have interpreted *Zaat* as a social commentary that provides keen insights into how Egypt has come to be the way it is today (Haist 2010; Johnson-Davies 2006). Zaat's daily struggles, life experiences and social relationships are juxtaposed with economic crises and social changes in Egyptian society. The novel highlights the ubiquitous corruption in society and state institutions, financial scandals, foreign debts, gender inequalities, and human rights violations. Her story is illustrated with extracts from newspapers – headlines, articles, captions, death notices, advertisements – narrating events in broader society as well (Johnson-Davies 2006).

It is impossible to confirm with certainty that women's rights is the animating theme of Ibrahim's novel. It is possible that the central figure in the novel, Zaat, represents Egypt, the nation. Indeed, the representation of Egypt as a woman is a common cultural image, as noted in Chapter 1. It emerged following women's participation in the 1919 uprising and flowered during the Nasserist regime. *Zaat's* author, Ibrahim, is known as a strong sympathizer of Nasser's nationalist regime.

Notwithstanding the absence of gender from a mainstream reading of the novel, my interviewee's gender reading of *Zaat* is, however, insightful, especially considering the popularity of the series. The popularity of *Zaat* suggests that the figure of the active female citizen is celebrated and "gracefully represented" when her activism and struggle are framed within the nationalist discourse. It is hard to imagine *Zaat*'s series gaining the same popularity if the "dosage of gender equality and sexuality was higher,"[44] another participant stressed. The televised reproduction of the novel toned down many of Zaat's questions regarding her sexuality and religiosity, although these themes are covered in great detail in the original novel.

Women's bodies and sexuality in the Middle East, and elsewhere, are a much-contested and debated discursive space (Al-Mahadin 2011; Hafez 2014; Mourad 2013). Salam Al-Mahadin (2011: 8) argues that it is the "'ultimate signifier' with a multitude of meanings that spill into various aspects of social, political, religious and economic life." In this sense, women and especially their bodies construct and reflect the social order in the Arab world. The status of a woman's body is a reflection of the moral status of the society. Other female characters in a number of television series aired in the same month as *Zaat* were, unlike Zaat, dressed liberally, had multiple love partners, and viciously ran businesses. I asked my participants why Zaat's agency was carefully displayed, while in other series aired at the same time, female characters were increasingly portrayed as powerful, even if in a misguided way. One of my participants explained that Zaat resembles the average Egyptian women: "you can relate to her in clothes, home, and profession."[45] Her actions and views, thus, "cannot be too liberal or too deviant" she argued, because Zaat is a role model, and role models need to be carefully constructed and represented.

Meanwhile, the liberal female characters in other series are clearly not a representation of the average Egyptian woman; their exceptionality is underscored and stressed in every single detail in the story. "You can thus play with this character," another participant attests; she is not "a potential role model, thus you can assign to her extreme actions, extreme views, an extreme liberal dress code and exceptionally powerful personality even if in a twisted way." Furthermore, the story line of these seemingly powerful women evolves in such a way

---

[44] Interviewee 32. Author's interview, Cairo, Egypt, August 2013.
[45] Interviewee 28.

that the audience ends up pitying some, despising others, but never adopting them as role models.[46]

Seen as such, women's false expression of liberation and agency – in their liberal way of dressing and their multiple sexual relations, all of which clashes with the predominant customs and traditions in Egypt – is a reflection of the malaise in Egyptian society rather than a manifestation of the powerful female citizen. Writing on the ideal forms of citizenship, Lisa Rofel (2007) suggests that "Citizenship, or belonging, is not merely a political attribute but also a process in which culture becomes a relevant category of affinity," and adds "Sex is a critical site where normalizations of cultural citizenship are being reformulated" (94–95). Appropriating Rofel's argument, the careful construction of Zaat's female agency and the framing of her activism along nationalist lines can thus be read as an attempt to articulate a certain image for the ideal female citizen. This image is integral to the process of constructing a gendered collective imagination of female heroines and activists.

Given the important role of the media in framing public discourse in Egypt, the media misrepresentation of women's movement in Egypt, I suggest, contributed in part to the framing of women's political activism. Gender-explicit approaches to women's rights and political participation have often been belittled in media productions and public discourse. The life story of feminist activists, as well, "has not made it to the podium of media commemoration."[47]

In mitigating these tensions involved in women's activism and political participation, women have tapped into the legacy of the nationalist discourse in Egypt in framing their participation. This nationalist discourse does not explicitly include gender issues and women's rights in its framing of collective action. Its supremacy in Egypt should also be situated within the unpopularity of identity politics in Egypt and the association of the women's rights movement with the agenda of the regime as well as Western/foreign pressures. It, thus, comes as no surprise that a gender-explicit frame to women's participation did not resonate with female protestors let alone the wider movement. The absence of gender from the framing of women's participation is thus the function of the political and cultural landscape of Egypt.

---

[46] Interviewee 30.
[47] Interviewee 45.

Notwithstanding the impact of this framing on the success of the uprising, this framing, I argue in the following section, had its own implications for limiting women's rights in the post-uprising period.

Women-Only Spaces: Friends of the Square

As noted, scholars within the tradition of collective action framing argue that an unfamiliar frame can alienate people and thus the movement will fail to gain popular support (Snow and Benford 1992; Snow et al. 2004; Tarrow 1998: 100). A frame that is nothing more than a reflection of the values in its society cannot also bring major changes to it (Tilly and Tarrow 2007: 110; see also Zemlinskaya 2009).

Several social movement scholars have extended this argument to consider how women have fared in the socialist regimes of Latin America in the aftermath of revolutions (Chinchilla 1994; Fisher 1993; Kuumba 2001; Noonan 1995). The influence of women's pre-transition frames in constraining and/or facilitating their demands for equality in the new nationalist states soon became the foci of numerous feminist studies in the 1980s and 1990s. Within this tradition, scholars have observed that women whose pre-transition frame incorporated gender equality achieve more gains under new democratic regimes (Jaquette 1973; Kampwirth 2002; Noonan 1995; Reif 1986).

Pre-transition frames can also constrain the success of later movements and limit women's rights. In Latin America, female protestors appropriated the authoritarian regimes' discourse of the pious woman and selfless mother in framing their political participation and struggle for democratic reform (Alvarez 1999; Okeke-Ihejirika and Franceschet 2002; Ray and Korteweg 1999). This framing, however, constrained women's activism in the period following the uprisings. New political actors used women's feminine framing to justify women's exclusion from the public space and to encourage female activists to return to the private sphere (Chinchilla 1994; Fisher 1993).

Within these studies, feminists have also observed that women achieve more gains if their collective action frames are accepted by broader society and also aligned with feminist demands (Alvarez 1999; Chinchilla 1994; Fisher 1993; Noonan 1995). The incorporation of gender in women's collective action frame benefited their organizations and in some cases produced strong women's movements in post-transition periods (Adams 2002; Baldez 2002; Molyneux 1985;

Noonan 1995). This is because women-only spaces – also dubbed women's free spaces (Evans 1986) and prefigurative groups (Polletta 1997) – are tolerated in movements that incorporate gender into their frames more than the ones that gloss it under nationalist or liberation discourses.

The presence of "conceptual" and "social" women-only spaces in ongoing movements, Sara Evans and Harry C. Boyte (1986) stressed in explaining Evans' then nascent term, is important to challenge gender inequalities. Other scholars also note the importance of these spaces in prefiguring "the society the movement is seeking to build" (Evans and Boyte 1986; Polletta 1997: 11; Taylor 1989). Evans and Boyte (1986: 102) attest that the presence of "women-only spaces" in the Southern civil rights movement gave rise to radical feminism in the USA in the 1970s. They explain how: "within the broader social space of the movement, women found a specifically female social space in which to discuss their experiences, share insights, and group strength as they worked in the office or met on the margins of big meetings" (Evans and Boyte 1986: 102; see also Allen 1970).

It is important to note that women's spaces in ongoing movements are not necessarily feminist spaces – in the Western liberal sense, that is, women do not necessarily join them to achieve gender equality. The narrative of individual and collective liberty, postcolonial feminists hold, does not exhaust the desires of women in these spaces (Abu-Lughod 1990; Ahmed 2012; Mahmood 2005; Nouraie-Simone 2005). These spaces are what their members make of them; they do not necessarily include discussions of gender issues and women's rights demands.

For instance, women's spaces within a revolutionary movement could differ between urban and rural sites. This is in part because women's oppression, several feminists note, is multicausal and mediated through a variety of different structures, mechanisms, and levels which may vary considerably across space and time (Mahmood 2005; Molyneux 1985; Nouraie-Simone 2005). I do not intend to tease out these differences in my study; rather, I argue that the absence of conceptual women-only spaces at the time of the Egyptian uprising contributed, in part, to limiting their rights.

This is because, in social movements, women's spaces offer women a safe haven to articulate greater consciousness of what makes them marginal and garner greater confidence in their ability

(Evans 1980, 1997; Gamson 1975; Polletta 1997). In her study of women-only spaces in the Southern civil rights movement, Francisca Polletta (1997) describes how in these spaces, women, feminist organizations, NGOs, unions, and political parties articulate gender concerns and build gender-awareness groups that eventually turn into a women's movement. In the context of the 2011 Egyptian uprising, participants argue that while there have been "physical" women-only spaces for female participants, gender issues were not discussed in these spaces. As such, there was no real "conceptual space" to garner gender-based coalitions and awareness.

In the case of Egypt, the young female participants, Ghada Lotfy – director at the Egyptian Center for Women's Rights – attests, "did not want to disrupt the unity"[48] that characterized the uprising. In fact, for quite some time following the uprising there has been a "juncture between the old generations of women's rights groups in Egypt and young female activists,"[49] to use the words of Maya Morsy, former regional gender practice team leader at the United Nations Development Program/Middle East Office (UNDP) and current president of the National Council for Women in Egypt. Many of the young activists, Maya explained, have sadly "ignored our calls for unity (Itiḥad)" during the uprising.[50] It is worth noting, though, that this juncture did not last long, a fact that Azza Soliman – founder of the Center for Egyptian Women's Legal Assistance (CEWLA) – emphasized to me.[51] This is evident as well in the number of women's rights groups and initiatives carried out by young activists and the collaborative projects put forward by older and newer waves of women's rights advocates in Egypt.

Charles Tilly (1975) concludes from his study of contention in Europe that it was not mobilization that produced reform. Reform was rather the result of realignments among the new political actors and the coalitions in power. It was triggered by mobilization and harnessed by skillful political players (1975: 184). In so doing, Tilly explains much of the variance in the outcomes of contention by intervening causal mechanisms rather than independent ones. In the

[48] Author's interview, Ghada Lotfy, director at the Egyptian Center for Women's Rights (ECW), Cairo, Egypt, July 2013.

[49] Author's interview, Maya Morsy.

[50] Ibid.

[51] Author's interview, Azza Soliman, founder of the Center for Egyptian Women's Legal Assistance (CEWLA), Cairo, Egypt, November 2014.

context of Blacks and Hispanics struggling for equality in American urban centers, Browning and his collaborators argue that participation in protest was not sufficient to introduce reforms and advancement in the status of minority groups (Browning, Marshal, and Tabb 1984). Reforms were the result of a widening in the political opportunity structure, mobilization, elections, and political realignments (Browning et al. 1984).

Sidney Tarrow and his collaborators, in a similar vein, argue that political change occurred not through protests or clashes between old and new paradigms in Western Europe and North America during the 1960s and 1970s (Tarrow 2012: 186; see also Tarrow 1993, 1996; McAdam et al. 2001) but through the competition between parties, unions, interest groups, and movements, through reform, and through the absorption of at least a proportion of the protestors into the party system after mobilization ended.

I do not suggest that since the absence of gender from women's collective action frame limits the effectiveness of women-only spaces, then gender inequality will inevitably follow contention. As I have already argued, the non-immediate and mediated outcome of participation in contention is significant regardless of the success or failure of the cycle of protest. Through their participation in these episodes, new female activists are trained and develop a repertoire of actions. These activists could then form new movements and might engage with parties and interest groups after the episode of contention is over. The significance of the women-only spaces is that in these spaces, conceptually, women sketch themes that the new movements would incorporate and coordinate. Their absence delays rather than obscures reform.

My analysis of women-only spaces is intended to highlight how the revolutionary moment might have contributed to the current gender order in Egypt. Thus, I do not claim to offer an exhaustive explanation for gender inequality in Egypt following the uprising. I argue that the absence of conceptual women-only spaces, notwithstanding their physical presence, limited women's rights but did not erode their activism in the post-uprising period. This analysis is significant as it not only complements but also better completes the discussion of women's collective action frame in the Egyptian uprising. Any discussion of women's framing of their participation would be incomplete without thinking about – or at least imagining – the implications of this framing on their rights and activism in the period after the uprising. Despite the limitations of my analysis, this analytical model can be explored across additional cases and in combination with other factors. The analysis is also meant to encourage future research on the meaning and significance of the growth in women's activism following the uprising.

Conclusion

I have just always felt that *the national unity talk is sometimes real but also and for sure partly orchestrated, particularly at times of contentions and political struggles.*[52]

This chapter opened up with the aforementioned statement, as it captures the dynamics that shaped women's collective action frame in the 2011 uprising. While the comment was made in the context of Copts' engagement in political struggles in Egypt, it can be applied to the different groups in Egyptian society. In the case of women, adopting the citizen frame was, I suggest, in part a strategic response by women to the supremacy of the historical national discourse in Egypt – a discourse that has traditionally emphasized the importance of national unity in staging political struggles and in communicating power to opponents. This framing facilitated their participation at the time of the uprising, but it also, arguably, limited their rights in the period after the uprising.

As I demonstrate, the nationalist discourse has framed Egypt's historical political struggles and women's political activism in the national collective memory and in popular accounts – as documented by the media and popular representations of these struggles. In contrast, a gender-explicit approach to women's activism and rights has often been the subject of critique and belittling in Egyptian society. Several female activists and women's rights organizations, I observe, have thus distanced themselves from an explicitly feminist label. In the absence of an alternative strong discourse for women's activism, the nationalist discourse represented one of the important cultural reservoirs that activists reflected on in the framing of their participation. This framing was modular and resonated with the cultural predisposition of Egyptian society. It thus dignified and energized collective action and

---

[52] Interviewee 31. Italics mine.

mobilization among women as well as other participants in the 2011 uprising.

My analysis suggests that the absence of gender secured women's participation in the uprising yet contributed to limiting their rights after the uprising. Espousing a political process approach, I argue that female protestors oriented their messages in relation to the existent opportunities and constraints. This framing temporally concealed differences and inequalities that had traditionally obscured women's participation in politics. However, from a feminist perspective, the absence of women-centered demands implies the absence of conceptual spaces for women. In these spaces, feminist organizations, unions, and political parties articulate gender concerns, and also build networks and gender-awareness groups that could eventually turn into a broader women's movement.

By offering a gender analysis of these early interactions, I attempt to advance an explanation of the nature and implications of their gender dynamics. The resulting analysis is temporally and spatially bounded. However, my focus on identifying the frame's limits and opportunities when analyzing it can be extended to other cases.

The significance of my approach to women's collective frame is that it reclaims women's agency and situates women's participation within the contentious and conventional politics in Egypt. Female protestors operated on the boundaries of constituted politics, embedded power relations, and established institutions. They are, in this sense, "strangers at the gates" (Tarrow 2012), demanding changes and reform but also accommodating inherited understandings and ways of doing things. Their repertoires and collective action frames are best read in light of their relation to conventional and contentious political discourses in Egypt.

4 | An Epicenter of Solidarity: Women's Recollections of the 18-Day Uprising*

It was Utopian.[1]
It was perfect.[2]
The place [Tahrir Square] was sacred (Moqadas).[3]
The best of Egyptians came out in those 18 days.[4]
Tahrir[5] seemed fenced off from the rest of the society.[6]
The [Tahrir] square embodied its own norms and values.[7]

The air in the square felt different. Outside the Tahrir square, people were fighting over an ailing country. Inside the square, protestors were celebrating the birth of a new Egypt.[8]

Protestors described in great pride the aura of equality that characterized the 2011 uprising. Tahrir Square, the epicenter of protests, was remembered as a place of solidarity and equality. The experience of collective action against government brutality created a shared feeling of community. The solidarity and equality that marked the 18-day uprising was still for all of my female interviewees a source of pride, notwithstanding their "agony"[9] over the current status of women's

---

* An abridged version of this chapter was presented at the American Political Science Association (APSA) Annual Meeting, Philadelphia, United States of America, September 1–4, 2016.
[1] Interviewee 23.
[2] Interviewee 53. Author's interview, Cairo, Egypt, June 2014.
[3] Interviewee 9.
[4] Author's interview, Mokhtar Amin – grandson of the late Qasim Amin the renowned Egyptian reformer and women's rights advocate, Cairo, Egypt, November, 2014.
[5] The reference here is to Tahrir Square, the epicenter of the January 25 demonstrations in Egypt that led to the ousting of Egyptian president Ḥusnī Mubarak in 2011.
[6] Interviewee 18.
[7] Interviewee 35. Author's interview, Cairo, Egypt, February 2014.
[8] Interviewee 18.
[9] Interviewee 45.

rights after the uprising. Women's subjective experience of solidarity and equality during these protests contributed to the absence of gender from their collective action framing.

Frame analysts describe framing as an emergent and context-specific social process (Gamson 1995: 90; McAdam, McCarthy, and Zald 1996: 6; Snow and Benford 1988: 199). The process is guided and constrained by the political culture and political discourse that surrounds it (Gamson 1988: 221–222; Gamson 1992: 135–136;McAdam, Tarrow, and Tilly 2001). In this chapter, I expand the contours of framing theory to consider the influence of women's lived experiences and their relations and interactions with other participants during contention on their collective action frame. In framing their participation, women embraced the nationalist cultural reservoir to negotiate tensions surrounding female political activism and to gain support for the wider movement in 2011. This reflexivity in framing their participation is not static. Participants are involved in ongoing framing articulation. They not only engage with the wider cultural predisposition in framing their participation but also continue to take cues from the surrounding environment during times of political struggles.

The solidarity and equality that marked the 18-day uprising were, however, short lived. To borrow the language of critical anthropologist Victor Turner, they were "liminal." Inequalities soon surfaced on the political and social landscape. In his book, *Drama, Fields, and Metaphors*, Turner (1974: 37–41) describes times of change as "liminal phases" in which social differences are temporally and spatially suspended and during which participants experience "communitas," that is, fellowship and an unexpected joy in sharing common experiences. Viewing the 2011 episode of contention as liminal allows us to reconcile women's accounts regarding the solidarity they felt during the Egyptian uprising with the resurgence of inequalities and harassment following the uprising.

In carrying out this analysis, I adopt a threefold approach. In the first section, I build upon my interviewees' accounts to elucidate the aura of solidarity that characterized demonstrations. Building upon framing literature, I demonstrate the influence of women's subjective experience during protests on their framing of collective action. I analyze this phase *au courant* that the nature of interactions during this episode was conjunctural. Notwithstanding that this experience was a conjuncture, I emphasize its significance on how women understood and presented their activism and engagement. I reconcile the true yet conjunctural features of this episode by appropriating Victor Turner's contribution to the study of contention dramas and by surveying the absence of sexual harassment during the eighteen days. I conclude by presenting the absence of sexual harassment during this initial episode of contention as a case study to emphasize the widespread gender equality during the uprising.

The analysis presented in this chapter is significant as it acknowledges that women's collective action frame was not merely a deliberate formulation in response to the legitimacy of the dominant framing of political struggles and women's political participation in Egypt. While accounting for these factors has provided women's collective action frames with resonance and credibility, women also continued to take cues from the surrounding environment during the uprising.

Tahrir Square: An Epicenter of Solidarity

Framing theorists maintain that the construction of frames in collective action is "situationally sensitive" (Steinberg 1999b; see also Gamson 1995: 90; Hunt, Benford, and Snow 1994: 192; Klandermans and Staggenborg 2002; McAdam, McCarthy, and Zald 1996: 6; Snow and Benford 1988; Tarrow 1992: 190–191). The process is interactive; it takes place in relation to the dynamics of collective action and is closely associated to broader cycles of protest (Hunt et al. 1994: 191–192; Klandermans and Staggenborg 2002; Staggenborg 2001; Steinberg 1999a).

In his study of the Berkeley free speech movement, Max Heirich (1971) convincingly demonstrates how a true reconstruction of reality took place during the "spiral of conflict" that developed at the time. The process of framing participation, thus, does not come to an end once individuals decide to join in collective action. The existent culture at the time of the uprising in this regard also has a dialectical character, both empowering and constraining the production and resonance of frames among participants.

Social movements' theorists determine the success of frames by their ability to resonate with the wider population and their understandings of the problem at hand. The resonance of different frames, they argue, is a function of their "narrative fidelity, experiential commensurability, and empirical credibility" (Snow and Benford 1988: 208; Steinberg 1999b: 738; see also Gamson 1988: 167–168; 1992: 135).

Frame resonance is thus a function of the participants' perceived reality as well as their lived experiences at the time of collective action.

Framing is therefore a dynamic process tied to not only a particular socio-historical context but also to the immediate context of collective action and to the participants' subjective experience in it. Hegemonic ideological packages and dominant public discourses have an influence on how participants frame their engagement, but this impact, Bert Klandermans (1992: 85) argues, is always filtered through social interaction. Writing on the social construction of framing, Klandermans (1992: 78) attests that it is "a crucial characteristic of these processes of signifying, interpreting and constructing meaning: that is, they are *social*, they take place in interaction among individuals, and thus they are conceptualized as the social construction of protest." These interactions are "the vehicle" of this process of framing collective action; they are, thus, integral to the formation of consensus and solidarity in social movements (Klandermans 1992: 78).

In the case of the Egyptian uprising, the widespread solidarity and equality that characterized interactions among participants explains in part why women actively framed their participation utilizing the citizen frame. Women's subjective experience of solidarity and equality contributed to framing their participation around their identity as "Egyptian." They participated and organized as citizens rather than specifically women of Egypt.

This frame was viewed by women as sufficient and inclusive to incorporate women's rights[10] and to fit within the post-uprising agenda.[11] The absence of gender from the framing of women's participation should not to be viewed as a sign of coercion – that is, the impression that women were coerced and silenced by their fellow men and discouraged from voicing their rights and demands. This claim was refuted by all of my participants during the interviews. Female protestors instead stressed that they were treated equally – in roles, leadership positions, and interactions – during the 2011 demonstrations.

Furthermore, the coercion argument holds no ground, I maintain, especially in the absence of clear leadership during the 18-day uprising (Abaza 2014; Al Aswany 2012; Al-Nagar and Abo-Dawood 2012; Amin 2012; Bameyah 2012; Bayat 2013; Korany and El-Mahdai

[10] Interviewee 19. Author's interview, Cairo, Egypt, July 2013.
[11] Interviewee 32.

2012; Said 2014). During the uprising, there was no leadership to channel people's demands and/or to sway women away from voicing their demands. Organizers and grassroots organizations can use times of contention to deliberately create consensus and solidarity among groups in social movements. However, even when organizers did not "exploit" collective actions to form consensus, participation in demonstrations had a tremendous influence on participants' political actions and participation (Klandermans 1992; see also Tarrow 1998; Tilly and Tarrow 2007).

Writing on the Independent Self-governing Labour Union "Solidarity" movement in Poland, Tarrow (1998: 121) describes how the very symbol of the movement, that is, Solidarity or *Solidarność*, was a product of their struggle. The designer of the *Solidarność* symbol later wrote:

I saw how Solidarity appeared among the people, how a social movement was being born. I chose the word [Solidarnosc] because it best described what was happening to people. The concept came out of the similarity to people in the dense crowds leaning on one another – that was characteristic of the crowds in front of the gate [of the Lenin Shipyard]. (Quoted in Laba 1990: 133)

Incorporating participants' subjective experience in times of contention is thus integral to understanding what actors meant by their actions and how their experience might figure in framing their resistance. After all, it is in struggle that "people discover which values they share, as well as what divides them, and learn to frame their appeals around the former and paper over the latter" (Tarrow 1998: 122).

A less emphasized and much under-theorized aspect of this episode in the uprising is the participants' focus on the present and the implication of this focus on their framing of collective action. This focus on the present, I hold, does have an influence on participants' framing. Unlike political parties, for instance, participants in social movements experience a sense of immediacy, urgency in action, where their actions are largely a response to the ongoing events. Writing on this immediacy and urgency experienced in social movements, social movement theorists argue that the temporal experience of networks in social movements is one where the future is not allowed to determine the present. This refusal to allow the future to determine the present is central to activists' rejection of the idea of a program and to their refusal to construct social models of future society – to the frustration of many commentators.

The refusal of representation, the temporality of the present, and the culture of immediacy are all features that were much present in the 18-day uprising. This produced a sense of urgency where actions were constructed in terms of contentious performances rather than carefully articulated interests. In her dissertation "The Concept of Body in Political Theory: A Case Study in the Conceptualization of the Self during the Egyptian Uprising,"[12] Marriam Mekheimar (2013: 129) captures this sentiment, describing how, "participants gathered around a common dream, they did not gather around common interests."[13] That is, participants were united by the dream of ousting former president Ḥusnī Mubarak. They did not necessarily articulate a vision of the future of the society and how the political system would be organized post-Mubarak. Many of the women and the youth I interviewed described how the hope among protestors was to institute democracy, a word they used interchangeably with freedom, equality, and even economic prosperity.

A constant theme in my interviews with activists was how "there was little discussion of a long-term plan,"[14] "there was little talk about how the future will look"[15] or "how the political system in Egypt will be reorganized."[16] The absence of these discussions has contributed to maintaining the harmony among protestors as it concealed their different interests and different visions. A debate over these different interests and visions in the court of public opinion would have disrupted "the aura of consensus" that marked discussions in the square.

Another common theme in my interviews was the equality that marked the 18-day uprising (see also Nunns and Idle 2011; Rizzo, Price, and Meyer 2012). This was a source of pride for all of the women I interviewed, notwithstanding their "agony"[17] over the current status of women's rights after the uprising. They described with great enthusiasm how the people seemed to have transgressed their social, class, and religious differences during the protests. The powerful and

---

[12] Unpublished dissertation. Original in Arabic, my translation.
[13] Original in Arabic, my translation.
[14] Interviewee 58. Author's interview, Cairo, Egypt, October 2014.
[15] Interviewee 47. Author's interview, Cairo, Egypt, June 2014.
[16] Interviewee 43.
[17] Interviewee 45.

potentially equalizing power found in crowds has been the subject of sociological and psychological research. It has been captured astutely by sociologist and Nobel laureate Elias Canetti in his 1960 book *Crowds and Power*.

Canetti moves away from early representations of crowds by theorists Gustave Le Bon, Gabriel Tarde, and others who were heavily influenced by the legacy of the French Revolution. In this early representation of crowds, a crowd is inherently irrational and dangerous. In contrast to this representation, Canetti conceptualizes crowds in a far more positive light. In unpacking the dynamics of crowds, Canetti emphasizes that in a crowd, "all are equal; no distinctions count, not even that of sex" ([1960] 1984: 15). He adds that equality within a crowd is

absolute and indisputable and never questioned by the crowd itself. It is of fundamental importance and one might even define a crowd as a state of absolute equality. A head is a head, an arm is an arm, and differences between individual heads and arms are irrelevant. It is for the sake of this equality that people become a crowd and they need to overlook anything which might detract from it. All demands for justice and all theories of equality ultimately derive their energy from the actual experience of equality familiar to anyone who has been part of a crowd. (Canetti 1962: 29)

This strong emphasis on equality in crowds was a familiar theme in my interviews with female protestors who participated in the Egyptian uprising. For instance, in describing the crowd during protests, one participant attested that "Women dressing in Louis Vuitton sat beside the vegetable vendors; both shared the same rationales, logic, and interpreted the events in similar fashion."[18]

Others were particularly impressed by the religious tolerance, where conservative men, "donning their beard," were chatting and sitting beside non-veiled female protestors[19]. One of my participants recounted a conversation between her and a conservative Salafi young man at Tahrir Square, "He told me: 'Sorry if this will sound offensive but your morals are high; I would have never thought so.'"[20] Women who do not don the veil are commonly stereotyped by some conservative Salafi Muslims as lacking piety and morals. She remembered jokingly responding "and your sense of humor is great, I would have

---

[18] Interviewee 12.
[19] Interviewee 38.
[20] Interviewee 29.

never thought so."[21] Religiously conservative men are commonly stereotyped as strict and lacking any sense of humor.

In addition to my participants' accounts, national and international media reporting as well as numerous scholars and analysts have hailed the equality and solidarity among participants (Al-Aswany 2012; Al-Nagar and Abo-Dawood 2012; Amin 2012; Frederiksen 2011; Korany and El-Mahdai 2012). Esraa Abdel Fattah, an Egyptian human rights activist, blogger, co-founder of the April 6 Youth Movement and Nobel Peace Prize nominee, described how "During the protests at Tahrir Square, women were organising, demonstrating, and calling for [President] Mubarak's ousting (*sic*). Many revealed their deep appreciation and respect for women as partners" (*The National* 2012). Esraa, however, contrasted this with the post-uprising backlash on women's rights and gender equality.

A similar sentiment was echoed in my interview with Dana, project coordinator at the Women and Memory Forum (WMF). A women-based organization, the forum is composed of a group of female academics, researchers, and activists concerned with negative representations and perceptions of Arab women in the cultural sphere. Through researching and documenting the role of women in history and contemporary Arab societies, the forum aims to promote gender-sensitive approaches to historical and cultural analyses of the Arab world. Among the projects carried out at the forum is developing an archive of Egyptian women's stories and accounts in the January 2011 uprising. Female participants interviewed as part of the archival project, Danna emphasized, still described their experience with great pride and nostalgia. Some of them "even described it as their first taste of what gender equality and women's rights felt like."[22]

Sharing her collection of uprising photos and images, one of my participants, a photographer and film director, recounted with great pride the feeling of solidarity and equality among male and female protestors. At the same time, she drew my attention to the media and the public preoccupation with using Western symbols of solidarity, such as the shoulder-to-shoulder metaphor. She notes that for some women "shoulder to shoulder was not always the norm" and further explains

---

[21] Interviewee 29.
[22] Author's interview, Dana, project coordinator at Women and Memory Forum (WMF), Cairo, Egypt, November 2014.

that, "in fact, the guy would apologize if his shoulder mistakenly touched yours."[23] She recounts how male protestors would shout "make room for women" to avoid physically protesting shoulder to shoulder.[24] Upon hearing this, I returned to her photographs, this time looking for instances of shoulder-to-shoulder contact between female and male protestors.

What stood out from her notes and my own survey of her collection is that, notwithstanding the dominance of "shoulder to shoulder" as a metaphor as well as in the images of the uprising, a careful unpacking of this frame reveals its limitations. That is, the frame potentially excludes the experience of some women, specifically religiously conservative ones who strictly observe gender segregation. I am aware that this reading could be viewed as a strict and/or narrow literal interpretation of a seemingly innocent symbolic metaphor. My objective of sharing my participants' critique is to highlight how capturing the experience of some groups of women requires reorienting the language used to describe solidarity and our understanding of its manifestations. This is one of the examples of the complexity and diversity of the experience of women in the uprising. It goes to show how uncontested and seemingly innocent symbols and frames can be alienating as well as contested in different contexts. In this case, the presence of solidarity and equality among participants is not the subject of contestation; the subject of contestation is how they experienced it and how they described it.

For instance, some protestors took pride in how they participated at the front lines, battling and fighting security forces – that is, taking a direct combatant role. Others limited their participation to caring roles – taking care of the wounded and preparing food and shelter for protestors. Both groups spoke with pride about their contribution, and most importantly both stressed that they had chosen their roles. They insisted that the division of labor between men and women, while present, was largely "sporadic"[25] (see also Snow and Moss 2014).

Participants would often emphasize how the opinions and views of women were respected and followed. One participant recounted, "The

---

[23] Interviewee 22. Author's interview, Cairo, Egypt, July 2013.
[24] Ibid.
[25] Interviewee 5.

idea of breaking pavements and using their stones to deter the security forces was proposed by a woman. An older lady."[26] Equality was in part a function and a reflection of the freedom of choice that participants experienced and enjoyed during demonstrations. Women were equal to men because they were not boxed in and limited to certain roles. Women felt equal because "they chose how to participate."[27] By shedding light on these specificities in women's experiences and – what could be considered by a Western observer – contradictions and/or inconsistencies, a more nuanced understanding of their experience and its influence is put forward.

To conclude, members of social movements construct resonant frames by utilizing familiar symbols and discourses (Gamson 1988: 222, 242; Gamson and Modigliani 1989: 3). Frames, however, are not free floating once constructed; their resonance can be either shifted or enhanced by developments on the ground. For instance, three weeks after the uprising, women went back to the street, this time to demand women's rights as gender inequalities began to surface at the political and public levels.

On March 8, 2011, International Women's Day in Egypt, women returned to the streets to advocate for gender equality and equal representation in the transitional period. By then, it was evident that women's rights were being pushed to the side. For instance, the transitional government did not include any female representation and women's rights did not figure squarely in the political debates. Activists, however, were beaten and harassed by mobs of angry men who chased them out of Tahrir Square, the square that three weeks before had been considered the epicenter of solidarity (Hatem 2011). In order to understand and explain this dramatic shift, it is necessary to build upon Victor Turner's work on symbolic and interpretive anthropology.

Liminal Solidarity

Turner's concepts of liminality and communitas are significant to account for the solidarity and unity that marked the 18-day uprising and how this state influenced, in part, women's collective

---

[26] Interviewee 7.
[27] Interviewee 40.

action frame. Turner's work on liminality draws from the French anthropologist Arnold van Gennep (1873–1957), specifically his triadic model of the *The Rites of Passage* (1960). Van Gennep identified three stages in the process of shifting from one social status to another: the disengagement stage, liminal stage, and post-liminal or reunion stage.[28] Inspired by the social movements of the 1960s, Turner closely analyzed the liminality phase – the second phase of Van Gennep's model. The word *liminality* is derived from the Latin word *limen*. It means threshold and is closely associated with the word *limes*, meaning "limit" (Westerveld 2010). In anthropology, a liminal phase refers to the transitional state of being "betwixt" and "in between"; in this phase participants step out of their identity and social differences and are on the verge of personal and social transformation (Turner 1969, 1983; see also Cultural Reader 2012). In his book, *Drama, Fields, and Metaphors*, Turner (1974: 37–41) describes these times as "liminal phases" in which social differences are temporally and spatially suspended. They emerge during times of political transformation and come to an end as reintegration or schism takes place among the different sides in a conflict (Turner 1969, 1977).

Besides factors such as the shifting opportunities and constraints, the popular slogans of the uprising, that is: "*Al-Sha'b Yurīd Isqat Al-Niẓam*" [The people want to overthrow the regime], "*Id Waḥda*" [One hand], and "*Nitjama' "* [Gather], I argue, reflect this liminal phase (Al Aswany 2012; Al-Nagar and Abo-Dawood 2012; Amin 2012; Korany and El-Mahdai 2012). The slogan captures the absence of categorical identities; it symbolically assigned participants a "prima materia" status (Turner 1974: 49) and – appropriating Plato's (1963) notion – a status of "androgyny." That is, there was no further distinction or stratification based on class, gender, or religion of the people who rallied under these slogans.

Sharing the details of her participation, one of my interviewees – a member of the now banned Muslim Brotherhood Organization – described how she had already joined protests before the organization

---

[28] Disengagement is the stage in which the individual is disengaged from society and his/her own identity. The liminal stage is the transitional stage from one status to another. The post-liminal stage is one in which the individual's new status is confirmed and he/she is reintegrated into society.

mobilized its members.[29] As she explained, "My friend called me in the morning of January 26th and encouraged me to join protests, not because I am a sister, but because I am an Egyptian, from the people not the Brotherhood." A similar sentiment was expressed in my interview with a senior female member of the Muslim Brotherhood[30] group. She described her response to a "comrade"[31] from the Brotherhood when he "commanded" her not to join the January 25 protest:

I told him, "Look, brother, I am not joining because of police brutality towards the organization or to personally avenge for the humiliation I suffered at their hands... I am joining because I want to reclaim my country and my rights and my family rights as citizens of this country... because the Ministry of Social Solidarity has been brutal to my family, denying us my father's full pension and thus forcing my mother to clean homes in her 70s."[32]

In fact, "Join because you are an Egyptian" became a significant mobilizing slogan over the internet and on social media pages a few days into the uprising (We Are Khaled Saiid). It "put power in the soul of protestors"[33] according to one female protestor. Most importantly, it served in glossing over social, political, and religious differences among participants. That is, it contributed, at least in part, to creating a sense of "communitas" among protestors.

According to Turner (1969, 1974), liminality brings about a state of "communitas." In the literary sense, *communitas* – a Latin noun – commonly refers to either an unstructured community in which people are equal or to the very spirit of community. Edith Turner (2012) recently built upon and expanded the concept defining communitas as "inspired fellowship, a group's unexpected joy in sharing common experiences" (xi), the "sense felt by a group when their life together takes on full meaning" (1). Turner shows how communitas is a driving force in history as it operates at the personal level and at all domains of life including in religion and in revolution. It is grounded in lived events, and may occur as the climax to a process that takes people to

---

[29] Interviewee 8. Author's interview, Cairo, Egypt, July 2012.
[30] Female members of the Muslim Brotherhood group often referred to themselves as the Sisterhood.
[31] Interviewee 11. Author's interview, Cairo, Egypt, July 2012.
[32] Ibid.
[33] Interviewee 12.

new structures. In *The Forest of Symbols*, Victor Turner (1967) defines communitas as a society which is based on equality and solidarity.

In media and participants' accounts, Tahrir Square was described using quasi-communitas features. As several female protestors described, the square seemed "fenced off from the rest of the society";[34] it embodied "its own norms and values";[35] it was "utopian,"[36] "perfect,"[37] and a "sacred place (Moqadas)."[38] Mariam Mekheimar describes Tahrir Square as evolving into a "self-sufficient republic" (2013: 129) during those eighteen days. Protestors, she illustrates, "organized spaces for eating, others for sleeping. The square even had its own hospital and its own prison"[39] (Mekheimer 2013: 129). A salient feature that is often cited in media and by protestors as a significant feature of this sacred and communitas-like character of the square is the absence of sexual harassment during the eighteen days.

The Absence of Sexual Harassment

Sexual harassment is an epidemic, a constant social problem that many women experience in public spaces on a daily basis in Egyptian society. A 2013 survey conducted by the United Nations Entity for Gender Equality and the Empowerment of Women reported that 99.3% of women in Egypt have experienced sexual harassment in their life at least once (UN Women 2013). In fact, women in Egyptian society adopt a more "tolerant" definition of sexual harassment compared to their Arab and Middle Eastern counterparts. In a recent study conducted by the Dignity without Borders initiative, Egyptian women defined sexual harassment as physical and overlooked its verbal manifestations; meanwhile their Tunisian counterparts included any form of "cat call" in their definition (Dignity without Borders 2013). This is, in my opinion, a signifier of how epidemic the problem of sexual harassment is in Egypt and how women have grown accustomed to verbal harassment.

---

[34] Interviewee 18.
[35] Interviewee 35.
[36] Interviewee 23.
[37] Interviewee 53.
[38] Interviewee 9.
[39] Original in Arabic, my translation.

The Arabic word *taharush*, which means "harassment," is relatively new in the Egyptian dictionary (Al-Jazeera 2013). It was recently adopted in the context of sexual assault as a result of mounting pressures from women's rights groups in Egypt. One of my participants, a volunteer with Operation Anti-Sexual Harassment (OpAntiSH) [Quwat did Al-Taharush], reminded me how the act of harassment was often considered a form of "flirting" and thus called "flirtation" [*mu'aksa*].[40] OpAntiSH is an activist group based in Cairo. The group is known for having intervened in sexual assaults by mobs in Tahrir Square during the protests. They also run hotlines and document cases of harassment. The term *flirtation* rather than *harassment* downplays the severity of the act and the violent nature that marks the assaults.[41] It implies that the act is consensual and that somehow the victim and the perpetrator are in mutual agreement. In so doing, the use of the term *flirtation* reproduces a discourse and a culture of blaming the victim (Al-Jazeera 2013). In an entrenched culture of blaming the victim, answering back to the harasser becomes unacceptable and unexpected, and can, in some instances, provoke violent reactions. For instance, in 2012, sixteen-year-old Eman Mostafa was shot dead by her attacker because she spat at him for touching her breasts (Al-Jazeera 2013).

During the 2011 uprising, however, no incidents of sexual harassment were reported. In fact, the absence of sexual harassment from the uprising came to dignify the uprising in the media coverage of it. Female protestors confirmed that they felt "respected"[42] and "dignified."[43] In an interview with one of the organizers of the first *human chain* against sexual harassment in Egypt, the activist explained that "the street was ours for few days."[44] The spirit of communitas, however, is liminal, spatially, and temporally limited, as Turner highlights. Sexual harassment did not disappear during the time of the uprising – consider the attack against the CBS news foreign correspondent Lara Logan. While it may not have been observed in Tahrir Square, women were still being harassed outside the square and they continue to be to this day.

---

[40] Interviewee 28.
[41] El-Mohandes, Amal, Siham Ali, and Mostafa Hamdey, "Launching of [*Kanon Nashaz*]," November 25, 2014, Cairo Egypt. Panel discussion.
[42] Interviewee 24. Author's interview, Cairo, Egypt, July 2013.
[43] Interviewee 29.
[44] Interviewee 23.

One of the protestors I interviewed described how "you need not step so far from the square before all the ridiculousness starts."[45] By ridiculousness, she was referring to the verbal harassment made by some men. Another protestor described how she "would be cat-called while waiting for a cab at Talat Harb,"[46] which is "not far away from the square as you can tell."[47] This spatial divide between inside the square and outside the square is further reinforced by the following conversation with one of the protestors:[48]

RESPONDENT: We joined protests as a group, me and a group of my friends. We wanted to be more vocal and louder so I went and I bought a big drum, similar to the Ultras drum. I would use the drum at the Tahrir Square to create a rhythm and make our slogans more vocal.

INTERVIEWER: Interesting. Were you mocked though? It is quite uncommon to see a female drumming at a public space in Egypt!

RESPONDENT: I would say that I was being mocked and ridiculed outside of the square while I am on my way to the protests just for carrying a drum! But once I entered the square, people were so friendly and encouraging and I felt ... I didn't feel strange; it didn't feel awkward drumming there.

It is clear that, despite the communitas evident inside Tahrir Square during the demonstrations, social and gender norms common in Egypt were not altered in society at large. Furthermore, the communitas-like features of the square were conjunctural in their own right. Following the 18-day uprising, the Tahrir Square that represented the epicenter of solidarity and equality became the epicenter of sexual harassment.

Understanding women's experience through the lens of Turner's concepts of communitas and liminality is significant, as it offers an explanation that does not omit the obvious and most recurrent assertion made by my female interviewees that they felt equal to men and were treated equally at demonstrations during the 2011 uprising. The concept of liminality, furthermore, captures the limitation and temporality of this state of communitas, as liminal phases are temporally and spatially limited (Turner 1969, 1974). They emerge during times

---

[45] Interviewee 3.
[46] Interviewee 10.
[47] Ibid.
[48] Interviewee 26. Author's interview, Cairo, Egypt, July 2013.

of political transformation and end as reintegration or schism takes place among the different sides in the conflict (Turner 1969). Viewing this episode of contention as liminal allows us to reconcile women's accounts regarding the solidarity they felt during the uprising with the resurgence of inequalities and harassment following the uprising after Mubarak's resignation.

Among the popular explanations for the "vicious return of sexual harassment"[49] is that those involved in the demonstrations were not the same. Protestors came from a different social class, namely middle and upper middle social classes. Following the uprising, it was the "poor"[50] and "illiterate"[51] who demonstrated. Notwithstanding its popularity in scholarly and popular accounts, this explanation did not resonate with many of my participants. A number of participants explained how patriarchal social norms are prevalent among the middle and upper social classes in Egypt. One interviewee cited the documentary *Virginities* as an example of how patriarchy is deeply rooted in society regardless of one's level of education and/or wealth.[52] In *Virginities* the director examines young men's views regarding monogamy and reveals how men are not likely to marry their girlfriends if they have slept with them before marriage. My interviewee described the director's shock and how he subsequently ended friendships with many of his male friends on account of their "patriarchal double standard views."

Other participants believed that protestors "were carrying their coffin"[53] – an expression that denotes one close to death in Egypt – in such moments, one protestor explained: "you fear God and remember after-life punishment."[54] A number of my participants did not agree with this religious reading as there were "relaxed moments"[55] during the uprising in which "we sat there and just chatted,"[56] and "women's opinions were not belittled then."[57]

---

[49] Interviewee 42.
[50] Interviewee 21. Author's interview, Cairo, Egypt, July 2013. Interviewee 34. Author's interview, Cairo, Egypt, February 2014.
[51] Interviewee 19. Interviewee 48. Author's interview, Cairo, Egypt, June 2014.
[52] Interviewee 23.
[53] Interviewee 18. Interviewee 20.
[54] Interviewee 30.
[55] Interviewee 28.
[56] Ibid.
[57] Ibid.

What I term the *equal partner argument* was the most salient among my participants. Some protestors believed that sexual harassment was absent because, in times of danger, women fought "shoulder to shoulder with men"[58] at the "front line of fire"[59] and were thus respected and dignified by their male counterparts and treated by them as equals, "not minors in need of protection."[60]

Those who supported the "equal partner" explanation were very critical of "male anti-harassment chains."[61] Following the spread of sexual harassment in demonstrations after the 18-day uprising, several male protestors formed male-chains surrounding female protestors to protect them during demonstrations. Some female protestors described this practice as "counterproductive"[62] as well as reproducing "gender hierarchies"[63] and "the patriarchal norms of the alpha male."[64] It conditions women's political participation on the presence of a man to protect her and introduces a limited private space for women within a supposedly open public space. As one of my participants stressed:

I should freely protest, like I did during the 18 days, without being harassed. If I am harassed, you should join me in punishing the harasser and kicking them out of our protests. Limiting my participation within a circle is still a form of constraint, instead of opening up public spaces we are creating closed-off spaces for women's participation. With all due respect to the efforts of these men, this practice creates limits on women's participation and defeats its purpose. It communicates a message that notwithstanding women's presence in a supposedly open public space, her participation will remain limited and fenced off by a circle.[65]

Another protestor mocked the practice, asking: "Do we need to move surrounded by a bubble in every public space?"[66] In-depth research on the phenomenon of sexual harassment in Egypt, such as the studies done by Nazra for feminist studies, see the resurgence of sexual harassment as an attempt to exclude women from the political

---

[58] Interviewee 32.
[59] Interviewee 17. Author's interview, Cairo, Egypt, July 2013.
[60] Interviewee 6.
[61] Interviewee 41. Author's interview, Cairo, Egypt, February 2014.
[62] Interviewee 37. Author's interview, Cairo, Egypt, February 2014.
[63] Interviewee 39. Author's interview, Cairo, Egypt, February 2014.
[64] Interviewee 35.
[65] Interviewee 9.
[66] Interviewee 12.

and public space and to break the movement as a whole (see also Rizzo et al. 2012). The name of the group "Nazra" means the gaze, and in line with its name, the group aims to direct the society's gaze to women's rights and gender issues. Through knowledge production and documentation, strategic litigation, networking, and advocacy for gender issues, the organization works toward building an Egyptian feminist movement with the understanding that feminism and gender are political and social issues. Building upon their extensive interviews with survivors of sexual assault, they concluded that the process is a "deliberate" and "organized effort"[67] carried out on behalf of some political sects in the society to exclude women from participating in the public sphere and to break the will of their male counterparts (Nazra 2012, 2013).

In an unpublished report titled "Tajmiʿ Shahadat ḥawl Al-Iʿtidaʾat Al-Jinsyah wa Al-Ightiṣab Al-Jamaʿī fi Midan Al-Tahrir wa Muḥituh Al-waqiʿa Ma Byn 2011–2013" [A Collection of Testimonies of Sexual Harassment and Rape Incidents in Tahrir Square and its Vicinity 2011–2013], researchers at Nazra, El-Nadeem Centre for Rehabilitation of Victims of Violence and the New Women Organization, compiled the testimonies of twenty-eight survivors of collective sexual assault and harassment that took place in the vicinity of Tahrir Square between 2011 and 2013.[68] The testimonies describe how women were being groped by tens of men and how the sexual assaults included raping women using knives.[69] The pattern is the same in all the testimonies: two circles form, one surrounding the victim and assaulting her and the other fence the group and push off anyone who might try to rescue the victim. The victim is unable to tell who is helping and who is assaulting, one survivor describes: "I didn't know who was trying to help and who wasn't. Some were really just helping and others were pretending to help but actually touching my body parts."[70] In the same report, another survivor illustrates: "they were not using sexual phrases as

---

[67] Original in Arabic, my translation.

[68] In 2014, The International Federation for Human Rights (FIDH), Nazra for Feminist Studies, the New Woman Foundation, and the Uprising of Women in the Arab World published a report titled "Egypt: Keeping Women Out." The document expanded on the unpublished report and presented over 250 cases.

[69] Ghada Lotfy, director at the Egyptian Center for Women's Rights (ECW) also described in our interview cases where victims had to be hospitalized for a bleeding womb because of being raped by knives.

[70] Original in Arabic, my translation.

you would expect; some kept repeating, 'you are like my sister, do not worry'; but these were the same people pulling down my pants!"[71]

A volunteer at the OpAntiSH explained how the operation had to change their rescue plans by assigning female rather than male volunteers to rescue and intervene in operations.[72] As part of the intervention and rescue force, female volunteers stepped into mob assaults and tried to rescue the victim. This is because, another volunteer at the OpAntiSH explained, "at this point, the victim is very suspicious of any man."[73] The level of violence involved as well, Salma El-Nakash, director of Women's Political Participation program at Nazra describes, is often extreme.[74] Ghada Lotfy, director at the Egyptian Center for Women's Rights (ECW), added that by analyzing the way the sexual assaults were committed, it became clear that they were orchestrated.

This view that the post-uprising assaults on women were orchestrated has been echoed by NGOs leaders and even state officials, and it was a constant theme in my interviews. The rationale is that those who carry out this crime know that they are not only breaking the women's will and sending them home away from protests, but breaking the will of the revolutionaries. The systemic and organized nature of the attacks implies, many believed, that they are used as a political tool to discredit protestors and to deter women from political and public participation. Sameeha Dwidar, director of the Penal Policy and Crime Research division at the National Center for Social and Criminological Research, also saw the episode of mass sexual harassment as part of the "political drama"[75] directed and staged by the Muslim Brotherhood and their supporters to demonize the protests against the former Muslim Brotherhood president, Muhammed Mursī. She cites how the human rights committee of the Shura Council addressed sexual assault in February 2013, when members of the committee blamed women for the attacks in Tahrir, and recommended that they should not attend protests. Indeed, one committee member from a Salafi party,

---

[71] Original in Arabic, my translation.
[72] Interviewee 26.
[73] Interviewee 28.
[74] Author's interview, Salma El-Nakash, director of Women's Political Participation program at Nazra, Cairo, Egypt, December 2014.
[75] Author's interview, Sameeha Dwidar, director of the Penal Policy and Crime Research division at the National Center for Social and Criminological Research, Cairo, Egypt, November 2014.

Adel Afifi, even declared: "The woman has 100 percent responsibility" (Al-Jazeera 2013).

Like rape and sexual violence in wars, the use of sexual harassment and assaults to deter political participation is not exclusively carried out by religious and/or extreme conservative groups in a society. Studying the use of rape in wars, Charlotte Watts and Cathy Zimmerman describe how sexual violence against women is "a deliberate strategy to undermine community bonds and weaken resistance to aggression" (2002: 1233). When staged in times of conflict, violence against women is thus a political tool grounded in political calculation and justification and used toward political goals; it is a form of "sexual terrorism (Irhab Jinsi)," one activist explained, "of no religion."[76] The assaults, a member of the now-banned April 6 Youth Movement recollects, occurred under Mubarak's regime as well, by the police-hired thugs in the 2005 protests against the regime.[77]

A similar tactic was carried out by the ruling Supreme Council of the Armed Forces (SCAF) in Egypt following the removal of President Ḥusnī Mubarak, a number of my participants pointed out.[78] As the demonstrations in Tahrir Square continued to call SCAF to account, the army-backed security forces found ways to humiliate and intimidate female activists and protestors. Consider, for example, included the notorious virginity tests in March 2011 and the public stripping and beating of a female demonstrator in December 2011 (Tripp 2014: 150).

It is worth noting, however, that while attacks are most prevalent and brutal in protests and demonstrations, they also occur outside of the political landscape. The assaults took place in concerts, on public transportation, in workplaces and at home, to cite a few. The problem as such has far deeper roots in the political, legal, and social dynamics in Egypt. Engy Gozlan, the cofounder of HarassMap, a societal awareness campaign that tracks sexual harassment across Egypt using an online interactive map, added that there is a culture of impunity at

---

[76] Interviewee 51. Author's interview, Cairo, Egypt, June 2014.
[77] Interviewee 18.
[78] Interviewee 36. Author's interview, Cairo, Egypt, February 2014.
Interviewee 50. Author's interview, Cairo, Egypt, June 2014.
Interviewee 57. Author's interview, Cairo, Egypt, October 2014.
Interviewee 63. Author's interview, Cairo, Egypt, October 2014.
Interviewee 68.

home, in the street, and at police and legal levels which, unfortunately, ensures that assailants rarely face consequence for their actions.[79] The extent of sexual harassment and political violence in Egypt is an important question which I do not intend to fully cover in this book. My point is to underscore the temporal and spatial suspension of sexual harassment during the 18-day uprising at Tahrir Square. I use the example of sexual harassment to highlight the liminal and communitas-like features of this phase of contention in which female protestors experienced solidarity and equality. This is an important aspect of women's experience in the uprising and is among the influential factors that shaped women's framing of their participation. This explanation is situated within women's lived experience during the 2011 uprising; it does not omit their testimonies regarding the equality and solidarity they felt. These testimonies are made by women who are deeply immersed in the debate surrounding sexual harassment in Egypt, and some of them are among the vanguards in supporting anti-sexual harassment campaigns. Viewing this episode of contention as liminal allows us to reconcile women's accounts regarding the solidarity they felt during the uprising with the resurgence of inequalities and harassment following the uprising.

Conclusion

To borrow from philosopher Mikhail Bakhtin, framing is a "dialogical" phenomenon; its essence resides "not within us, but between us" (Medvedev and Bakhtin 1978: 8; Todorov 1984). Interactions among a movement's participants are thus important elements in framing and shaping their participation. These interactions are contextual and develop in the process of mobilization and action (Steinberg 1999b). They shape participants' subjective experience during collective action. The experience of women during the uprising is an important element in understanding how participants frame their participation in collective actions.

Expanding framing theory as I have tried to do in this chapter allows us to consider the ways in which collective action frames are shaped by the subjective experience of participants during times of

---

[79] Author's Interview, Engy Ghozlan, cofounder of HarassMap, Cairo, Egypt, December 2014.

contention. During this phase, the unity and solidarity among participants were ostensibly real and felt by female protestors. I use the case of the absence of sexual harassment to demonstrate the prevalence of the sense of communitas and to highlight the temporal limitation of this liminal phase. I argue that, given the prevalence of equality and solidarity during the 18-day uprising, women actively framed their participation utilizing the citizen frame. This frame was viewed by women as sufficient to incorporate gender equality rights and to sit comfortably in the post-uprising agenda.

In line with postcolonial feminist scholarship, the analysis presented in this chapter aims to capture the experience of female protestors in its entirety, presenting a *tertium datur* (third alternative) to the respective views of Western observers and Arab narrators. It seeks to emphasize the true yet conjunctural experience of equality and solidarity during the uprising while explaining the ways in which it influenced women's collective action frame. In so doing, I present "an archeology of women's recollections" in which I highlight overt ambiguities, ruptures, and shifts in women's experience.

The openness emerging from this analysis is not to be confused with cultural relativism; rather, it is driven by a burning need for "sincerity toward my interviewees." After all, recollection, as Haruki Murakami describes it in his novel *Kafka on the Shore* (2002), is "the only proof that I have lived." Indeed, recollection is the "trace" – appropriating Jacques Derrida's concept – that people leave behind in time. In preserving their trace and out of the need for sincerity toward my interviewees, I convey their recollection to the reader while keeping and – in fact – highlighting all the fragmentary splinters that marked their engagement and framing of the uprising.

5 | "Intu Bito' Sūzān" (You Are Suzanne's Clique): Gender and Political Opportunities in the 2011 Uprising*

The association between feminist groups and the regime advanced women's rights on limited fronts. The regime, however, ignored acknowledging the efforts and struggles of independent feminists and their role in advancing women's rights. This has contributed in part in viewing activists demanding gender equality post the uprising as 'Bito' Sūzān' [Suzanne's clique].[1]

In the shifting political landscape that accompanied the 2011 Egyptian uprising, voices speaking up for women's rights were often cast out as "Baqaya Al-Niẓam, Foloul [remnant of the old corrupt regime]"[2] and/or called, as Maya Morsy attests, "bito' Sūzān" in reference to being a clique of Suzanne Mubarak – Egypt's former first lady. Suzanne Mubarak appeared to take on the role of championing women's rights and advocating for gender equality through policies and initiatives. Legislation and laws promoting gender equality were therefore increasingly called "Sūzān's laws." Furthermore, Morsy adds, in this context the regime eliminated any feminist movement that existed in opposition to the state. Where feminist organizations did exist, they often had to act in accordance with the state's political priorities. Some women's rights groups traded their independence for visibility as the state, through policies of state-sponsored feminism, promised the movement limited gains and salience. Mubarak's government was heavily criticized, moreover, for systematically and explicitly exploiting the agenda of women's rights for political priorities narrowly linked to

* An abridged version of this chapter was presented under the title "Women's Collective Action Frame in the 2011 Egyptian Uprising" at the 111th 2015 American Political Science Association (APSA) Annual Meeting, San Francisco, USA, September 3–6, 2015.
[1] Author's interview, Maya Morsy, former regional gender practice team leader at the United Nations Development Program/Middle East Office (2014–2015) and current president of the National Council for Women, Cairo, Egypt, October 2014.
[2] Interviewee 60. Author's interview, Cairo, Egypt, October 2014.

enhancing the image, prestige, and ideological sustainability of the authoritarian regime (Elsadda 2011; Morsy 2014).

The close association between women's rights and Mubarak's regime had negative implications for women's issues, particularly at times of regime change and political transformation. Since the old regime appropriated the issues of women's rights in service of maintaining the status quo, rejecting the old regime entailed, at least in part, rejecting these regime-sponsored advancements. The absence of complete autonomy for feminist groups, the policies of state-sponsored feminism, and the place of gender in other political groups thus served as an important component of the political opportunity structure of the 2011 uprising. In the social movement paradigm, political opportunities are defined as the social, political, economic, and subjective conditions that allow the movement to emerge, expand, and resonate (Kitschelt 1986; Kries 1989, 1995; Jenkins and Perrow 1977; McAdam 1982; McAdam, McCarthy, and Zald 1996; Tarrow 1983, 2012; Tilly and Tarrow 2007). Within the tradition of the political opportunity approach, scholars have further focused on the opportunity structure of different groups such as women and how they emerge, expand, and change over time (Abdel Rahman 2012; Kuumba 2002; McAdam 1990, 1992; Noonan 1995).

In understanding women's engagement in the uprising, I apply an explicit gender lens to the political opportunities model. A gender-conscious approach to political process (Kuumba 2002) focuses on gender structures and women's experiences as important elements of the political opportunity structure (Abdel Rahman 2012; Kuumba 2002; Noonan 1995, to cite a few). Unlike conventional approaches to political process, a gender-explicit approach uncovers the gender inequalities and systematic divisions between women and men in political struggles. That is, it makes these inequalities central in our analysis and study (Kuumba 2001). This approach, I demonstrate, is appropriate for understanding and explaining women's activism in this initial episode of contention.

Utilizing a gender-conscious approach to the political process model, this chapter uncovers the political opportunities and constraints that framed women's engagement in the 2011 uprising from the standpoint of women. First, in elucidating the challenges to women's mobilization, I reveal how women negotiated sexism and ageism directed at young women in order to participate in demonstrations. Unlike conventional approaches to political process, this gender-explicit approach to political structure reveals the deep divisions and institutionalized inequalities between women and men and how it affected their engagement positively and negatively (Abdulhadi 1998; Kuumba 2001, 2002; Noonan 1995). Second, I trace women's agency and activism in the period prior to the uprising by very briefly surveying women's activism and participation in labor unions and philanthropic organizations at this time. Women's forms of participation in these venues are among the political opportunity structures that contributed to the mobilization and politicization of women. In making this argument, I expand notions of women's activism within Egypt's political structure and cultural context where the routes of women's empowerment projects were largely appropriated by state forces.

Locating Political Opportunities

The political process model emphasizes the social, political, economic, and subjective conditions that provide movements with the opportunity to surface, expand, and resonate. Favorable political opportunities provide space and momentum for social movement mobilization and increase the likelihood of success (Jenkins and Perrow 1977; McAdam 1982; McAdam et al. 1996; Tarrow 1983). Political opportunities cluster around three factors: shifts in the political opportunity structure, the organizational strength and resources of the participants, and their consciousness and perceived probability of success (Goldstone 2001; Meyer and Staggenborg 1996; Tarrow 2012). The political opportunity structure generally refers to the interplay between external institutionalized power relations and the social movement. Among the commonly cited political structures are: the openness of the system, the stability among elite networks, and the capacity for repression (Kuumba 2001; McAdam 1982; Tarrow 1996). According to the theory, shifts in the political structure combined with the movement's ability to galvanize organization and the participants' perceived likelihood of success catalyze protests.

The idea that the relative openness of the system encourages protests was initially put forward by sociologist Peter Eisinger. In his analysis of different municipal structures in the United States, Eisinger (1973) argued that the relationship between protests and political opportunities is curvilinear. Protests are most likely to take place in structures characterized by "a mix of open and closed factors" (1973: 15). This is particularly significant in the context of non-democratic regimes. The narrower the pre-existing avenue to participation, the more likely each new opening is to produce new opportunities for contention (Tarrow 1998: 78). In the case of Egypt, the appearance of movements such as the Kefaya and April 6 movements is often cited as significant in giving activists a site in which they could engage in action, access participation, and thus trigger wide contention.

In addition to these sites, Craig Jenkins and Charles Perrow (1977) argue that the appearance of influential allies is crucial for the emergence and spread of contention. Influential allies, I argue, are not limited to national actors; international powers are also powerful and necessary friends. International actors are equally important allies especially in an increasingly interconnected world and specifically in a strategic geopolitical region such as the Middle East. In the case of Egypt, the success of the Tunisian uprising and the de-certification of the Mubarak regime by the United States contributed to widening contention. It communicated a message to protestors that the US administration "blessed their uprising."[3] It is worth noting that many protesters were not initially "looking for approval from Western countries,"[4] and in fact many activists deliberately distanced themselves from Western discourses as these framings could have potentially "cast doubts on their agendas"[5] and discredited their "nationalist sentiment"[6] and "loyalty."[7]

The American de-certification of the Mubarak regime was, however, significant as it delegitimized the regime and left it powerless and vulnerable in the face of a mounting opposition. The implications of this new image of the regime as powerless and lacking support were significant. Among these implications was encouraging further mobilization among participants, who now believed that the success of the uprising was possible. Most importantly, it deepened divisions among national elites as seen in the defection of the Egyptian army (Ketchley 2014; Nassif 2012). This is significant in light of the long history of

---

[3] Interviewee 63.
[4] Interviewee 44.
[5] Interviewee 49.
[6] Interviewee 9.
[7] Interviewee 50.

the Egyptian army's economic dependency on the US administration (Abul-Magd 2011). This dependency dated back to the 1978 Camp David Accords that established the peace terms between Egypt and Israel under the sponsorship of Jimmy Carter's administration and led directly to the 1979 Egypt–Israel Peace Treaty ("Camp David Accords 1978" n.d.; Telhami 1990). As part of the negotiation, the United States committed several billion dollars' worth of annual subsidies to the Egyptian army (US Department of State 2009–2017).

Divisions and fractures among political elites offer strong motivations for resource-poor groups to engage in collective action and widening the circle of conflict (Tarrow 1998). In the case of Egypt, elite defection can be seen, as the army initially refused to violently suppress protests. Images of army protecting protests and the slogan of the "The Army and People Are United" [*Al-Jīsh wa Al-Sha'b Id Waḥda*] marked this episode of protests (Korany and El-Mahdi 2012; Lynch 2013). By seizing the role of "tribune of the people" (Tarrow 2012: 80), the army ensured that it preserved and increased its own political influence. This move had other implications: mobilizing more protestors and legitimating the uprising at large. This move therefore generated political opportunities for activists and groups in the uprising.

Repression is another, unlikely, factor that has ostensibly widened contention in Egypt (Korany and El-Mahdi 2012; Lynch 2012; Tarrow 2012, to cite a few). While repression could be viewed as a factor that deflates mobilization, in the case of Egypt, in the famous "Battle of the Camel" where the regime attacked and killed peaceful protestors in the early days of the demonstrations, it enraged the population. It increased the size of demonstrations and the scope of mobilization. Della Porta and Reiter (1998) suggest that it is easier to mobilize against violent and capricious police who throw sincere and peaceful protesters into jail than reasonable-sounding public authorities and security forces. This is particularly true in the case of Egypt. The early acts of police brutality in suppressing protesters who were initially calling for reform of the security forces resulted in turning people's resentment into more solid opposition. It turned moderate dissenters into opponents of the regime and forced them to demand the regime's overthrow as the condition for reform.

As the above analysis demonstrates, the political opportunity approach offers valuable insights into understanding the spread of contention in Egypt. Notwithstanding the significance of the above-surveyed aspects of opportunities in mobilizing protesters and encouraging participation in collective action, these factors did not directly translate into opportunities for women's engagement. That is, these opportunities did not equally encourage and facilitate women's participation in the uprising. Women continued to negotiate cultural and social constraints limiting their activism. Salient among these constraints were gendered forms of ageism toward youth. In the following section I elaborate the implication of these factors on women's activism and how they were able to negotiate these constraints. In so doing, I demonstrate the gendered nature of political opportunities. Specifically, I uncover how the same political opportunities do not equally encourage activism among both women and men and the ways in which gendered relations promote or constrain female activism and engagement in political struggles.

Gendering Political Opportunities

Feminist scholars have extended the political opportunity approach to consider gender structures and the ways in which political opportunities are gender differentiated (Noonan 1995; see also Abdulhadi 1998; Blackstone 2004; Kuumba 2001; McAdam 1990, 1992). As opposed to the larger political structure affording potential activists undifferentiated opportunities to rebel, Bahanti Kuumba (2001) explains that the differential experiences and structural locations of women and men in society affect their engagement and participation in political struggles (see also Barnett 1993; Robnett 1997; Walker 1991). In her study of the Montegro movement and anti-pass movements, Kuumba (2001) argued that global gender relations and class-based systems of power contribute to constraining and motivating social movement activities. Political opportunities, Rita Noonan (1995) elucidates in the same line, do not open up equal political spaces for men and women (Noonan 1995; see also Kuumba 2001; McAdam 1990). In this section I build upon this fledgling body of literature and demonstrate the ways in which sexism and ageism toward youth and young adults shaped and constrained women's activism, notwithstanding the leverage afforded by the political opportunities that opened up at the time of contention.

Young protestors made up the majority of participants in the uprising (Hoffman and Jamal 2012; Osman 2012). The uprising has often been dubbed in scholarly and popular accounts as the "Youth Uprising." However, the age of participants was often an obstacle to their participation. Several participants complicated the picture of their engagement by introducing the age factor as a constraint to political activism. Many noted how the political participation of youth broadly is conditioned on their parents' consent.

The literature on youth civic engagement echoes this point. The activism and political engagement of young people is constrained in ways that differ from adults (Lucas 1998; Sibley 1995; Westman 1991). They often face obstacles related to their age and their dependency. This is not only the case in the Middle East and North Africa, where youth stay longer within the family and remain largely dependent on their parents. Jack C. Westman (1991) introduces the term "juvenile ageism" to describe the different layers of discrimination that the youth face at the institutional, interactional, and individual-level by a variety of adult social actors in different societies.[8] To participate in social movements all young activists have to navigate adult power. The gendered nature of some of these challenges is, however, less studied in the literature on youth and civic engagement. Apart from a number of important contributions, the ways in which systems of gender shape younger people's activism in the public sphere remain largely under-researched (Gordon 2008; Yates and Youniss 1999; Youniss et al. 2002). Studying the ways in which gender and age shape the experience of female activists is important in Arab societies, as young women, especially unmarried ones, are expected to live with their parents regardless of their age until they get married and move out to their husband's place.[9]

---

[8] Another participant underscored the age factor in influencing young people's political participation sharing with me a popular joke at the time of the uprising. Young people, the joke goes, found it easier to confess to their parents that they had failed in school exams than that they had joined a demonstration.

[9] Married women also continue to face constraints imposed by their parents in addition to their spouses. According to one of my participants, a married woman is often more constrained and even more harshly criticized for her political activism. A married woman, she explained, is expected to "look after her home, husband, and kids rather than protesting in the streets." This view speaks to the widely accepted private–public divide in Egyptian society and stems from the misguided assumption that care work is the sole responsibility of women in Egyptian families.

Recollecting their experience in the uprising, many female protestors emphasized their parents' reluctance – and many times outright refusal – to allow them to participate in protests. Many protestors confessed to simply withholding information to avoid their parents' worry over their safety. "Sneaking out" was a very common strategy among my participants. Sneaking out often meant making up stories, lying about their whereabouts, skipping work or university to participate. Fully 61 percent confessed to participating often in protests without their parents' knowledge. Some, however, used a confrontational approach; one participant describes how, initially, during the early episodes of demonstrations, she participated behind her parents' back but then "got tired of leading this double life" and confessed to them.[10] While her family did not support her participation, they ultimately did not stop her.

Another intriguing theme raised by several participants was the contrasting views displayed by their parents regarding virtual versus on-ground activism. A female protestor had described her parents as very supportive of what she called "domesticated activism."[11] That is, they admired her political views, engaged with her in political discussions, and shared her political updates over Facebook. They even re-tweeted her political views. However, she described how they opposed her participation in on-ground protests. Their rejection to her on-ground activism, she explains, was because "they feared for my safety."[12] This fissure between the virtual and the street in parents' views of their daughters' activism was echoed by a number of participants.

Several female protestors described how their families were receptive and often took pride in their daughters' activism on social media. However, parents often displayed great opposition when their daughters took their activism to the public space. Parents' differential view surrounding virtual versus on-ground activism complicates our views regarding challenges to women's political participation in Middle Eastern societies. It reveals that these challenges are not always a sign of women's oppression or inferiority in their societies; rather, it is often situated and rooted in larger and more complex sociocultural relations

[10] Interviewee 26.
[11] Interviewee 58.
[12] Ibid.

and anxieties.[13] These sociocultural relations and anxieties were displayed not only by fathers but also by mothers and other male family members – such as husbands and brothers.

It is, however, worth noting that these anxieties and sociocultural constraints are often mediated by women's positionality and socioeconomic background. Even if virtual activism opened up a narrow space and opportunity for women's political activism, this opportunity was not accessible to all women. For instance, while in my interviews participants from the middle and upper middle class, particularly from Cairo – the capital city of Egypt – had no problem accessing internet activism, many other participants from the conservative rural town of Al-Fayoum did not enjoy this privilege, because of a stronger belief in this rural setting that "chatting with men and strangers was 'a wrong doing' (*'ib*), even if it was on a non-physical platform, like the internet."[14] Thus, although new information technologies allowed some young women to access the Internet and carry out forms of online activism and assert their political presence, this accessibility varied according to the woman's socioeconomic background and positionality. Furthermore, the significance of women's online activism was limited given that online communication is not a substitute for the on-the-ground participation in social movements (Christensen 2011; Gladwell 2010; Gordon 2008; Morozov 2011; Newsom and Lengel 2012; Rich 2011; Shirky 2008).

Like other activist groups, it is integral for young female activists to access public spaces and political organizations to participate in social movements (Westman 1991). However, this mobility is often challenged and obscured because of their age and gender. This "public" aspect of social movement activities, whose importance for collective action Jürgen Habermas (1989) emphasized, was often not as accessible as the virtual aspect for female protestors. While the Internet contributed to expanding women's engagement and activism,[15] their

---

[13] In her essay "Under Western Eyes" (1984) Chandra Talpade Mohanty criticizes the tendency of Western feminists to view "Third World" women as a singular group and all as victims of traditional culture. According to Mohanty, this view pays scant attention to historical context and cultural differences within the different societies and entrenches Western feminism as the norm while overlooking the agency and voices of "Third World" women.

[14] Interviewee 84. Author's interview, Al-Fayoum, Egypt, November 2014.

[15] In the case of Egypt, women were indeed very active in internet political activism. For instance, Israa Abdel-Fattah, also known as Facebook Girl,

activism needed to be grounded in real life and in public space to make any change. Some participants even emphasized that limiting your activism to the Internet "won't take your cause so far."[16]

Few participants emphasized that they participated with their parents' blessing and knowledge. This, however, was rarely the case with other female protestors in my study. A female protestor in her late twenties acknowledged that privilege and her family's attitude toward her activism were not representative of the conventional perspective in Egyptian society.[17] She explained how this attitude stemmed from her parents' long history of political activism, a history that dated back to the 1970s. It was an activism, she added, that had earned her father several years in prison.

Although some protestors cited how their parents influenced their political principles and were even their inspiration for participation, parents did not always support their daughters' public activism. Parents often opposed their daughters' activism not because they supported the ousted regime, but, rather, because they were concerned with their daughters' safety and security. For instance, an activist explained how while her parents did not allow her to spend the night at Tahrir Square, they did not judge the young women who did.[18] A number of female protestors also described how their parents strongly believed in the uprising and viewed it as "an ideal";[19] however, they utterly rejected "self-scarifying for an ideal." Explaining her parents' initial reluctance toward her participation in the 18-day demonstrations, a protestor described her parents' stance stressing that:

They strongly believed that people were unjustly suffering under Mubarak's regime. They strongly believed in the revolution, and that something had to be done to amend this unjust situation. They, however, were far from

helped to found Egypt's April 6 Youth Movement in 2008. Also, Asmaa Mahfouz, among others, was credited with sparking the uprising after posting a video blog mobilizing Egyptians to protest on January 25. For a detailed discussion of Asmaa Mahfouz's role in the 2011 uprising, see Wall and El Zahed 2011.

[16] Interviewee 42.
[17] Interviewee 60.
[18] Interviewee 42.
[19] Interviewee 9.

ready to risk their daughter's safety and well-being for the sake of this cause, regardless of its significance.[20]

However, parents' concerns over their daughters' activism was also deeply embedded in overlapping gender and social contexts. One participant – whose activism dates from before the uprising – explained how parents are concerned about not only their daughters' personal safety but about "safe-guarding [their] reputation in the neighborhood."[21] They worry, she adds, about "what the doorman will say if you returned late, what neighbors will think if they saw you participating in a sit-in or marching in a protest."[22]

Another protestor stressed that while her family supported her activism, the "street did not."[23] She recalled how the taxi driver who was driving her to Tahrir Square kept asking "what's in it for you?" and took the liberty to condemn her actions as "inappropriate for a decent young woman."[24] These forms of community surveillance are carried out by both men and women. One of my participants recalled how on her way to protests and while riding the Women-Only Metro carriages,[25] some female passengers insulted her for participating in demonstrations.[26] As my interviewee explained, they could often tell that she was on her way to demonstrations, as she would be carrying Egyptian flags with her. She remembers her shock when one of the women called her "a slut" and accused her of joining demonstrations to "hook up with men."[27] This perspective is deeply rooted in the social norms emphasizing the value of female virtue and modesty in Egyptian society, as well as nurtured and fostered by the ruling regime's practices and discourses and broader ideas of family honor, and community forms of surveillance of behavior.

Women in Egyptian society are at the forefront of ongoing debates over culture, religion, and the interpretation of Sharia. Such debate

---

[20] Interviewee 10.
[21] Interviewee 23.
[22] Ibid.
[23] Interviewee 60.
[24] Ibid.
[25] On all Cairo Metro trains, two passenger cars of each train are reserved for women. This policy was introduced as a way of protecting women from sexual harassment on crowded train lines.
[26] Interviewee 18.
[27] Ibid.

had its impact on their political activism. Hence, as men confronted security authorities, women confronted social, political, cultural, and religious authorities and constraints. In the context of Egypt, and to varying degrees in other Middle Eastern and North African societies, certain interpretations of Sharia law have contributed to limiting woman's political and public participation as she is represented as an incomplete human in constant need of protection and supervision (Abouzeid 2009; Abu El-Komsan 2012; Booth 2001; El Saadawi 1997, 2007). Egyptian reformers tried to show that it was not the tenets of Islam that subordinated women but rather an incorrect interpretation of it. Their efforts date back to the time of Sheik Rifa'a al-Tahtawi (1801–1871), Sheik Mohamed Abdu (1849–1905) and his disciple, Qasim Amin (1895–1908) – the intellectual reformer. On the basis of texts from the Qur'an, these leading religious intellectuals and reformers argued that female seclusion and subjection was un-Islamic (Amin 1992; El Saadawi 2007; Jayawardena 1986; Philip 1980). A hundred years later, discussions over women's position in Islam and in society still remain widely disputed in Egypt. Amina Shafiq, the first and only female secretary-general of the Egyptian Press Syndicate (1989–1993), as well as a symbol of 1960s leftism in Egypt, explains in a personal interview that this remains the case given the growing religious and conservative influence in society over the past few decades.[28]

This increase in the influence of conservatives is a function of at least two interrelated factors: the return of Gulf emigrants and the rise of popular Islam. First, in the late 1980s Egypt witnessed mass economic migration to the Gulf countries. The migration coincided with the oil boom in the Arab Gulf countries and the resulting demand for labor. This regional migration has often been temporary, that is, families eventually returned and settled in Egypt (Gruntz and Pagès-El Karoui 2013; Reichert 1993). Sociological and psychological studies that have been carried out on Egyptian migration to the Gulf countries, however, emphasize the impact of this experience on the migrants' value system (Gruntz and Pagès-El Karoui 2013; Reichert 1993). Specifically, Amina Shafiq argues that migrants brought with them the Gulf norms of female segregation and religious conservatism to Egyptian society.

---

[28] Author's interview Amina Shafiq, founder of left-wing Tajammu' Party, Cairo, Egypt, November 2014.

Second, the increase in the influence of the conservative religious tide is also a function of the distinction – and often contradiction – between what Baqer S. Alnajjar (2014) terms popular religion and official religion. According to Alnajjar, popular religion is imparted by families, neighbors, and friends. Meanwhile official religion is an integral part of the state, engaging in political discourse and legitimizing political regimes. Popular religion, I would further add, is increasingly acquired through the electronic medium as well as through private religious television. These channels, however, lean toward a proliferation in the production and dissemination of a radical religious intolerance within Islam and between Muslims and non-Muslims (Alnajjar 2014).

The distinction between official and popular religion produced various configurations in Egyptian society, where official religion was increasingly viewed as regime propaganda. Meanwhile, popular religion with its conservative leanings claimed a position of legitimacy above and over official religion. This strand of religion presented itself as unbiased/objective and closer to the heart and essence of Islam, "not tainted by the hands of the corrupted regime," that is not manipulated to support the regime's policies. The official religious messages and teachings communicated through its educational syllabus and state-owned channels were viewed as part of the regime apparatus. Thus, popular religion with its conservative message gained more resilience and popularity among the poor as well as the upper classes (Alnajjar 2014: 290–293). This influence was even strengthened by the Muslim Brotherhood proliferation across the poor classes in Egypt in its bid for votes and support in elections. Beyond its political wing, the Muslim Brotherhood has garnered support among the population for its decades of experience in providing social services to the poor segments of the population (Lynch 2013).

The ruling regime fostered and nurtured these conservative views and cultural norms regarding women's role and status by employing sexual harassment against female protestors to deter and sanction women's political activism and anti-regime activism at large. In a society where family honor is defined in large part by its females' honor, women's participation in protests was deemed to harm not only her reputation but also that of her entire family. Nehad Abu El-Komsan (2012) argues that the security forces made use of this culture by sexually harassing female political activists. Abu El-Komsan (2012) reads intentionality behind the media coverage of the incidents of sexual harassment that targeted female protestors by "regime-hired thugs" in the protest that took place in 2005 against the National Democratic Party – the ruling party at that time. She explains:

Cameras captured and aired the carrying out of gang harassment for political reasons. The goal was to terrorize Egyptians, the female protestor was not the goal but a means to breaking the protestors and to sending a message via the television to all Egyptians who dared to go out against the will of the ruling party or even to just criticize it. (Abu El-Komsan 2012: 44)

In that sense, sexual harassment became the regime's weapon to break the will of the activists, both male and female. The incapacity of the movement to protect its female supporters embarrassed the movement. Furthermore, families who watched the acts of sexual harassment became even stricter in preventing female members from participating in any form of political activism.

As such, despite the perceived relative openness of Egyptian society, the prevailing culture continued to deal with women as the weaker person constituting a potential threat to family honor and in need of constant supervision and protection. Women's engagement in the public and political sphere was thus often challenged and opposed by the family and broader society on the basis of love. Underpinning this argument are paternal forms of control and discrimination, which often have originated in customs and traditions, more than religion per se. The extent to which these norms prevail, however, varies relatively across different classes and communities in Egypt, as well as within specific families, as noted.

As a response to the security vacuum that marked the period after the uprising, Rania Ramadan, a facilitator at the Population Council project's Niqdar Nisharik [We Can Participate] in Al-Fayoum, notes that many families forced their young daughters to get married as a way of protecting them.[29] The same observation was made by another female participant from El-Mahalla. She, too, noted that a growing number of young girls – as young as 14 and 15 years old – got married to older men following the uprising.[30] She, however, argues that this is because of the deteriorating economic condition, and corruption – where the legal age of marriage

---

[29] Author's interview. Rania Ramadan, a facilitator at the Population Council project's Niqdar Nisharik [We Can Participate], Al-Fayoum, Egypt, November 2014.

[30] Interviewee 78. Author's interview, Al-Mahala, Egypt, November 2014.

is not enforced. These create the conditions which may allow some families to get away with marrying off their girls at a young age.

In this section, I have demonstrated how the immediate political opportunities were insufficient to mobilize women and facilitate their participation in the uprising. An opening in the political structure was not a sufficient condition for women's participation. Women still negotiated societal constraints that governed their participation. Salient among these constraints is navigating parental worry and power. While this can be said to have affected both male and female youth broadly, women were often more influenced by this factor than their male counterparts. I have thus argued that women's understanding of parental power and their negotiation with their parents affected how they benefited from the political opportunities at the time of the uprising. An understanding of young women's activism and engagement thus necessitates analyzing the effect of gender dynamics, parental control, and women's access to public space.

Shifting Opportunities and Constraints

In their study of historical and modern movements, Tilly and Tarrow (2007) observe that opportunities signaled to "some" are also available to "many," and that the different sectors of movements experience opportunities differently (Tarrow 1998: 77; see also McAdam et al. 2001; Tilly 1978). This is because, I suggest, the nature of opportunities follows the inclination of the early vanguards, who initially contributed to cracking the structure and thus creating opportunities. Furthermore, political opportunities are a by-product of the immediate policy environment as well as the regime's relations with different groups.

In the 2011 uprising, the vanguards – such as the April 6 Youth Movement and Kefaya – were largely social movement organizations with diverse backgrounds and cross-sectional affiliations. They were in a sense a movement of movements. Donatella Porta (2005) writes extensively about the significance and nature of this "movement of movements" emphasizing how these movements are characterized by their loose rather than rigidly structured nature. Groups and individuals within the movements are weakly linked and feel part of a collective effort (Della Porta et al. 2005). The April 6

Youth Movement in 2008, and Kefaya before it, are movement of movements as they created a new model of political opposition. They built a diverse and youthful movement by collaborating with different groups and working across diverse dialogical lines (see Shorbagy 2013; Singerman 2013). The significance of this movement of movements' model is that it broadened participation and thus generated an impact on the regime.[31]

In these organizations, activists who were at the time of the interviews members in the April 6 Youth Movement elaborate: women's rights were part of a broader agenda;[32] they were never explicitly articulated as a standalone objective.[33] The absence of women's rights from this model contributed to sidelining gender issues from the political opening. While these sites are significant for locating women's agency, their impact on pushing forward the agenda of women's rights in Egypt is largely contested. This is particularly the case as the vocabulary of women's rights and gender equality was not explicitly prominent in their agenda. The agenda of women's rights, as such, continued to be appropriated and institutionalized by the corrupt ruling regime in Egypt.

I do not wish to deemphasize the significance of the Kefaya and April 6 movements in effectively challenging an authoritarian regime. The Egyptian regime was more effective at co-opting weak opposition parties, dividing NGOs, and imprisoning independent oppositions (Hassan 2010; Lim 2012; Shorbagy 2013; Singerman 2013). Unlike these formal institutions, Kefaya and the April 6 Youth Movement

---

[31] In line with several Middle East scholars and commentators, I view the Egyptian 18-day uprising as post-ideological and post-Islamist (Bayat 2011a; Dabashi 2012; Mahdavi 2014). This paradigm shift was largely brought about by the failure of Islamist and nationalist projects and the development of new forms of political participation and expressions; it has resulted in the emergence of a new kind of Arab public and politics in which the language of human rights, democracy, and dignity is central (Bayat 2013). It is, however, important to note that while these uprisings were in many aspects "post," there are elements of the "past" in the "post," I contend. Indeed, writing on the process of construction and reconstruction, Derrida (1973) holds that something new in thinking can be evoked only by supplementing something already given. In this sense, the supplement does not erase the established meaning but writes over it, and thus is always bound to it. Collective action frames are therefore not woven from brand new cultural and political cloth; they incorporate elements from the past and the post.

[32] Interviewee 18.

[33] Interviewee 20.

were "movement of movements," as their network was loose and their membership was informal. The regime was thus less successful in tracking members and completely destroying and/or dividing the movement (see Singerman 2013).

My point is that the weakness of Kefaya and the April 6 Movement lies in its inability to open up political and public discussion of women's rights and to create new language and mechanisms for gender equality. The name of the movement, Kefaya (the Egyptian word for "enough") embodied a clear message and articulated a strong master frame (Singerman 2013). Egyptians were fed up with Mubarak's regime, they had had "enough" of political corruption, economic calamities, and police brutality (Lim 2012; Shorbagy 2013; Singerman 2013). As Diane Singerman (2013) eloquently argues, the word "enough" implicitly conveyed the target of discontent (the Mubarak regime) and was able to motivate some people to join collective action. Its weakness was that "enough" did not propose an alternative plan beyond ousting the Mubarak regime (Singerman 2013) and, I hold, did not explicitly include gender equality in its agenda.

The agenda of women's rights in Egypt is, in fact, rife with complexities and tensions. The framing of women's rights as a dimension of liberation has always been challenged in Egypt. Before the uprising, women's rights, as already discussed, were identified with policies of state-sponsored feminism. However, the agenda of gender equality, Sholkamy argues, was the "pet project of the regime" (2012a: 156). The National Council for Women in Egypt, which is the national machinery for the empowerment of women, was commonly perceived as the "regime mouthpiece (Boq Al-Niẓam),"[34] explains Fatma Khafaga, director of the Alliance for Arab Women and former director of the Office of Women's Complaints, National Council for Women, 2000–2002. She criticizes the Council for its role in circumscribing independent feminist organizations and competing against them for funding. The crisis and isolation of the feminist movement was apparent in the first few months after the 2011 uprising. Elham Aidarus, legal representative of the Bread and Freedom Party, highlighted this crisis and isolation, citing the mounting calls to dismantle the Council in the period immediately following the uprising and adding that

---

[34] Author's interview, Fatma Khafaga, director, Alliance for Arab Women, Cairo, Egypt, November 2014.

"some young feminists refrained from becoming members in it."[35] Legislative victories secured by the Council have also been attacked and called "Suzan's Laws," even though they were the result of a decades-long struggle by feminists and women's rights advocates.[36]

In addition to isolating the feminist movement from the masses, the policies of state-sponsored feminism yielded modest and class-differential improvements in the status of women in Egypt (Abu-Lughod 2001; Ahmed 2012; Badran 1988; Baron 2005; Dawood 2012; Hatem 1994, 2011; Sholkamy 2012a) because the policies were largely instrumental and politically motivated. Consider, for instance, the approval of a women's quota in the 2010 parliament and the allocation of sixty-four seats to women. On the surface it appeared as advancement for women, while in reality fifty-six seats went to the ruling party, reinforcing its domination over the political landscape ("Official Results," 2010). Policies of state-sponsored feminism did not, as such, necessarily deliver real cultural changes and/or substantial gender equalities.

This is "the classic trap for feminist movements in Third World countries" (Abd El-Hameed 2013), as authoritarian governments attempt to constrain the feminist movement without offering genuine gains.[37] In the case of Egypt, notwithstanding the relatively progressive laws and policies criminalizing female genital mutilation or women trafficking, poor working class women and women from rural areas continued to pay the heaviest price for political corruption and sexual violence (Egyptian Initiative for Personal Rights 2013; ECWR Egyptian Women's Status Report 2010).

The implication of this full control in conjunction with the cosmetic advancements in women's rights was that it distanced the discourse of women's rights from its grassroots bases and associated it with the regime in power (Sholkamy 2012a). The regime blocked every independent initiative and appropriated "gender issues" under its name (Sholkamy 2012a; Sorbera 2013). Even long, daunting struggles

---

[35] Author's interview, Elham Aidarus, legal representative of the Bread and Freedom Party, Cairo, Egypt, November 2014.

[36] Author's interview, Maya Morsy, regional gender practice team leader at the United Nations Development Program/Middle East Office (UNDP), Cairo, Egypt, October 2014. Author's interview, Elham Aidarus, legal representative of the Bread and Freedom Party, Cairo, Egypt, November 2014.

[37] I am thankful to Dr. Martina Rieker director of the Cynthia Nelson Institute for Gender and Women's Studies at the American University in Cairo for directing me to this body of literature, November 2014, Cairo, Egypt

carried out by women's rights groups and activists against the regime were omitted. Victories following the long struggles with the regime were not attributed to women's groups and their struggle but rather presented as a grant from the regime. A case in point is the appointment of female judges in Egypt's legal system. The appointment came, Maya Morsy explains, following extensive debates between the regime and several women's right groups and advocates.[38] These struggles went unnoticed and unacknowledged.

The Islamist opposition and labor movements, meanwhile, have been effective in mobilizing the lower classes, for whom the discourse and vocabulary of feminism seems alien in terms of class and culture (Meriwether and Tucker 1999; Nelson 1991; Sholkamy 2012a; Sorbera 2013; Zuhur 1992). The Muslim Brotherhood's approach to the agenda of women's rights and the status of its female members in the organization is an illustration of this. Their approach is informed and largely based on the teachings and ideological premises of Hassan al-Banna (1906–1949), the Islamist theorist and founder of the Muslim Brotherhood in Egypt. In al-Banna's article published in 1940, entitled "The Muslim Woman" [Al-Mar'a Al-Muslima], al-Banna prescribed a strict gender role for men and women based on biological differences (1984). He emphasized the primary role of women as responsible for childbearing and motherhood and rejected their presence in the public space, describing it as contradicting Islam and its decrees.[39] This gendered construction of women's role continued to mark the Muslim Brotherhood's approach to women albeit in a more subtle and concealed way. The organization recognized the significant role of women in sustaining the movement and carrying out its outreach activities through religious and welfare programs. The group adopted a twofold utilitarian approach toward women and its female members. The crux of this approach was utilizing women' and their ability and access to secure support and recruit voters to support the movement during elections. Meanwhile, the group granted women only limited access to leadership positions.

[38] Author's interview, Maya Morsy, October 2014.
[39] See Mariz Tadros' (2011) discussion of the Hassan al-Banna discourse and its influence on the Muslim Brotherhood's approach to the agenda of women's rights and their status in Egypt.

For instance, while Zaynab Al-Ghazali (1917–2005) was highly respected and honored by the organization for her roles and sacrifices,[40] she was never a member of the Guidance Bureau. Al-Ghazali was the founder of Jama'at Al-Saīdat Al-Muslimat, the Muslim Ladies Association in 1936. While al-Ghazali stressed upon the independence of her organization from the Muslim Brotherhood, she was closely affiliated with the larger Islamist organization (al-Ghazali and Farouk 2012: 14). It is worth noting, however, that the roots of al-Ghazali's activism and formulation should be traced to her participation and membership in the Egyptian Feminist Union in Egypt. At the age of 16, al-Ghazali joined the union, but she soon left it and established the Muslim Ladies Association that promulgated a strand of Islamic feminism, encouraging women to seek religion as a means to agency and advancement. The status and role of al-Ghazali in the Muslim Brotherhood offers us a glimpse of the place of women in the Brotherhood discourse and framework. Female members are not allowed to occupy leadership positions inside the organization and their commitment to the organization rather than their activism in the area of women's rights takes center stage in collective memory.

Trade unions in Egypt are far from being egalitarian or explicitly profeminist either (Beinin 2010; Duboc 2013). While women are involved in trade unions, they are often relegated to the backroom rather than leadership positions.[41] In the trade union elections of 2001–2006, women secured only 4 percent of the local union committee positions, 1.5 percent of the local union presidencies, and 2 percent of the positions on the executive boards of general unions (Badr 2007: 73). In the 2006–2011 elections, the former Minister of Manpower and Migration (2006–2011), Aisha Abd al-Hadi, announced that women won 1,000 out of 18,000 seats, approximately 5.5 percent, on local union committees (International Labor Conference 2008, cited in Beinin 2010: 75). The status of female leadership in Egypt's trade unions is not an exception; feminist scholars emphasize the ways in which trade unions are often restrictive of women's differences, leadership, and rights (Connaughton 2013; Parker and Foley 2010; Warskett 2001).

---

[40] In her memoir, Al-Ghazali narrated how she was subject to vicious and brutal torture after her imprisonment between 1965 and 1971, under the Nasserist regime, for her association and service with the Muslim Brotherhood.
[41] See Joel Beinin's (2010) discussion on women's status in trade unions in Egypt.

Besides the limited presence of female leadership in trade unions, the identity of women and their demands are often tangential in debates about workers' solidarity and collective bargaining in Egypt. Women's rights and gender equality claims are not central in the discourses and frames utilized by the union and its female members (Alexander 2012; Morsi 2008). In framing their claims and collective action, female members often deliberately distance themselves from "accusations" (Morsi 2008) of being feminists and instead emphasize the wider resonance of their demands among workers. Trade unions in Egypt, thus, are not often receptive spaces for the development and articulation of a strong women's rights discourse and explicit feminist activism.

An example of the absence of explicit gender issues from the labor movement was the El-Mahalla strike. The strike is now acknowledged in popular and scholarly accounts to have represented the "first flutters" of a popular rebellion (Duboc 2013). The workers of El-Mahalla initially went on strike to demand disbursement of an overdue annual bonus. Marie Duboc (2013: 29) in her ethnographic study of the protests comments that the strike "began when female workers mobilized and chanted the slogan, 'Where are the men? Here are the women!' to shame their colleagues into joining the strike."

Women such as Fatma Ramadan joined unions struggling for freedom of association and the right of collective action. Ramadan has spent more than a decade in courts fighting for the right to membership in unions and workers' committees (Sholkamy 2012a). Women expressed some grievances related to "matrimony permission required from management"[42] and even "harassment."[43] The movement's strategy, however, focused primarily upon the more traditional labor issues motivating the strike, issues that clustered mainly around the anti-unionist attitude of management and the concerns over working conditions (Duboc 2013). The main discourse of the strike relied on the classical framing of class struggle, emphasizing precarious working conditions and the violation of the right to organize (Amar 2011: 40–41; Duboc 2013). Less emphasized, though, were women's specific grievances and gender inequalities on the factory premises.

An equally important channel for mobilizing and politicizing female participants is their involvement in charitable organizations and

---

[42] Interviewee 78.
[43] Interviewee 79. Author's interview, El-Mahalla, Egypt, November 2014.

community development initiatives. These organizations and initiatives, studies have shown, have grown exponentially in Egypt since the 1990s (Daly 2010; Haddara et al. 2013).[44] In line with the literature, I argue that these organizations are important sites for empowering and politicizing youth and particularly young women (Bayat 2010; Daly 2010; Ibrahim and Sherif 2008; Mahmood 2005; Pruzan-Jørgensen 2012). In my view, these sites are significant for a number of reasons. In authoritarian regimes, these seemingly apolitical sites are tolerated and often encouraged by the state as they step in to fill the state's economic and social role by providing goods and services for the poor. As such, they are perceived as "agents maintaining the status quo," Shaheda El-Baz, director of the Arab and African Research Center contends.[45] In a personal interview, she explains how, by satisfying some of the basic needs of the poor segments of the population, these organizations contribute to assuaging the masses' anger and frustration against the government.

A contrary view, however, is advanced by Asef Bayat in his book *Life as Politics* (2010). In it, Bayat draws our attention to how these sites are political, telling us about the "art of presence" and "agency in times of constraints" (2010: 15). Barbra Ibrahim (2008) further unpacks the implications of political constraints on civil society and youth activism in Egypt. Analyzing civil society in Egypt, she stresses how traditional venues for participation and activism may not be available in an authoritarian political climate such as in Egypt. In line with these modes of thinking, I contend that these sites are an umbrella under which new challengers are often formed and actors are politicized.

Many of my participants describe how their involvement in charities and community volunteering transformed them. It particularly brought them closer to the regime's injustices evident in "the dire poor condition suffered by many segments of the population."[46] Through their involvement, activists were exposed to the "plight of poverty"[47] that marked the life of the majority of the population. Activists were

---

[44] I am thankful to Dr. Mona Amer, Associate Professor at the American University in Cairo, Egypt, for directing me to this body of literature, December 2014, Cairo, Egypt.

[45] Author's interview, Shaheda El-Baz, director of the Arab and African Research Centre, November 2014.

[46] Interviewee 61.

[47] Interviewee 53.

further politicized in these sites as the latter served as a space to debate politics and share information. For instance, one of my participants described how "her journey to politics"[48] started at a community organization working on poverty reduction. She describes how she did not really follow the news before the uprising; however, it was through her involvement in charity work that she became aware of "the stories of the regime's corruption."[49] The informing function of these organizations was underscored in a number of my interviewees. The discussions in the organization meetings and among members about the politics of state corruption and injustices became one of the major sources of trusted information for them.

Access to these informal, and ostensibly apolitical, sites is particularly significant for women's mobilization. In her book *Avenues of Participation*, Diane Singerman (1995) launches a searing critique of political theory that narrowly locates political power in state institutions. For women in the Arab Spring who were largely marginalized from the formal political structures, the civic domain and social life became sites for the cultivation of agency (Singerman 2013; see also Bayat 2010, Bilge 2010; Jaunzems 2011; Mahmood 2005; McLarney 2015; Winegar 2012; Zaatari 2006). Several of my interviewees stressed how the seemingly apolitical nature of these sites offered women important opportunities to access information and public participation.

This is particularly significant for young women, as volunteering is an acceptable way to network and make new friends away from family supervision.[50] In fact, society often encourages women to get involved in social activism and philanthropy, and women performing such roles are always highly regarded. This, undoubtedly, plays on gender stereotypes and the essentialist representation of women as caregivers. For instance, one of my participants mockingly described how her parents made sure to mention her charity work to prospective grooms, and specifically that they mentioned her volunteer activities to show that she had a "kind heart and motherly feminine quality."[51] Another interviewee

---

[48] Interviewee 41.
[49] Ibid.
[50] Interviewee 63.
[51] Interviewee 35.

contrasted her parents' pride in her volunteer and charity work with their anger and rejection of her activism in unions.[52] While charity work could be interpreted as an extension of women's care jobs and roles in domestic space, these sites were important outlets for women's social and political engagement. The emancipatory features of these activities were emphasized by several participants. They described how their involvement in these organizations and initiatives allowed them to "push the limits with their parents"[53] and negotiate some of the restrictions, such as "extending the curfew"[54] and "traveling to dis-privileged locations"[55] – which are often seen as unsafe for women. It thus allowed activists to renegotiate the limits of young women's activism.

However, the success of labor movements, charities, and Islamic opposition in mobilizing women for the organizations' agenda, Sorbera (2013) argues, fostered a view of feminism by the majority of the population as an elitist movement, sometimes accused of being incapable of producing grassroots activities. The movement was often perceived as elitist given the history of its evolution and development. By the late nineteenth century, females from the elite and aristocratic class led the movement and channeled women's demands. In modern times, the oft-cited "first lady" syndrome also contributed to framing the feminist movement as elitist. The prevalent public perception, Hoda Elsadda (2011) rightly argues, has long associated women's rights groups and their activities with the former first lady, Suzanne Mubarak, and her entourage.

The association of women's rights with the old corrupt regime in Egypt explains in part why protestors distanced themselves from the discourse of gender equality in the framing of their demands in the 2011 uprising (Sholkamy 2012a). As such, the uprising expanded political opportunities for women to participate and voice their demands as citizens of Egypt. However, it was not an opportunity to voice gender-specific demands. Political opportunities, as I have already argued, were situated within the group's prior relation with the former regime and its tradition of activism.

---

[52] Interviewee 31.
[53] Interviewee 23.
[54] Interviewee 18.
[55] Interviewee 27. Author's interview, Cairo, Egypt, July 2013.

Conclusion

In his analysis of political opportunities, Sidney Tarrow describes opportunity structures as the "basic grid within which movements operate" (2012: 85), but, as Tarrow emphasizes, this grid is "seldom neutral between social actors." This chapter has offered a survey of the political opportunities that served as the grid for the 2011 uprising in Egypt, with an eye to how gender mediated women's access to these new openings in the system. Specifically, I highlighted the ways in which sexism and ageism toward young women shaped and constrained their activism notwithstanding the leverage afforded by political opportunities at the time of contention. Furthermore, I uncovered how the agenda of women's rights faced challenges in the political environment of the 2011 uprising and situated this within the group's prior relations with the regime. The chapter thus offers a nuanced view of political opportunities, a view that situates them in a system of gender inequalities and relations with immediate and distant conventional and contentious politics.

Writing about women's experience in the Arab Spring, John Davis (2013) describes how things that happened to women as women did not happen in a vacuum. Rather, women's experiences are related to gender, class, and cultural structures. This occurs within a system of constructed expectations about women's public activism that explain, express, reinforce, and sometimes reproduce gender divisions and differential access. The character of opportunities, I further suggest, is situated within this overall structure and relation between the state and different groups. This relation has an influence on the articulation of the movement's demands and the framing of participation by its different groups. I am not implying that this influence is detrimental; a movement's agenda can be influenced by its different subgroups. The influence of different groups, however, is determined by their available resources, the resonance of their message and frame, and the opening of new opportunities. Political opportunities are a system of "openings and closures" that both isolates demands and makes the same demands possible by triggering further openings and opportunities (Tarrow 2012: 77–92; see also Kuumba 2001; Noonan 1995).

Notwithstanding the limits of political opportunities that gave rise to the 2011 Egyptian uprising, the uprising had a significant mediating effect on women's agency and activism. Collective action, regardless of its outcome, often expands opportunities to other groups (Tarrow 2012: 89). Protestors demonstrate the significance of collective action, they encourage other groups to mobilize, display contentious repertoires and introduce new issues and demands (Tarrow 2012; Tilly 2007). As we will see in the concluding chapter, the 2011 Egyptian uprising expanded the doctrine of dignity and rights that later became the master frame of the women's movement. It showed the movement, in a dramatic way, the path for change and reform.

6 | *What Holds Next? The Politics of Hope and Disappointment**

This book opens with an optimistic and forceful statement given by Tawakkol Karman, the Nobel Peace laureate and Yemeni activist, on women's leading role in the Arab uprisings of 2010/2011. In the years separating Karman's statement from the current political reality, a lot has happened that has fundamentally changed and challenged this aura of optimism that marked the initial phase of the uprisings. In Egypt, women have been largely marginalized from the political process and violence against women not only resumed but also escalated to unprecedented levels. Disappointing gender outcomes persisted throughout the transitional period, under SCAF's interim rule as well as under the former president, Muhammed Mursī, the Muslim Brotherhood presidential candidate.

The virginity tests[1] carried out by military doctors against female protesters (Amnesty International 2011) and the brutal beating and exposing of the "girl in the blue bra" became the hallmarks of SCAF's violence against female activists (Reuters 2011). Gender discrimination and violence against women became further institutionalized and intensified under the regime of Mursī, and the Muslim Brotherhood. The constitution and the elected parliament institutionalized deep-seated inequities and gender discriminations. Women's rights advocates heavily scrutinized the constitution of 2012 for its violations

---

* An abridged version of this chapter was published at the London School of Economics Middle East Centre blog under the title "What Holds Next? The Politics of Disappointment." The full article can be found at: http://blogs.lse
.ac.uk/mec/2015/08/11/what-holds-next-the-politics-of-disappointment/.

[1] Samira Ibrahim and at least six other female protesters were subjected to virginity checks performed by a military doctor in March of 2011. The military claimed that this was a standard procedure to shield the army from later accusations of rape. Ibrahim filed a legal complaint against the military and the court ruled decreeing the illegality of the practice. However, a military court acquitted the doctor charged with performing the tests in March 2012.

of women's rights. The contentious constitution was accused of jeopardizing women's personal liberties and civil rights (McLarney 2013; NCW and Dokhan 2015; Ottaway 2013). Furthermore, the members of the parliament displayed great resistance toward calls for gender equality and its members, particularly those from Al Noor Salfaist Party and the Muslim Brotherhood's Freedom and Justice Party, often came under fire for their overtly patriarchal and misogynist stances (McGarth 2012; NCW and Dokhan 2015; Tadros 2012). The agenda of women's rights continued to stumble following the overthrow of Mursi's regime in June 2013. The current military-backed regime of President Abdel Fattah el-Sisi seemingly advocates the agenda of women's rights while curtailing the freedom of independent women's organizations.

For many observers these mixed gender outcomes following the uprising are signs that the grand visions of the uprising are gone; more dramatically, that the "Egyptian Spring"[2] was a false hope in a better tomorrow that we could not control and that politics now is one marked with disappointment. I palpably felt that disappointment was the overarching and bitter emotion that characterized the last rounds of my field research in Egypt.

Disappointment emerges as people compare the expectations of the uprising to the post-uprising realities. It also emerges as people contend with the murkiness and contingency of political agency under such conditions (Greenberg 2014: 8; see also Gould 2001, 2009). Jessica Greenberg, in her study of the experience of activists in the post-uprising period in Serbia, defines disappointment as "a condition of living in contradiction, of persisting in the interstitial spaces of expectation and regret" (2014: 8). While disappointment often leads to political detachment and inaction, it may also give rise to pragmatic hope (Gould 2001, 2009; Greenberg 2014; Tarrow 2001). This sense of pragmatic hope is born out of confusion over what reform is and how it can be sustained amid a climate of authoritarianism. In this chapter, I map the field in which the politics of disappointment and hope unfolded among women's groups after the 2011 Egyptian uprising. Specifically, I argue that disappointment does not mark the end of politics; rather, it may give rise to pragmatic hope and activism. My analysis suggests that notwithstanding the prevalence of disappointment

[2] Interviewee 70.

among women's groups, action and activism continue nonetheless to take place despite a sense of dismay or even perhaps futility.

In pursuing this argument, I adopt a twofold approach. In the first section, I offer a dynamic explanation of the challenges that emerged during the transitional period and how activists dealt with failures and navigated this difficult sociopolitical terrain. I build upon participants' accounts and experiences to highlight the influence of deep state, democratic deficiency, state-sponsored feminism, and authoritarian resilience on activists' experiences. The survey of these forces encourages us to moderate our expectation and appreciate the diminutive forms of sustained activism that managed to develop and emerge against all the odds. In the second section, I highlight some of the ways in which female activists reconfigure their actions, demands, and strategies. I argue that female activists maintain their activisms and the memory of resistance through participation in creative social and/or artistic initiatives, engagement in critical debates over long-standing taboos, and reformulation of their vocabulary and forms of activism. This survey is significant as the failure to consider and analyze the changing spaces for mobilization and the nature of activism in the Middle East and North Africa blinds scholars and policymakers to the important changes taking place on the ground and contributes to stereotyping the region as stagnant and women as passive.

Studying the politics of disappointment is momentous as disappointment can be eliminated in the experience of many new – as well as older – democracies in the Middle East and North Africa (MENA) region and beyond (Amanat 2012; Brownlee, Masoud, and Reynolds 2013; Byman 2012; Doran 2011; Tabaar 2013). "All, all dead," Thomas Jefferson, American Founding Father, wrote to a friend near the end of his life (Wood 1993: 368). Jefferson's disillusionment, historian Gordon S. Wood explains in his book *The Radicalism of the American Revolution*, resulted not from activism itself, but from the ambitiousness of his vision for America and the revolution's actual outcome (Wood 1993: 368). The same was true following historical and modern episodes of contention in Europe. Following the Russian revolution and World War I, a reverse wave of authoritarianism advanced slowly over the course of the 1920s and 1930s notwithstanding the initial course of democratization of 1918/1919 (Huntington 1993; Weyland 2016).

Furthermore, studying the politics of disappointment is meaningful, as disappointment is a powerful force with significant influence on political engagement and participation. As a result of being disappointed in the political process, individuals may self-censor their actions and distance themselves from activism and political engagement. In understanding the puzzle of collective action and inaction, economist Albert Hirschman writes about the "rebound effect" which describes how individuals who participated with enthusiasm in political activism return to private life with a degree of disgust proportional to their effort during collective action (2002: 80; see also Tarrow 2012). Disappointment in the political process and its outcomes following episodes of contention is thus a huge force in curbing – not only inducing – activism and thus contributes to explaining setbacks following major political transformation.

Finally, and more specifically in line with the crux of my research, women are the group most likely to experience disappointment following political struggles and regime change. This seemingly disappointing outcome is evident in the mixed gender outcomes of regime change and democratic transition throughout history and across different societies in the MENA region and beyond. Indeed, more than any other recent movements and scholarships, the women's movement and feminist studies have recognized and explored the force of emotion and affect in social movements (Tarrow 1998: 112; Taylor 1995: 226–229). This chapter builds upon and contributes to this body of scholarship. It highlights some of the ways in which emotions such as disappointment and hope emerge among activists groups and how such emotions shape the way people respond to structural inequalities and generate different experiences.

The Politics of Disappointment in Post-Uprising Egypt

Underpinning the argument that disappointment is an important aspect in studying post-uprising politics is a view of feelings and emotions as fundamental to political life (Gould 2009; Greenberg 2014; Taylor 1995). They are important not in the sense that they overtake reason but, as Gould (2009: 3) argues, in the sense that they are an "affective dimension to the processes and practices that make up the political, broadly defined." The significance of emotions in social movements has recently gained scholarly attention among social movements analysts and theorists. Particularly within the tradition of political process, scholars offer "a multifaceted picture of human beingness" (Gould 2009: 17). They recognize emotion as "a ubiquitous feature of human life" that influences and brings meaning to political action and inaction (Gould 2009: 17; see also: Ahmed 2004; Aminzade and McAdam 2001: 17; Goodwin and Jasper 2004). In line with Gould (2009: 16–19), I contend that activism includes not only common feelings in the realm of activism, like hope, pride, and solidarity, but also those like fear, shame, guilt, desperation, and disappointment that might be less expected.

In this section, I survey how emotions of disappointment, despair, and even guilt emerged during the transitional period. The analysis presented highlights the influence of deep state, authoritarian resilience, democratic deficiency, and state-sponsored feminism on activists' experience. The survey highlights how these factors closed off some forms of political actions and created possibilities for new kinds of women's participation and disappointments in politics.

Deep State, Authoritarian Confidence, and Patriarchal Essence

During my conversation with activists in Egypt, many participants described their frustration over the old guard's strong grip on power and institutions in Egypt. The object of frustration was the military control and its ongoing sanctioning and criminalization of political dissent. As an activist eloquently explained, understanding the complex unfolding of post-uprising politics in Egypt should begin by analyzing the speech of the former Egyptian president Ḥusnī Mubarak that was delivered by his vice president, Omar Suleiman, on the night of February 11, 2011. In the former president's resignation speech, Suleiman announced that Mubarak "has *charged* [italics mine] the high council of the armed forces to administer the affairs of the country" (CNN 2011). According to my interviewee, a prominent activist and a vocal women's rights supporter who wished not to be identified, the speech should be read as a "delegation" rather than "resignation" speech. Even as Mubarak resigned, she explains, "he still gave himself the right to delegate state authority to the army rather than leaving it to the parliament or the constitutional mandate." The speech is a symbolic reflection of the power of the deep state in Egypt; activists had to hurdle these powers even as they celebrated what appeared to be a concession by the regime and a victory against it. In the years following the uprising, the power of the deep state continued to gradually and systemically resurface and manifest itself in judiciary, administration, and executive branches (Kandil 2012; Makara 2016).

Writing on the post-contention challenges of democratic transition, scholars argue that reactionaries who have a vested interest in maintaining the status quo continue to pursue their retrograde plans in a gradual yet systematic fashion (Sperber 1994; Weyland 2016). These reactionaries are often the old guards of the regime and agents of the deep state. Their actions are believed to be driven by fear of losing their grip on power and wealth.

The persistent power of the security state in Egypt also added to the disappointment among the activist communities. The regime used accounts of the violence that was breaking out in Libya, Syria, and Yemen to warn the public against a similar trajectory and to justify their oppressive policies and practices against oppositions (Abdelrahman 2017; Lynch 2015). State officials framed regional and national unrest as part of a broader conspiracy to bring down Egypt and its military force (Abdelrahman 2017; Lynch 2015). In the face of the increase in terrorist attacks in Egypt, the government often played on the security versus human rights discourse, placing them at two irreconcilable ends. This discourse, several participants felt, is alarming as it bears a definite resemblance to the old repressive order of Mubarak's security state.

The security discourse is also pervasive in shaping and justifying the regime's responses to flare-ups of contention carried out by the masses. Once a respected and acclaimed symbol of resistance and political engagement, flare-ups of contention became increasingly framed as disruptive and destructive during the transitional period. Framing them as disruptive legitimates their suppression – sometimes violently. As many segments of the population grew tired of the economic and political burden of contention, they then showed support for the government's repressive acts against activists and political dissidents. By showing such support, they contributed to creating what I describe as a form of "authoritarian confidence." Under authoritarian confidence, the government's violent response to political dissidence is largely justified and often unchecked. Female participants and activists suffered under this emerging trend of authoritarian confidence that also

embodied and openly displayed a patriarchal and misogynist undertone. The public and official discourse often blamed female activists
who were harassed and assaulted in protests (Al-Masry Al-Youm
2013). A culture of blaming the victim and trenching her reputation
became all too common in media coverage and in the state response to
sexual harassment and violence against female oppositions.

My observation regarding the rise of authoritarian confidence with
its patriarchal undertone is not intended to essentialize Egyptian society and/or paint it with an Orientalist brush. Growing impatience with
dissidence and contention is a defining character of post-uprising politics in Western and non-Western societies. Writing on the waves of
collective action from 1845 revolutions onwards, Tarrow (1998: 160)
notes the spread of "exhaustion" and disappointment as the cycle of
contention winds down. Zolberg (1972) goes even further writing,
"what we remember most," after the intoxication of protest cycles,
"is that moments of political enthusiasm are followed by bourgeois
repression or by charismatic authoritarianism, sometimes by horror
but always by the restoration of boredom" (205). Exhaustion, disappointment, and the return of authoritarian confidence following
episodes of major contention are thus important areas of study for
future research on social movements and democratic consolidation. A
close analysis of the dynamics and tensions underlying these issues is
important if we are to understand the complex field of action in which
the post-uprising politics unfolds in often contradictory ways.

Stakes of Hope and Despair in Egypt's Civil Society

An important and underresearched issue that demands equal attention in the drive to understand gender politics in the period after the
uprising is that of how civil society organizations and their members
contributed to the changing Zeitgeist in Egypt. During my fieldwork,
several activists described how their experience in the newly emerged
organizations and political groups did not live up to their expectations and was marked by disappointment. Examining what I term the
"democratic deficiency" in civil society organizations is an important
analytical venture, as it forces a self-reflexivity in assessing the stakes
of hope and despair that came out of the uprising. While political
structures influence and sanction our choices and options of activism, scholarly analysis would be incomplete without accounting for

our own actions and (in)actions. This is significant not only for academic research but, most importantly, for the lives and the future of the masses in the region.

During the round of my field research in Egypt in 2014, several of my participants revealed how their experience of post-uprising activism was not devoid of the very challenges that gave rise to the uprising. Robert Michels' iron law of oligarchy is relevant to understanding the issue of democratic deficiency in newly emerged political organizations. Observing the governance of political parties and trade unions in 1911 in Europe, Michels famously argued that "Who says organization, says oligarchy" (1915: 15). He observed how leaders of organizations tend to take more power than the members who selected them and once in power they are not influenced by the opinions of members.

Others explained how the dynamics among group members were often marked by struggles for power and sometimes even animosities. A generational gap between the older and younger members of the movement also persisted and widened among women's groups. The gap, some argued, closed to some extent under the regime of the Muslim Brotherhood, as women's rights came under serious threat.[3] Different groups came together to defend the National Council for Women, and to pressure the state to respect women's rights and its commitment to international conventions safeguarding women's rights.

Under the regime of Mursī and the Muslim Brotherhood, the agenda of women's rights suffered major setbacks. After the 2012 election that brought the Muslim Brotherhood to power, the number of women in the first People's Assembly was only 9 out of 508 (NCW and Dokhan 2015). Members of the parliament often came under fire for their misogynist stance; they unsuccessfully called for reducing the legal age of marriage to the age of 12 and abolishing women's rights to initiate divorce (Culberston 2016; NCW and Dokhan 2015; Nowaira 2013). They also unsuccessfully pushed for abolishing the mother's right under divorce to keep the custody of her children to the age of 15 and reducing it to the age of 7 in the case of boys and 9 in the case of girls (NCW and Dokhan 2015). The

---

[3] Interviewee 112. Author's interview, Cairo, Egypt, March 2017; Interviewee 118. Author's interview, Cairo, Egypt, March 2017.

constitution of 2012 was also criticized for not safeguarding women's rights in Egypt. Salient among these criticisms was the omission of the proposed clause banning the trafficking of women (NCW and Dokhan 2015). The constitution also reduced the size of the court from eighteen judges to ten. Critics viewed the decision as vindictive, suggesting that it was tailored to remove Brotherhood critics from the court; salient among them was the only female judge, Tahani al-Gebali, a vocal critic of the regime (CBC 2013). The party's members also condemned the UN Commission on the Status of Women's declaration entitled "End Violence against Women," accusing it of undermining Islamic ethics and destroying the family (Ikwanweb 2013). The party also objected to the criminalization of female genital mutilation and petitioned Egyptian courts to lift the ban on it (Tadros 2012).[4]

Where before there was discord, the arrival of Mursī and his policies resulted in women's rights organizations and different groups displaying unity, one of my interviewees, a women's rights consultant, attested.[5] This reconciliation, however, was short-lived and soon came to an end. Members had a very different approach to the "most democratic" way to structure organizations, and the "most effective" way to represent women's interests and interact with state institutions (Fadl 2014; Sadiqi 2016; Shams al-Din 2015a, 2015b; Tadros 2016). Contentions and problems appeared among members not because of their differences but, rather, because of their inability to move beyond their diverse and sometimes competing views and reconcile them.

This is the case not only for women's groups; the activist community in Egypt at large has been increasingly criticized for suffering from the replication of authoritarianism in their processes and discussions. It is not self-evident how this corrupt political culture affected and translated into particular kinds of exclusionary (authoritarian) practices among opposition and social movement members. This, however, might be explained as a function of the decades of authoritarian rule that have corrupted political culture in Egypt. The political regime

---

[4] The National Council for Women (NCW)'s report on "Women and Terrorism," published in January 19, 2015, as part of the proceedings for the "Women and Terrorism Conference," reported that the Freedom and Justice Party offered subsidized medical services for FGM in Minya as a part of the party's election campaign.

[5] Interviewee 118.

tolerated criticism from the opposition forces, as is evident from the growing number of opposition newspaper and media outlets; however, state security forces heavy-handedly punished any attempts at collaboration and collective action across different oppositional forces. Activists and political opposition forces were not, thus, ostensibly accustomed to working together and reconciling their political differences in order to construct a viable and sustainable political project.

Increasing dissension and internal divisions among groups and major political organizations were often the result of disagreements over leadership, the appropriate relation with Islamist parties, and resurgence of forces from the old regime. Parties and politicians also constantly failed to mature beyond rhetoric and develop policy platforms; rather, they engaged in constant vilification of the other (Mohamed and Momani 2014). This constant vilification stripped many politicians, parties, and revolutionaries of their initial popularity and credibility and contributed to the aura of despair and disappointment among many activists (Alaa 2015; Allam 2015; El-Raggal 2015; and Fadl 2014).

The Islamist oppositions, who in 2011 were largely considered the only credible political options, were also increasingly viewed with cynicism and distrust once in power. In addition to the challenges posed by reactionary forces, the parties' political missteps and their failure to respect women's rights and resolve chronic social and economic crises contributed to distancing the parties from their base support (Boukhars 2015; Mohamed and Momani 2014). In Egypt, the Muslim Brotherhood's ideological rigidity, exclusionary practices, and damaging battles over identity and individual freedoms stripped the party from its initial popularity (Boukhars 2015).

It would definitely be an overstatement to generalize the aforementioned observations and ascribe it to every oppositional group, social movement organization, and/or NGO in Egypt's civil society. First, the observation is in itself a bold statement, and activists who made this observation conveyed it in an "off record" milieu. This is in sharp contrast to their outspoken revolutionary persona; indeed, the same activists were largely open to voicing their opinions and views on various other and, most importantly, politically sensitive matters. How a group of activists who view themselves as fundamentally democratic can produce practices that seem exclusionary and undemocratic is thus a tough question to ask and – not surprisingly – difficult to answer. It is, however, an incredibly important question for understanding the challenges of transition and tracing the enduring effects of authoritarianism on political culture. This analytical venture promises to explain the experience of revolutionaries and activists as they try to navigate a post-revolutionary present and distance themselves from past legacy.

The Revival of State-Sponsored Feminism

The revival of state-sponsored feminism under the current regime of President el-Sisi also contributes to the politics of disappointment. The policies yield mixed developments, yet also setbacks for the movement and the agenda of women's rights in Egypt. During my 2017 fieldwork, participants often quoted the state's celebration of Mother's Day as the latest manifestation of the regime's schizophrenic approach to the agenda of women's rights in Egypt. The state honoured a number of female figures and "role models par excellence" on Egypt's Mothers' Day, March 21, 2017. Honourees came from diverse fields to reflect and "supposedly" capture women's success and service in different realms. The celebration honored actresses, academics, athletes, professionals, and mothers of army and police martyrs. The list of honourees, however, did not include any independent feminist figure or vocal women's rights advocate.

As a single event, this might not seem a deliberate oversight. After all, the honored women are indeed role models in their respective fields and their success certainly gives women's groups every good reason to celebrate. However, a less benign narrative emerges when situating this omission within the current landscape that surrounds the agenda of women's rights in Egypt. It raises some unsettling questions about the overt and covert interests that this image serves. The image of the ideal mother and woman, the message seems to be, is one that is most importantly apolitical and loyal to the regime.

The topic of the celebration often came up in my conversations with my interviewees. This was definitely a function of the timing of my fieldwork, which coincided with the celebration. But several participants also viewed it as the most recent example of the regime's recent attempt to co-opt the women's movement in Egypt. The approach seems well suited for the regime's dual objective of curtailing freedoms while seemingly advocating for women's rights. Consistent with the regime's objective of polishing its image, the cabinet includes a number of high-profile female ministers and eighty-nine women sit in the current parliament (El-Behary 2016). Notwithstanding these much-celebrated and publicized developments in the agenda of gender equality, women's rights organizations have languished in the current political climate.

A case in point is the controversial NGO law, passed in 2017. The law threatens and eliminates advocacy and the charitable work carried out by women's rights organizations along with other civil society groups. Furthermore, a number of women's rights organizations are subject to asset freezes, and its staff and leaders face travel bans and ongoing interrogations. Among those facing ongoing legal litigations are Mozn Hassan, the director of Nazra for Feminist Studies; Azza Soliman, the director of the Center for Egyptian Women's Legal Assistance (CEWLA); and Aida Seif al-Dawla, the cofounder of the Nadeem Center for Rehabilitation of Victims of Violence (Mada Masr 2017).

The conflict between the state and independent women's rights organizations is not merely over the agenda of women's rights or to curb potential challengers and imminent threats but over the issue of control and consolidation. Similar to the approach of former president Gamal Abdel Nassar, the aim is to consolidate the power of the regime by establishing full control over social groups and weakening, if not abolishing, their ability to organize.

While for some this might mark the beginning of the politics of disappointment among women's groups, the politics of hope, I hold, has not disappeared (Allam 2015, 2016). Notwithstanding the mixed developments and disappointments on the ground, activists continue to maintain hope and sustain their activism through experimenting with different venues for change, action, and reform.

Beyond Disappointment: Activism at Times of Constraints

Whereas the mass uprising was followed by challenges and disappointments, it opened up new spaces for activism and left its mark on protestors' agency. The politics of disappointment, I believe, in line with social movement theorists, is a "complex political" and affective form in its own right (Greenberg 2014: 11; Tarrow 1998: 169). Contrary to the grim picture of quiescence, activists, I hold, continue to crave a space for dissent and action notwithstanding their disappointment in the political process.

The section is not intended to offer a comprehensive list of the initiatives or a complete picture of the field of activism and resistance in Egypt since the uprising. Rather, I offer several examples and highlight some areas for locating hope while inviting the reader to expand on the list. This survey is significant as the failure to consider and analyze the changing spaces for mobilization and activism in the Middle East and North Africa leads to stereotyping the region as politically stagnant (Khatib and Lust 2014) and women as passive. This view further blinds scholars and policymakers to the important changes taking place on the ground (Khatib and Lust 2014; Pace and Cavatorta 2012). Michele Pace and Francesco Cavatorta (2012) rightly point out that the Arab Spring took the scholarly community by surprise, as the community was too narrowly focused on analyzing state and elite politics to pay proper attention to the changes occurring within the broader society. A focus on these subtle changes promises to enhance our understanding of the unfolding of events after the uprisings and opens up new ways of understanding the process of regime change and democratic transition.

Artistic and Social Initiatives

Women's rights groups in Egypt continue to fight for formal representation in political institutions and legal rights in the constitution in addition to increasingly focusing on bringing to light issues of gender inequality across Egyptian society. Thus, rather than the top-down approach that has often been adopted by women's rights groups during the last decade, the younger generation of women's rights activists that has emerged following the 2011 uprising emphasizes rooted and localized activism that takes shape in non-conventional initiatives.

In these emerging forums of activism, gender issues figure squarely and centrally. Salient among these initiatives are anti-sexual harassment campaigns, women's oral history projects, as well as visual and literal arts productions. For instance, among the memorable moments of my field work in Egypt in the fall of 2014 was attending a participatory theatrical play on the issue of female genital mutilation at the Swiss Club in Al-Kitkat neighborhood in Cairo, Egypt. The play was among a number of grassroots initiatives launched to celebrate the International Day for the Elimination of Violence Against Women. The show narrates the life and daily struggles of Hania, a young middle-class Egyptian girl as she confronts harassment and gender discrimination at school and home. The story reaches its climax as Hania's parents decided to circumcise her, and the play closes with Hania's emotional cry as she is pushed to the floor, strangled by her mother, and approached by the midwife holding a knife.

"And everything froze," I wrote in my field notebook, "the silence seemed so loud in the crowded room where over 200 people were watching the play." The heavy silence continued as the director took to the stage asking for the audience's reactions as well as what they thought Hania should do. The first to speak was a middle-aged Sheik; speaking in a confident voice, he insisted that female genital circumcision is a religious obligation rooted in Islam and dictated in its teachings. Before he could finish his sentence, the majority of the women in the room raised their voices in dismay, shouting that the practice was inhumane, and some even challenged the Sheik's religious view outright, insisting that FGM is rooted in patriarchal systems.

It is worth noting that the act was being played at Al-Kitkat neighborhood in Egypt, one of Egypt's poorest slums. Unemployment, violence, crime, and radicalization are among the long list of socioeconomic ills that are salient in the neighborhood. I thus found it surprising – yet promising – that the show was held there. Indeed, Magy Nabil, an actress in the play, emphasized in our interview following the play that the group deliberately staged their plays in rural and poor areas of the country as part of their effort to reach out to the poor and disadvantaged segments of society, who may be among those more likely to still practice FGM.[6] Women's assertive reaction to the Sheik's statements took me by surprise as well. I left with a sense that change and social transformation are indeed possible, and that they can take place when and where we least expect.

Another markedly hopeful project is BuSSy; a storytelling initiative. The theater group holds storytelling workshops and thematic performances across the country. The ostensibly benign apolitical nature of these mundane forms of advocacy is a path out of the political and social dilemmas, past and present, posed by Egypt's contentious politics. Members of these artistic initiatives are also often viewed above the fray of messy politics and thus better able to represent the interests of women and introduce subtle social change.

---

[6] Author's interview, Magy Nabil, actress in "One Voice" Theatrical Group, Cairo, Egypt, November 2014.

Politics, as one of my interviewees astutely described, has been given "a bad name."[7] The hyper-politicization of everyday politics in Egypt and the media[8] treatment of "politics as entertainment"[9] has contributed to the loss of momentum. The public Zeitgeist also changed because of the ways in which the official discourse constantly vilified oppositions and how civil society organizations could not move beyond constantly denouncing each other.

Beyond the creative and localized approach of these initiatives, these forms of activism and engagement hold great potential as they are often, but not always, tolerated by the regime. They potentially may escape altogether the radar of state censorship and security surveillance. In an increasingly narrow political space, these venues thus hold potential for sustaining engagement and pushing for social change. Furthermore, these initiatives are significant in raising consciousness about gender inequality and women's rights among female citizens as well as broader Egyptian society. This is significant as awareness of one's own interests is a prerequisite for democratic representation and claim-making (Greenberg 2014). Furthermore, by carving a space outside of politics for grassroots activism and social empowerment, activists chart a potentially democratic project in a politically sensitive context.

Individual Salvation

The political rupture and the unfolding of events following the uprisings have profoundly influenced the nature and cause of activism among women's groups. Activists turned to the social and artistic milieu to make demands and mobilize around social issues in lieu

---

[7] Interviewee 108. Author's interview, Cairo, Egypt, March 2017.

[8] The media that helped to launch the uprisings also contributed to driving polarization, fear, and demobilization following the uprising. Islamists were pitted against anti-Islamists and revolutionary against reactionaries, each followed different television channels, Facebook groups, and Twitter feeds. On social media, like-minded individuals self-segregated into ideological clusters, which contributed to diminishing common ground and driving politics into mutually uncomprehending camps (Lynch 2015). The residues of the old regime also continued to control mainstream state media and sought to resurrect the old order by invoking traditional themes of patriotism, law, and order, as well as some of the social concerns raised by the uprisings.

[9] Interviewee 115. Author's interview, Cairo, Egypt, March 2017.

of direct political action. They further developed new language to be resilient, effective, and flexible.

HarassMap is one example of how women's rights groups reformulate a new language to make their claims heard. The organization, founded in 2010, tracks and maps cases of sexual harassment in Egypt. Amid a tense political climate and increasingly curtailed freedoms, their performance currently rests on negotiating the proper role and image to make their claims heard. In response to the current climate of censorship, they claim the image of experts, rather than activists, reproducing evidence to inform corporate strategies and state policies. This reformulation, I hold, is a language of hope.

As activists face an increasingly narrow political space and threats of suppression, initiatives such as HarassMap and BuSSy hold potential for sustaining engagement and pushing for social and subtle political change. The threats of suppression did not completely hinder collective action, as threats are not the flip side of opportunities. Social movement theorists define threats as not only the costs that social groups will incur if they do take action but also the costs that they expect to suffer if they do not take action (Goldstone and Tilly 2001:183; Sewell 2001). Threats can recede but also encourage actions if the cost of not acting is too high or exacerbated.

A focus on these forms of activism is important as it complicates and expands our understanding of activism under politics of disappointment. It encourages a view of activism as a result of multiple emotions. In line with social movement theorists, I hold that the emotions that may lead people to join in a movement may not be the same emotions that keep them within the movement (Aminzade and McAdam 2001: 39). The sympathy and empathy of bystanders are crucial for the movement to grow and expand. However, as the movement declines the focus shifts to maintain affective solidarity among a small number of activists who sustain the struggle through the years of decline (Aminzade and McAdam 2001; Taylor 1995).

It is true that activism is becoming more restricted in Egypt. However, the essence of this research is ignited by participants' affirmation that their experience in the uprising has changed them, and that, notwithstanding their disappointment over the turn of events, "things cannot go back to the old days."[10] Many of the activists whom I met in

[10] Interviewee 95. Author's interview, Cairo, Egypt, November 2015.

Egypt stressed that the experience of contention will continue to mark them for life. The significance of the experience of collective action on participants' activism and agency has been underscored and analyzed in social movement literature. Writing on the significance of participants' experience during Freedom Summer camp, Douglas McAdam describes their experience as the "most emotionally intoxicating and socially connective experience one can have" (Aminzade and McAdam 2001: 43). He notes the distinctive influence of this experience on volunteers' life-course choices and how they disseminated these norms to the wider population long after the decline of collective action.

Indeed, the effect of youth experience during collective action can be seen not only on their activism and political engagement but also on their life and career choices. The experience, several participants attest, gave them a sense of purpose and hope. This sense waxes and wanes, but it is never completely gone. It, I thus argue, created a political generation, borrowing Karl Mannheim's influential concept. Writing on the role of demographic and life-course events on youth, Mannheim ([1923] 1952) observed how a generation with distinctive consciousness emerges when particular birth cohorts are exposed to highly distinctive life experiences during adolescence or young adulthood.

As scholars within the tradition of social movement attest, distinctive experiences such as political unrest and collective action may give participants a sense of potency as a political and social force (Tarrow 1998, 2001). These experiences make them candidates for future collective action and social change. Writing on the experience of the new left in the United States during the 1960s, Goldstone and McAdam observe how activists fashioned new life-course alternatives and developed repositories of the "60s experience" (2001: 219). These alternatives were inspired by activists' experience and fashioned to what they came to regard as more just and personally fulfilling alternatives to the traditional life-course (Goldstone and McAdam 2001: 218–219).

During the 2011 Egyptian uprising, protestors experienced a very different political and social culture. Several interviewees describe how their experience during contention gave them the strength and grit to express and voice different political and social values even after the decline of collective action. There is less conformity to taken-for-granted concepts, authorities, and life courses. For instance, a number of participants attribute the change in their career to their experience during the uprising.[11] One of my interviewees describes how she left her well-paid position at the corporate world following her participation in protests and started an organization to combat sexual harassment against kids.[12] Her experiences during contention, she explains, made her believe in her capacity in instilling change and value herself as well as the inherent right of human beings to dignity and respect regardless of age.[13]

A number of participants attribute their focus on self-advancement and development to their experiences during the uprising. This focus on individual rather than community salvation, while not selfless, is not completely selfish, many of my interviewees were quick to point out. It is a way to "keep the memory of resistance alive."[14] In light of the current neoliberal forms of governmentality, this neoliberal vocabulary of the self and individual rather than the collective and community is often, if not always, tolerated by the regime. Shifts in the relationship between citizens and state necessitate these kinds of pragmatic approaches to activism and reform.

A counterculture of defiance and heterogeneity among the younger generation is also unmistakeable in Egypt. Strolling through Cairo's bustling libraries, I could not help but notice the expansion in provocative and critical publications. Several recent publications revisit and refute classic religious texts, while others demystify the aura surrounding historical figures, nationalist leaders, and key events. During my interviews, several participants also cited the rise of atheism and openly self-described sexual minorities as a manifestation of this culture.[15] It is impossible to identify with any degree of certainty the number of atheists or members of the lesbian, gay, bisexual, and transgender (LGBT) community in a conservative society like Egypt, or even in a more secular one like Tunisia. Many stay anonymous and limit their activism strictly to online forums. It is not clear whether the growing online presence of atheists after the uprising in Egypt reflects a rise in their number or whether more individuals are openly declaring it.

---

[11] Interviewee 12. Interviewee 26. Phone interview with Tunisian activist 6, March 2016.

[12] Interviewee 27.

[13] Ibid.

[14] Interviewee 115. Author's interview, Cairo, Egypt, March 2017.

[15] Author's interview with Ahmed Ben Amor, the vice president of Shams, phone interview, February 2016; Interviewee 44; Interviewee 56; and Interviewee 61.

Several participants attested that it is a combination of both.[16] Others stressed that the missteps of Islamist oppositions in the period following the uprisings is what prompted some to question their beliefs.[17] Many youth, they explain, questioned their beliefs as they saw how Islamist parties used religion for their own motives.

Irrespective of whether the number of atheists and sexual minorities has risen or they became more visible, I argue that the uprising created an opening in our public debate. It is this opening, rather than the ideas, that I am interested in. In this opening, different ideas are exchanged and long-standing taboos are questioned. These openings, I argue, are significant for the future of democratic transition, as they encourage freedom of speech and promise to produce a critical polity that can engage, discuss, and dissect competing thoughts and opinions. "A tiny splash of color in a largely plain toile," as one of my interviewees eloquently describes it.[18] It does not mean that diversity is achieved, but that the society is nudged to contemplate its foundations.

Conclusion

In this chapter I argue that attention to the politics of disappointment and hope is significant for understanding women's experience and the unfolding of gender politics following regime change in Egypt. The analysis presented is not intended to heroicize women's groups or any other groups for fighting against the odds. Rather, it is to draw the lesson that small changes and reforms can happen even in the face of disappointments. This approach encourages us to locate not only the causes of disappointment and democratic setbacks but also to emphasize women's agency and actions amid these challenges and uncertainties.

Exhaustion, disappointment, and the return of authoritarian confidence following episodes of major contention, I hold, are important areas of study for future research on social movements. A close analysis of the dynamics and tensions underlying these issues is significant for understanding the challenges that face female activists and the

---

[16] Interviewee 44; and Interviewee 61.
[17] Interviewee 34.
[18] Interviewee 104. Author's interview, Edmonton, Canada, September 2016.

women's movement following the uprising. This is not a call for disappointment or an attempt to write the uprising's obituary. By analyzing the bleak side of the uprising, we will properly appreciate the subtle, mundane forms of activism on the ground and moderate our hope of what is really possible within the limits of Egypt's political system.

While the more imminent result of disappointed expectations is political apathy and populist tendencies, disappointment does not mark the end of politics. In the post-uprisings era, as I demonstrated, female activists continued to develop their skills and sustain the memory of resistance. The chapter briefly surveyed these creative experiences and emphasized the ways in which activists negotiate the limitations of the processes of regime change and transition. It elucidated how these reform initiatives and actions have the potential to gradually open up spaces that can be occupied by social actors struggling against dominant gendered and power relations.

In the long run, the nodes of hope surveyed in this chapter might become part of effective repertoires of women's activism in the next cycles of contention. The relations and dynamics among women's groups, broader society, and the state are continuously recreated and negotiated; they give rise to hope and disappointment.

Conclusion

The absence of gender issues from women's collective action frame in the 2011 Egyptian uprising was not a sign of coercion, passiveness, or misguided activism. Rather, it was a function of frame resonance, political opportunities, and women's subjective experience during the eighteen days of the revolution. This view of women's collective action frames is significant as it analyzes women's engagement with an eye to their agency. Underlining this analysis is a view of agency as inevitably ambiguous and often involving contradictory aspects that cannot easily be disentangled (Charrad 2010; see also Mahmood 2005). Women's positionality as well as their interests, demands, and identities are not constant; rather, they are constantly remade as women interact with other participants and negotiate complex structures and relations. Women's collective action frame thus should be understood in relation to the complex context of broader structures and interactions in given moments, situations, and places.

This book provides an oral history of women's participation in the 2011 Egyptian uprising, a key historical moment in Egypt's politics. My focus, however, has been not only on documenting their accounts but also on situating their experience within the historical trajectories, as well as the contentious and conventional politics of Egypt. The book puts forward a narrative of women's experiences, knowledge, and recollections of their engagement in the Egyptian uprising. This narrative of knowledge emphasizes the influence of history, politics, and institutions in framing and mediating women's experience in the uprising.

The analysis presented emphasized how women's political engagement has often been excluded from the collective memory or remembered only selectively at key moments when it served symbolic purpose. Despite what seemed a disappointment relation between women and political struggles, these struggles had liberating consequences on women's activism in Egypt. For instance, notwithstanding the different regimes' hostile attitude toward independent feminist activists, women's experiences and struggle provided a strong base of experienced activists, and established national and international networks and collaborations.

Continuity in the framing of women's activism in Egypt's political struggles was ascertained in the media coverage of women's engagement in the 2011 uprising. My analysis of media coverage in key national and international newspapers suggested that traditional motifs of passiveness coexisted alongside new ones of feminine agency in their coverage of the 2011 uprising. By evoking the myth of female passiveness and framing women's activism within a feminine framework, the coverage assuaged the effect of women's activism in challenging traditional gender stereotypes. The analysis also explicated the variation and multiplicity involved in the practice of othering and the ways in which the participation of women was erased from the main discourse as a result of patriarchy and/or Orientalism. The representation of women in the media coverage of the uprising was a paradigmatic example of what Gramsci called "the trenches and fortification" of the existing order (Gramsci 1971, cited in Tarrow 2012: 2). It exposed some of the tensions that were a backdrop to women's activism and also revealed some of the ways in which power relations and gendered dynamics are exercised in society through media discourses.

Women's framing of their engagement, I thus argue, was not simply a reflection of external influence but also a response to inherited cultural materials as well as dominant and historical framings of political struggles. In the absence of a strong discourse for women's activism, the national unity frame represented an important cultural reservoir for framing women's engagement in past and modern struggles. This framing was modular, as it resonated with the cultural predisposition of Egyptian society. It thus encouraged collective action among women and also broad participation in the 2011 uprising.

Furthermore, given the widespread ethos of equality and solidarity during the 18-day uprising, women actively framed their participation utilizing the citizen frame. This framing was viewed by many women as sufficient to guarantee their rights in the aftermath of the uprising. Building upon my participants' accounts, I argued that women's subjective experience of solidarity during the eighteen days of protests contributed to the absence of gender from their collective action framing.

The mobilizing – as well as constraining structures – that influenced women's engagement and experience in the uprising are further explicated in the book's analysis of the political opportunities and constraints that shaped women's engagement. This explicit gender approach to political structure revealed the deep divisions and institutionalized inequalities between women and men and how it affected their engagement (Abdulhadi 1998; Kuumba 2001, 2002; Noonan 1995). For instance, in addition to the formal oppressive political structures that sanctioned and limited political participation under the former regime, female protestors negotiated sexism, parent's control, and past relations of co-optation with the regime. Their participation in philanthropic and informal political venues was one of the political opportunity structures that have contributed to the mobilization and politicization of women. This view expands notions of women's activism and political engagement within Egypt's political structure and cultural context where the routes of women's political participation were appropriated by state forces.

The findings presented in the book add to our stock of knowledge on the Arab Spring and particularly the gendered processes of regime change. They also enrich the study of women's engagement in nationalist struggles. Specifically, the analysis presented contributes to expanding debates on women's participation in national struggles beyond reductionist accounts that view them as misguided or passive. By offering a nuanced view of women's engagement in modern and historical political struggles in Egypt, I problematized the mainstream literature's tendency to theorize a single, common relationship between nationalist movements and women's rights. This tendency obscures the complexity of the issue and overlooks the positive influence of women's experience during contention on their activism, agency, and sense of empowerment. The book, as such, contributes to de-essentializing the category of women by highlighting their different experiences. I also suggest areas for continuities and junctures in the assumed relationship between women and political struggles.

Beyond the gender politics of the Middle East and North Africa, the book makes a significant contribution to the field of political science more broadly. It highlights affective motivations and challenges to women's political activism and engagement in contentious episodes. In so doing, I uncovered some factors that make political action conceivable, and others that make some forms of activism unimaginable (Gould 2009: 3–9). Answering these questions is important for the discipline of political science, as it contributes to uncovering the processes through which power is exercised and reproduced in our forms and frames of activism. It also promises to reveal the ways in which a prevailing or hegemonic political discourse might be challenged and transformed.

The book also contributes to postcolonial feminist studies. The analysis presented opens up a space in our research for the "subaltern to speak," appropriating the critical theorist Gayatri Chakravorty Spivak's connotation. It challenges and deconstructs Orientalist and/or patriarchal frames and discourses that have often dominated the representation of non-Western women in the literature on women's engagement in national struggles. The resulting organic and situated knowledge is important for understanding women's different and specific experience in political struggles in authoritarian societies and for locating their agency rather than their plight.

The book also adds to research in the field of media studies and political communications. An analysis of the media framing of women's activism illuminates the ways in which gender stereotypes are embedded within and make themselves manifest in text. Such analysis is significant as it draws critical attention to some of the dominant frames that women negated in framing their experience, and reveals some of the ways in which covert gender stereotypes are embedded in the media representation of women's activism in national struggles.

This analytical exercise is also significant given the implications of media on the social schisms in society and its centrality in demarcating cultural difference as well. In this regard, the image of women, I elaborate, corresponds to Egypt's social context and the representational history of women in Western media. Despite the significance of this topic, the question of women's representation in Arab media is an under-researched area in Middle Eastern studies. The book, thus, contributes to filling this scholarly void.

Finally, the book advances social movement theory by applying the political process model to non-Western cases and expanding the contours of its political opportunities and framing thesis to integrate gender structures and frames. While the literature on social movements offers many valuable insights and interesting lines of inquiry, studying women's engagement in the 2011 Egyptian uprising brought to light the present omissions and shortcomings of the literature. The analysis uncovers the ways in which collective action frames are not merely a deliberate formulation in response to the social culture and the legitimacy of the dominant framing of political struggles. While accounting for these factors provides collective action frames with the necessary resonance, activists continue to take cues from the surrounding environment during political struggles. This book thus complements social movement scholarship by foregrounding the important role of gender structures in movement processes and the ways in which issues of interpretation are central to the story of all social movements.

Concluding Comments

Throughout my book, I sought to demonstrate that women's engagement in the 2011 Egyptian uprising existed in relation and sometimes tension with existing political structures, deep-seated social relations, and embedded cultural practices. Their activism continued under the shadow of the public's sense of uncertainty and insecurity in the period following the uprising. In their struggles with the regime, and the public at large, women attempted to authorize their participation and engagement despite these messy histories and disappointing realities.

The analysis offered is thus animated by the knowledge that the politics of gender and women's rights are influenced by competing structures and rooted in multiple contexts simultaneously. Women's political activism and engagement in the uprising and after the uprising, remained fundamentally diverse, with multiple meanings and histories. This view encourages us to consider women's political activism as subject to constant reinterpretation and reframing in ways that can make the work of studying it incredibly important and deeply challenging.

This conclusion is not, however, an imminent *cri de cœur*, sad reflection, or cry of disappointment. Disappointment is not the end of politics (Greenberg 2014: 11; Gould 2009; Tarrow 1998: 169). Rather, it is an invitation to researchers to consider significant and hopeful sets of questions about the possibility of change, and the future of women's rights and gender equality in the Middle East and North Africa. These questions should be explored through the quest to locate women's agency rather than plight.

Bibliography

Ababneh, Sara. 2014. "The Palestinian Women's Movement versus Hamas: Attempting to Understand Women's Empowerment Outside a Feminist Framework." *Journal of International Women's Studies* 15 (1): 35–53.

Abaza, Mona. 2014. "Post January Revolution Cairo: Urban Wars and the Reshaping of Public Space." *Theory, Culture & Society* 31 (7–8): 163–183. doi:10.1177/0263276414549264.

Abd El-Hameed, Dalia. 2013. "The National Council for Women: State Feminism Seeking to Contain Revolutionary Feminism." Egyptian Initiative for Personal Rights, October 2013. http://eipr.org/en/blog/post/2013/10/02/1832.

Abdal Majid, Laylá. 2007. *al-Mar'a al-Miṣrya w-al-i'lam [Egyptian Women in Media]*. Cairo: Markaz Qaḍaya al-Mar'a al-Miṣrya

Abdel Haleem, Nora. 2012. "58 Years after July Revolution ... The Story of Women." *Al-Ahram*, June 19. Accessed February 20, 2013. http://digital.ahram.org.eg/articles.aspx?Serial=197812&eid=1515.

Abdel Maksood, Ahmed. 2011. "Um Sayida" [Sayida's Mother]. *Al-Ahram*, February 10. Accessed February 4, 2013. www.ahram.org.eg/archive/439/2011/02/10/12/62183/219.aspx.

Abdel Nasser, Gamal. 1954. *The Philosophy of the Revolution*. Cairo: National Publication House Press.

Abdelrahman, Maha. 2012. "A Hierarchy of Struggles? The 'Economic' and the 'Political' in Egypt's Revolution." *Review of African Political Economy* 39 (134): 614–628. doi:10.1080/03056244.2012.738419.

2017. "Policing Neoliberalism in Egypt: The Continuing Rise of the 'Securocratic' State." *Third World Quarterly* 38 (1): 185–202. doi:10.1080/01436597.2015.1133246.

Abdulhadi, Rabab. 1998. "The Palestinian Women's Autonomous Movement: Emergence, Dynamics, and Challenges." *Gender and Society* 12 (6): 649–673.

Abouzeid, Leila. 2009. *Year of the Elephant*. Austin: University of Texas Press.

Abu El-Komsan, Nehad. 2012. *The Freedom of the Square: Reflections on the Course of the Egyptian Revolution and the Participation of Women.* United Nations Entity for Gender Equality and the Empowerment of Women (UN Women).

Abu-Laban, Yasmeen. 2008. "Gendering the Nation-State: An Introduction." In *Gendering The Nation-State: Canadian and Comparative Perspectives*, 1–20. Vancouver: UBC Press.

Abu-Lughod, Lila. 1990. "The Romance of Resistance: Tracing Transformations of Power through Bedouin Women." *American Ethnologist* 17 (1): 41–55. doi:10.1525/ae.1990.17.1.02a00030.

——— 1998. *Remaking Women: Feminism and Modernity in the Middle East.* Princeton, NJ: Princeton University Press.

——— 2001. "Orientalism and Middle East Feminist Studies." *Feminist Studies*, no. 1: 101–113.

——— 2002. "Do Muslim Women Really Need Saving? Anthropological Reflections on Cultural Relativism and Its Others." *American Anthropologist* 104 (3): 783–790. doi:10.1525/aa.2002.104.3.783.

——— 2005. *Dramas of Nationhood: The Politics of Television in Egypt.* University of Chicago Press.

——— 2013. *Do Muslim Women Need Saving?* Cambridge, Mass.: Harvard University Press.

——— 2014. "On and Off-Camera in Egyptian Soap Operas: Women, Television, and the Public Sphere." In *On Shifting Ground: Muslim Women in the Global Era*, ed. Fereshteh Nouraie-Simone, 67–87. New York: The Feminist University Press.

Abul-Magd, Zeinab. 2011. "Al-Jeish wa Al-Iqtiṣad Fi Br Maṣr" [The Army and the Economy in Egypt]. *Jadaliyya*, December 23. www.jadaliyya .com/pages/index/3732/the-army-and-the-economy-in-egypt.

Adams, Jacqueline. 2002. "Gender and Social Movement Decline: Shantytown Women and the Prodemocracy Movement in Pinochet's Chile." *Journal of Contemporary Ethnography* 31 (3): 285–322. doi:10.1177/0891241602031003002.

Afshar, Haleh. 1985. *Iran: A Revolution in Turmoil.* Albany: State University of New York Press.

Agah, Azadeh, Sousan Mehr, and Shadi Parsi. 2007. *We Lived to Tell: Political Prison Memoirs of Iranian Women.* Toronto: McGilligan Books.

Åhäll, Linda. 2012. "The Writing of Heroines: Motherhood and Female Agency in Political Violence." *Security Dialogue* 43 (4): 287–303. doi:10.1177/0967010612450206.

Ahmed, Leila. 1992. *Women and Gender in Islam: Historical Roots of a Modern Debate.* New Haven, Conn.: Yale University Press.

2012. *A Quiet Revolution: The Veil's Resurgence, from the Middle East to America*. New Haven, Conn.: Yale University Press.

Ahmed, Maryam. 2010. "Women and the 1919 Revolution: Egyptian Women and Revolution (1)." Egyptian Centre for Monitoring Women's Priorities, Cairo. www.mramcenter.com/page3.php?id=289scond=7. Accessed June 20, 2012.

Ahmed, Sara. 2004. *The Cultural Politics of Emotion*. New York: Routledge.

Al-Ahram. 2010. "Official Results: 16 Opposition, 424 NDP, 65 'Independents.'" *Ahram Online*, December 6. http://english.ahram.org .eg/NewsContent/1/5/1321/Egypt/Egypt-Elections-/Official-results— opposition,—NDP,—independents.aspx.

Al-Ali, Nadje. 2000. *Secularism, Gender and the State in the Middle East: The Egyptian Women's Movement*. Cambridge University Press.

2012. "Gendering the Arab Spring." *Middle East Journal of Culture and Communication* 5 (1): 26–31. doi:10.1163/187398612X624346.

Al-Aswany, Alaa. 2012. *Hal Akhṭa't Al-Thawra Al-Maṣrya?* [Did the Egyptian Revolution Go Wrong?]. Cairo: Dar al-Shorok.

Al-Bady, Doaa, Soha Salah, and Salah Sharaby. 2011. "Aṭfal al-thawra" [Children of the Uprising]. *Al-Wafd*, February 8. Accessed February 4, 2013. https://goo.gl/9W5vc2.

Al-Banna, Hassan. 1984. "Al Mar'a Al-Muslima" [The Muslim Woman]. In *Al Mar'a Al-Muslima* [The Muslim Woman], ed. Mohamed Nasr Al-Din Al-Albany. Cairo: Dar al-Kotob al-Salafia.

Al-Faqi, Mustafa. 1985. *Al-aqbat fī al-siyasa al-Miṣriyya* [Copts in Egyptian Politics]. Cairo: Dar al-Shorok.

Al-Ghazali, Zainab, and Amr Farouk. 2012. *Ayam Min ḥayaaty* [Days of My Life]. Cairo: Kenouz.

Al-Jazeera. 2013. "Egypt's Sexual Assault Epidemic" [by Bel Trew]. *Al-Jazeera*. August 14. www.aljazeera.com/indepth/features/2013/08/201381494941573782.html.

Al-Kazendar, Mohamed. 2015. "Rad 'la Bilal Fadl: Hal ḥaqn Khasirna Al-Ma'raka qabl An Tabda'?" [A Response to Bilal Fadel: Did We Really Lose the Game before It Started?]. *Mada Masr*. Accessed September 28, 2015. www.madamasr.com/ar/opinion/politics/.

Al-Maaitah, Rowaida, Hadeel Al Maaitah, Hmoud Olaimat, and Muntaha Gharaeibeh. 2011. "Arab Women and Political Development." *Journal of International Women's Studies* 12 (2–3): 7–26.

Al-Mahadin, Salam. 2011. "Arab Feminist Media Studies." *Feminist Media Studies* 11 (1): 7–12. doi:10.1080/14680777.2011.537018.

Al-Mahdy, Hoda. 2011. "Mesh Bas Taghir Siyasi" [Not Only Political Changes]. *Al-Ahram*, March 17. Accessed February 4, 2013. www .ahram.org.eg/archive/443/2011/02/14/16/62693/219.aspx.

Al-Malki, Amal, David Kaufer, and Suguru Ishizaki. 2012. *Arab Women in Arab News: Old Stereotypes and New Media*. London: Bloomsbury Academic.

Al-Mansi, Shaimaa. 2011. "Shyokh Al-Qada' Wa Zawgatohum Fi Yom Al-Ghadab" [The Judges and Their Wives at the Day of Rage]. *Al-Wafd*, January 27. Accessed February 4, 2013. https://goo.gl/xhj1Dl.

Al-Masry, al-Youm. 2010. "Minimum Wage Protest." *Egypt Independent*, August 11, sec. News. Accessed June 20, 2012. www.egyptindependent .com/node/231168.

2013. "Shura Council Committee Says Female Protesters Should Take Responsibility, If Harassed." *Egypt Independent*, February 11. www .egyptindependent.com/news/shura-council-committee-says-female-protesters-should-take-responsibility-if-harassed.

Al-Nagar, Zaghloul, and El-Sayed Abo-Dawood. 2012. *Midan Al-Taḥrir: Al-Taḥawolat fi Maṣr Byn Jozor Al-Madi wa Afaq Al-Mustaqbl* [Tahrir Square: Changes in Egypt between the Historical Roots and the Future]. Cairo: Dar Nahḍa Miṣr.

Al-Qasimi, Noor. 2010. "Immodest Modesty: Accommodating Dissent and the 'Abaya-as-Fashion in the Arab Gulf States." *Journal of Middle East Women's Studies* 6 (1): 46–74. doi:10.2979/MEW.2010.6.1.46.

Al-Rafei, Abdel-Rahman. [1937] 1949. *Al-Thawrat Al-'urabi wa Al-Ihtilal Al-Inglizi* [Urabi Revolution and British Colonialism]. Cairo: Al-Nahḍa.

Al-Saji, Alia. 2009. "Muslim Women and the Rhetoric of Freedom." In *Constructing the Nation: A Race and Nationalism Reader*, ed. Mariana Ortega and Linda Martín Alcoff, 65–91. Albany: State University of New York Press.

Al-Shamy, Doaa. 2011a. "Fatayat Al-Ghaḍab ... Maṣriyat Biḥaq wa ḥaqiqi" [Girls of Anger ... True Egyptians]. *Al-Wafd*, January 27. Accessed February 4, 2013. https://goo.gl/MDAOwy.

2011b. "Zaghrouta Hilwa Rant Fi Al-Midan" [A Wedding Celebration at the Square]. *Al-Wafd*, February 9. Accessed February 4, 2013. https:// goo.gl/GTzryI.

Alaa, Bilal. 2015. "Limadha Yanjaḥ Al- 'askar Wa Yanhazim Al-Agharwun? " [Why Does the Army Succeed While Others Fail?]. *Mada Masr*. Accessed September 28, 2016. www.madamasr.com/ar/opinion/politics.

Albrecht, Holger. 2012. "Authoritarian Transformation or Transition from Authoritarianism? Insights on Regime Change in Egypt." In *Arab Spring in Egypt: Revolution and Beyond*, ed. Bahgat Korany and Rabab El-Mahdi, 251–270. American University in Cairo Press.

2015. "Does Coup-Proofing Work? Political–Military Relations in Authoritarian Regimes amid the Arab Uprisings." *Mediterranean Politics* 20 (1): 36–54. doi:10.1080/13629395.2014.932537.

Alexander, Anne. 2012. "Egypt: Women Workers Speak out – Introduction." *MENA Solidarity Network*, March 13. https://menasolidaritynetwork.com/egyptwomen-2/.

Alinsky, Saul David. 1972. *Rules for Radicals: A Practical Primer for Realistic Radicals*. New York: Vintage Books.

Allam, Nermin. 2013. "Abla Al-Kahlawy." *The Oxford Encyclopedia of Islam and Women*. New York: Oxford University Press.

2014a. "Arab Revolutions: Breaking Fear / Blesses and Curses: Virtual Dissidence as a Contentious Performance in the Arab Spring's Repertoire of Contention." *International Journal of Communication* 8: 853–870.

2014b. "Activism and Exception in Covering Egypt's Uprising: A Critical Reading of *The New York Times*' Representation of Female Protestors." *Sociology of Islam* 2 (3–4): 310–327. doi:10.1163/22131418-00101001.

2015. "What Holds Next? The Politics Of Disappointment." *London School of Economics and Political Science Middle East Blog*. August 11. http://blogs.lse.ac.uk/mec/2015/08/11/what-holds-next-the-politics-of-disappointment/.

2016. "Locating Hope: Women's Activism in Post-Uprising Egypt." *AlbertaPoliBlog*, March 31. http://albertapoliblog.blogspot.com/2016/03/locating-hope-womens-activism-in-post.html.

Allam, Rasha. 2004. "Image of Women as Portrayed in the Egyptian Media: A Content Analysis Study of Al-Masry Al-Youm and Nahdat Misr." American University in Cairo.

2014. "Egypt – Media Landscape | European Journalism Centre (EJC)." *European Journalism Centre (EJC)*. July 10. http://ejc.net/media_landscapes/egypt.

Allen, Lori. 2003. "Political-Social Movements : Revolutionary : Palestine." In *Encyclopedia of Women & Islamic Cultures: Family, Law, and Politics*, ed. Suad Joseph and Afsaneh Najmabadi, 655–657. Leiden; Boston: Brill.

Allen, Pamela. 1970. *Free Space: A Perspective on the Small Group in Women's Liberation*. New York: Times Change Press.

Allison, Katherine. 2013. "American Occidentalism and the Agential Muslim Woman." *Review of International Studies* 39 (3): 665–684.

Alloula, Malek. 1987. *The Colonial Harem*. Manchester University Press.

Alnajjar, Baqer S. 2014. "Formation of Religious Leaders and Impact of Enlightened Imams." In *Arab Human Development in the Twenty-First Century: The Primacy of Empowerment*, ed. Bahgat Korany, 285–324. American University in Cairo Press.

Alsultany, Evelyn. 2012. *Arabs and Muslims in the Media: Race and Representation after 9/11*. New York University Press.

2013. "Arabs and Muslims in the Media after 9/11: Representational Strategies for a 'Postrace' Era." *American Quarterly* 65 (1): 161–169. doi:10.1353/aq.2013.0008.

Alvarez, Sonia E. 1999. "Advocating Feminism: The Latin American Feminist NGO 'Boom.'" *International Feminist Journal of Politics* 1 (2): 181–209. doi:10.1080/146167499359880.

Amanat, Abbas. 2012. "The Spring of Hope and Winter of Despair." *International Journal of Middle East Studies* 44 (1): 147–149. doi:10.1017/S0020743811001292.

Amar, Paul. 2011. "Middle East Masculinity Studies: Discourses of 'Men in Crisis,' Industries of Gender in Revolution." *Journal of Middle East Women's Studies* 7 (3): 36–70.

Amin, Qasim. 1992. *The Liberation of Women: A Document in the History of Egyptian Feminism*. Trans. Samiha Sidhom Peterson. American University in Cairo Press.

Amin, Samir. 2012. *Thawrat Miṣr* [Egypt's Revolution]. Cairo: Dar Elain Publishing House.

Aminzade, Ronald, and Doug McAdam. 2001. "Emotions and Contentious Politics." In *Silence and Voice in the Study of Contentious Politics*, ed. Ronald Aminzade, Jack A. Goldstone, William Jr. Sewell, Sidney G. Tarrow, Charles Tilly, and Elisabeth Perry, 14–50. Cambridge University Press.

Amnesty International. 2011. "Egyptian Women Protesters Forced to Take 'Virginity Tests.'" *Amnesty International*. www.amnesty.org/en/press-releases/2011/03/egyptian-women-protesters-forced-take-e28098virginity-testse28099/.

Amos, Valerie, and Pratibha Parmar. 1984. "Challenging Imperial Feminism." *Feminist Review* 17 (1): 3–19. doi:10.1057/fr.1984.18.

Amrouche, Fadhma A. M. 1988. *My Life Story: The Autobiography of a Berber Woman*. London: Women's Press.

Anderson, Benedict. 1991. *Imagined Communities: Reflections on the Origin and Spread of Nationalism*. London: Verso.

Anderson, Lisa. 2011. "Demystifying the Arab Spring: Parsing the Differences Between Tunisia, Egypt, and Libya." *Foreign Affairs* 90 (3): 2–7.

Arafa, Mohamed Gamal. 2011. "Naṣa'iḥ Thowar Tunis Lel Maṣrīn" [Tunisian Protestors' Advice to Egyptians]. *Al-Wafd*, January 26. Accessed February 4, 2013. https://goo.gl/STGeqb.

Armstrong, Cory L., and Michelle R. Nelson. 2005. "How Newspaper Sources Trigger Gender Stereotypes." *Journalism & Mass Communication Quarterly* 82 (4): 820–837. doi:10.1177/107769900508200405.

Awad, Abir. 2013. "A Girl Called Zaat: A TV Drama for a Turbulent Egypt." *BBC Media Action*. www.bbc.co.uk/blogs/bbcmediaaction/entries/b0ff8860-02ce-30d6-accb-79abe0f57865.

Awwad, Julian. 2010. "The Postcolonial Predicament of Gay Rights in the Queen Boat Affair." *Communication and Critical/Cultural Studies* 7 (3): 318–336. doi:10.1080/14791420.2010.504598.

Azari, Farah. 1984. *Women of Iran : The Conflict with Fundamentalist Islam*. London: Ithaca Press.

Badr, Intisar. 2007. *Nisaʾ Fi Suq Al-ʿamal: Al-ʿamilat Wa Siyasat Al-Khaṣkhaṣa* [Women in Labor Market: Female Workers and Privatization Policies]. Giza: New Women Foundation.

Badran, Margot. 1988. "Dual Liberation: Feminism and Nationalism in Egypt, 1870s–1925." *Gender Issues* 8 (1): 15–34.

1991. "Competing Agenda: Feminists, Islam and the State in Nineteenth- and Twentieth-Century Egypt." In *Women, Islam and the State*, ed. Deniz Kandiyoti, 201–236. Philadelphia: Temple University Press.

1995. *Feminists, Islam, and Nation: Gender and the Making of Modern Egypt*. Princeton, NJ: Princeton University Press.

2005. "Between Secular and Islamic Feminism/s: Reflections on the Middle East and Beyond." *Journal of Middle East Women's Studies* 1 (1): 6–28.

Bakhtin, Mikhail M., and Pavel N. Medvedev. 1978. *The Formal Method in Literary Scholarship: A Critical Introduction to Sociological Poetics*. Baltimore, Md.: Johns Hopkins University Press.

Baldez, Lisa. 2002. *Why Women Protest: Women's Movements in Chile*. Cambridge University Press.

Bamyeh, Mohammed A. 2012. "Anarchist Philosophy, Civic Traditions and the Culture of Arab Revolutions." *Middle East Journal of Culture and Communication* 5 (1): 32–41. doi:10.1163/187398612X624355.

Barnett, Bernice McNair. 1993. "Invisible Southern Black Women Leaders in the Civil Rights Movement: The Triple Constraints of Gender, Race, and Class." *Gender and Society* 7 (2): 162–182.

Baron, Beth. 1988. "The Rise of a New Literary Culture: The Women's Press of Egypt, 1892–1919." Ph.D dissertation, University of California, Los Angeles.

1997. *The Women's Awakening in Egypt: Culture, Society, and the Press*. New Haven, Conn.: Yale University Press.

2005. *Egypt As a Woman: Nationalism, Gender, and Politics*. Berkeley: University of California Press.

Baron, Beth, and Sara Pursley. 2005. "National Insignia, Signs, and Monuments: Arab States." In *Encyclopedia of Women & Islamic Cultures: Family, Law, and Politics*, ed. Suad Joseph, 523–524. Boston: Brill.

Bayat, Asef. 2007. *Making Islam Democratic: Social Movements and the Post-Islamist Turn*. Stanford, Calif.: Stanford University Press.

2010. *Life as Politics: How Ordinary People Change the Middle East.* Stanford, Calif.: Stanford University Press.

2011a. "A New Arab Street in Post-Islamist Times." *Foreign Policy,* January 26, 2011. Accessed July 2, 2016. http://foreignpolicy.com/ 2011/01/26/a-new-arab-street-in-post-islamist-times/.

2011b. "Arab Revolutions and the Study of Middle Eastern Societies." *International Journal of Middle East Studies* 43 (3): 386. doi:10.1017/ S0020743811000468.

2011c. "Paradoxes of Arab Refo-Lutions." *Jadaliyya,* March 3. Accessed August 21, 2012. www.jadaliyya.com/pages/index/786/paradoxes-of-arab-refo-lutions.

2013. "The Arab Spring and Its Surprises." *Development and Change* 44 (3): 587–601. doi:10.1111/dech.12030.

Bayoumi, Moustafa. 2010. "The God That Failed: The Neo-Orientalism of Today's Muslim Commentators." In *Islamophobia/Islamophilia: Beyond the Politics of Enemy and Friend,* ed. Andrew Shryock, 79–93. Bloomington: Indiana University Press.

Beinin, Joel. 2010. *The Struggle for Worker Rights in Egypt: A Report by the Solidarity Center.* Washington, DC: Solidarity Center. www.solidarity center.org/wp-content/uploads/2015/02/pubs_egypt_wr1.pdf.

Beinin, Joel, and Frédéric Vairel. 2011. *Social Movements, Mobilization, and Contestation in the Middle East and North Africa,* ed. Joel Beinin and Frédéric Vairel. Stanford Studies in Middle Eastern and Islamic Societies and Cultures. Stanford, Calif.: Stanford University Press.

"Bel Tawfir: Tudir Al-Mar'a Al-Miṣrya Shw'un Baytaha" [With Prudence: Egyptian Women Can Manage the Family Budget]. 2011. *Al-Ahram,* February 1. Accessed February 4, 2013. www.ahram.org.eg/archive/ 430/2011/02/01/3/61072/219.aspx.

Benford, Robert D. 1993. "'You Could Be the Hundredth Monkey': Collective Action Frames and Vocabularies of Motive within the Nuclear Disarmament Movement." *Sociological Quarterly* 34 (2): 195–216. doi:10.1111/j.1533–8525.1993.tb00387.x.

1997. "An Insider's Critique of the Social Movement Framing Perspective*." *Sociological Inquiry* 67 (4): 409–430. doi:10.1111/ j.1475-682X.1997.tb00445.x.

Benford, Robert D., and Scott A. Hunt. 1992. "Dramaturgy and Social Movements: The Social Construction and Communication of Power." *Sociological Inquiry,* 6.

Benford, Robert D., and David A. Snow. 2000. "Framing Processes and Social Movements: An Overview and Assessment." *Annual Review of Sociology* 26 (1): 611–639. doi:10.1146/annurev.soc.26.1.611.

Berkovitch, Nitza, and Valentine M. Moghadam. 1999. "Middle East Politics and Women's Collective Action: Challenging the Status Quo." *Social Politics: International Studies in Gender, State & Society* 6 (3): 273–291. doi:10.1093/sp/6.3.273.

Bernal, Victoria. 2001. "From Warriors to Wives: Contradictions of Liberation and Development in Eritrea." *Northeast African Studies* 8 (3): 129–154.

Bier, Laura. 2005. "Political Social Movements: Revolutionary: Egypt." In *Encyclopedia of Women & Islamic Cultures: Family, Law, and Politics*, ed. Suad Joseph, 648–650. Leiden; Boston: Brill.

2011. *Revolutionary Womanhood: Feminisms, Modernity, and the State in Nasser's Egypt.* Stanford, Calif.: Stanford University Press.

Bilge, Sirma. 2010. "Beyond Subordination vs. Resistance: An Intersectional Approach to the Agency of Veiled Muslim Women." *Journal of Intercultural Studies* 31 (1): 9–28. doi:10.1080/07256860 903477662.

Blackstone, Amy. 2004. "'It's Just about Being Fair': Activism and the Politics of Volunteering in the Breast Cancer Movement." *Gender & Society* 18 (3): 350–368. doi:10.1177/0891243204264092.

Blommaert, Jan, and Chris Bulcaen. 2000. "Critical Discourse Analysis." *Annual Review of Anthropology* 29 (1): 447–466. doi:10.1146/ annurev.anthro.29.1.447.

Boehmer, Elleke. 2005. *Stories of Women: Gender and Narrative in the Postcolonial Nation.* Manchester University Press.

Bon, Gustave Le. 1897. *The Crowd: A Study of the Popular Mind.* London: T. Fisher Unwin.

Booth, Marilyn. 2001. "Woman in Islam: Men and the 'Women's Press' in Turn-of-the-20th-Century Egypt." *International Journal of Middle East Studies* 33 (2): 171–201.

Botman, Selma. 1991. *Egypt from Independence to Revolution, 1919–1952.* Syracuse, NY: Syracuse University Press.

Boukhars, Anouar. 2015. "The Reckoning: Tunisia's Perilous Path to Democratic Stability." *Carnegie Endowment for International Peace.* April 2. http://carnegieendowment.org/2015/04/02/reckoning-tunisia-s-perilous-path-to-democratic-stability/i5cj.

Braden, Maria. 1996. *Women Politicians and the Media.* Lexington: University Press of Kentucky.

Brown, Nathan J. 2013. "Egypt's Failed Transition." *Journal of Democracy* 24 (4): 45–58. doi:10.1353/jod.2013.0064.

Browning, Rufus P., Dale Rogers Marshall, and David H. Tabb. 1984. *Protest Is Not Enough: The Struggle of Blacks and Hispanics for Equality in Urban Politics.* Berkeley: University of California Press.

Brownlee, Jason, Tarek Masoud, and Andrew Reynolds. 2013. "Tracking the Arab Spring: Why the Modest Harvest?" *Journal of Democracy* 24 (4): 29–44.

Brynen, Rex, Bahgat Korany, and Paul Noble. 1995. "Political Liberalization, Gender and the State." In *Political Liberalization and Democratization in the Arab World*, 187–210. Boulder, Colo.: Lynne Rienner Publishers.

Bullock, Katherine. 2002. *Rethinking Muslim Women and the Veil: Challenging Historical and Modern Stereotypes*. London: International Institute of Islamic Thought.

Bunce, Valerie. 2003. "Rethinking Recent Democratization: Lessons from the Postcommunist Experience." *World Politics* 55 (2): 167–192.

Burke, Edmund, and David Prochaska. 2008. *Genealogies of Orientalism: History, Theory, Politics*. Lincoln: University of Nebraska Press.

Busby, Linda J. 1975. "Sex-Role Research on the Mass Media." *Journal of Communication* 25 (4): 107–131. doi:10.1111/j.1460-2466.1975. tb00646.x.

Butler, Judith. 1990. *Gender Trouble: Feminism and the Subversion of Identity*. New York: Routledge.

Byman, Daniel. 2012. "Regime Change in the Middle East: Problems and Prospects." *Political Science Quarterly* 127 (1): 25–46. doi:10.1002/j.1538-165X.2012.tb00719.x.

Canetti, Elias. 1962/1984. *Crowds and Power*. Trans. from the German by Carol Stewart. New York: Viking Press; repr. Farrar, Straus and Giroux, 1984.

CBC. 2013. "Former Top Court Judge Challenges Egypt's New Constitution." *CBC News*, January 8. www.cbc.ca/news/world/former-top-court-judge-challenges-egypt-s-new-constitution-1.1390698.

Centre of Arab Women for Training and Research (CAWTAR). 2006. "Arab Women and the Media : Analytical Study of Research Conducted between 1995 and 2005." Tunis: CAWTAR and United Nations Development Programme.

Charrad, Mounira. 2001. *States and Women's Rights: The Making of Postcolonial Tunisia, Algeria, and Morocco*. Berkeley: University of California Press.

——— 2010. "Women's Agency across Cultures: Conceptualizing Strengths and Boundaries." *Women's Studies International Forum*, Special issue: Women's Agency: Silences and Voices, 33 (6): 517–522. doi:10.1016/j.wsif.2010.09.004.

Charrad, Mounira, and Amina Zarrugh. 2014. "Equal or Complementary? Women in the New Tunisian Constitution after the Arab Spring." *The Journal of North African Studies* 19 (2): 230–243. doi:10.1080/13629387.2013.857276.

Chinchilla, Norma Stoltz. 1994. "Feminism, Revolution, and Democratic Transitions in Nicaragua." In *The Women's Movement in Latin America: Participation and Democracy*, ed. J. S. Jaquette, 177–197. Boulder, Colo.: Westview Press.

Christensen, Henrik Serup. 2011. "Political Activities on the Internet: Slacktivism or Political Participation by Other Means?" *First Monday* 16 (2). http://firstmonday.org/ojs/index.php/fm/article/view/3336.

Clarke, Killian. 2014. "Unexpected Brokers of Mobilization: Contingency and Networks in the 2011 Egyptian Uprising." *Comparative Politics* 46 (4): 379–397. doi:10.5129/001041514812522770.

CNN. 2011. "Egypt Uprising: Mubarak Steps Down." *CNN*. www.cnn.com/TRANSCRIPTS/1102/11/bn.04.html.

Cohen, Roger. 2011. "Facebook and Arab Dignity." *New York Times*, January 24, sec. Opinion. www.nytimes.com/2011/01/25/opinion/25iht-edcohen25.html.

Collins, Patricia Hill. 1990. *Black Feminist Thought: Knowledge, Consciousness, and the Politics of Empowerment*. Boston: Unwin Hyman.

Connaughton, Paula. 2013. "Women, Trade Unions and Solidarities." *Concept* 4 (3): 12.

Crozat, Matthew, David S. Meyer, and Sidney G. Tarrow, eds. 1997. *The Social Movement Society: Contentious Politics for a New Century*. Lanham, Md.: Rowman & Littlefield Publishers.

Culbertson, Shelly. 2016. *The Fires of Spring: A Post-Arab Spring Journey Through the Turbulent New Middle East – Turkey, Iraq, Qatar, Jordan, Egypt, and Tunisia*. New York: St. Martin's Press.

Cultural Reader. 2012. "Victor Turner on Liminality and Communitas: Summary and Analysis." March 25. *Cultural Reader*. http://culturalstudiesnow.blogspot.com/2012/03/.

Cusack, Tricia. 2000. "Janus and Gender: Women and the Nation's Backward Look." *Nations and Nationalism* 6 (4): 541–561. doi:10.1111/j.1354-5078.2000.00541.x.

Dabashi, Hamid. 2006. "Native Informers and the Making of the American Empire." *Al-Ahram Weekly*, no. 797 (June).

2012. *The Arab Spring: The End of Postcolonialism*. London; New York: Zed Books.

Daily Mail Online. 2011. "How the Internet Refused to Abandon Egypt: Authorities Take Entire Country Offline … but Hackers Rally to Get the Message out." *Daily Mail Online*, January 30. www.dailymail.co.uk/news/article-1351904/Egypt-protests-Internet-shut-hackers-message-out.html.

Dalacoura, Katerina. 2012. "The 2011 Uprisings in the Arab Middle East: Political Change and Geopolitical Implications." *International Affairs* 88 (1): 63–79. doi:10.1111/j.1468-2346.2012.01057.x.

Daly, Sunny. 2010. "Young Women as Activists in Contemporary Egypt: Anxiety, Leadership, and the Next Generation." *Journal of Middle East Women's Studies* 6 (2): 59–85.

Davis, John. 2013. *The Arab Spring and Arab Thaw: Unfinished Revolutions and the Quest for Democracy.* Burlington, VT: Ashgate.

Dawoud, Aliaa. 2012. "Why Women Are Losing Rights in Post-Revolutionary Egypt." *Journal of International Women's Studies* 13 (5): 160–169.

Dearden, Lizzie. 2014. "Mubarak Trial: Egyptian Court Drops All Charges against Ousted President." *The Independent,* November 29. www .independent.co.uk/news/world/africa/hosni-mubarak-trial-egypt-court-drops-charges-against-former-president-of-ordering-killing-of-9892394.html.

Della Porta, Donatella. 2014. *Mobilizing for Democracy: Comparing 1989 and 2011.* Oxford University Press.

Della Porta, Donatella, and Lorenzo Mosca. 2005. "Global-Net for Global Movements? A Network of Networks for a Movement of Movements." *Journal of Public Policy* 25 (1): 165–190. doi:10.1017/ S0143814X05000255.

Della Porta, Donatella, and Herbert Reiter. 1998. *Policing Protest: The Control of Mass Demonstrations in Western Democracies.* Minneapolis: University of Minnesota Press.

Della Porta, Donatella, Massimiliano Andretta, Lorenzo Mosca, and Herbert Reiter. 2006. *Globalization From Below: Transnational Activists and Protest Networks.* Minneapolis; London: University of Minnesota Press.

Denzin, Norman K., and Yvonna S. Lincoln. 2000. *Handbook of Qualitative Research.* 2nd edn. Thousand Oaks, Calif.: Sage Publications.

Derrida, Jacques. 1973. *Speech and Phenomena, and Other Essays on Husserl's Theory of Signs.* Evanston, Ill.: Northwestern University Press.

Deutsch, Karl W. 1966. *Nationalism and Social Communication: An Inquiry into the Foundations of Nationality.* 2nd edn. Cambridge, Mass.: MIT Press.

Dhruvarajan, Vanaja, and Jill Vickers. 2002. *Gender, Race, and Nation: A Global Perspective.* University of Toronto Press.

Dignity Without Borders. 2013. "Women's Rights in Egypt: The Anti-Sexual Harassment Movement." *Muftah.* Accessed September 23. http:// muftah.org/womens-rights-in-egypt-the-anti-sexual-harassment-movement-and-empowerment/.

Dijk, Teun A. Van. 1991. *Racism and the Press.* London: Routledge.

1993. "Principles of Critical Discourse Analysis." *Discourse & Society* 4 (2): 249–283. doi:10.1177/0957926593004002006.

1997a. *Discourse as Structure and Process.* Thousand Oaks, Calif.: Sage Publications.

1997b. *Discourse as Social Interaction.* Thousand Oaks, Calif.: Sage Publications.

Doran, Michael Scott. 2011. "Heirs of Nasser: Who Will Benefit from the Second Arab Revolution." *Foreign Affairs* 90: 17.

Doumato, Eleanor Abdella, and Marsha Pripstein Posusney. 2003. *Women and Globalization in the Arab Middle East: Gender, Economy, and Society.* Boulder, Colo.: Lynne Rienner Publishers.

Downing, John, Ali Mohammadi, and Annabelle Sreberny. 1995. *Questioning the Media: A Critical Introduction,* ed. John Downing, Ali Mohammadi, and Annabelle Sreberny-Mohammadi. Thousand Oaks, Calif.: Sage Publications.

Duboc, Marie. 2013. "Where Are the Men? Here Are the Men and the Women! Surveillance, Gender, and Strikes in Egyptian Textile Factories." *Journal of Middle East Women's Studies* 9 (3): 28–53. doi:10.2979/jmiddeastwomstud.9.3.28.

Durkheim, Émile. [1912] 1968. *The Elementary Forms of the Religious Life.* New York: Free Press.

Duyvendak, Jan Willem, Marco G. Giugni, Ruud Koopmans, Hanspeter Kriesi, I. Welsh, Dieter Rucht, Carl Strikwerda, and Lomey Singh. 1995. *New Social Movements in Western Europe: A Comparative Analysis.* Minneapolis: University of Minnesota Press.

"Early Reflections of a Historian on Feminism in Egypt in Time of Revolution." 2014. *Anna Lindh Foundation,* May 2. www.annalindhfoundation.org/publications/early-reflections-historian-feminism-egypt-time-revolution.

Ebeid, Ahmed Hassan. 1964. "National Policy and Popular Education in Egypt, 1919–1958." D.Phil. dissertation, University of Oxford.

Edmonds-Cady, Cynthia. 2009. "Mobilizing Motherhood: Race, Class, and the Uses of Maternalism in the Welfare Rights Movement." *WSQ: Women's Studies Quarterly* 37 (3–4): 206–222.

"Egypt Artists 'Reopen' Street by Graffiti Protest." 2012. www.deseretnews.com/article/765564100/Egypt-artists-reopen-street-by-graffiti-protest.html.

"Egyptian Constitution 1923." n.d. *International Institute for Democracy and Electoral Assistance (International IDEA).* www.constitutionnet.org/files/1923_-_egyptian_constitution_english_1.pdf.

"Egyptian Women's Status Report 2010." *The Egyptian Center for Women's Rights (ECWR).* Accessed September 28, 2016. http://ecwronline.org/?p=4569.

Eisinger, Peter K. 1973. "The Conditions of Protest Behavior in American Cities." *American Political Science Review* 67 (1): 11–28. doi:10.2307/1958525.

El-Amrani, Issandr. 2012. "Sightings of the Egyptian Deep State." *Middle East Research and Information Project*, January 1. www.merip.org/mero/mero010112.

El-Behary, Hend. 2016. "Women's Representation in New Parliament Highest in Egypt's History." *Egypt Independent.* January 5. www.egyptindependent.com/news/women-s-representation-new-parliament-highest-egypt-s-history.

El-Raggal, Aly. 2015. "Al-General Wa Al-Parlaman: 'an Al-Nafy Al-Siyasa Wa ḥoḍor Al- 'askara" [The General and The Parliament: On the Absence of Politics and the Presence of Militarization]. *Mada Masr.* Accessed September 28, 2015. www.madamasr.com/ar/opinion/politics/.

El-Rashidi, Yasmine. 2010. "'Hire a Thug' and Other Campaign Expenditures." *Al-Ahram*, December 15. http://english.ahram.org.eg/NewsContent/1/5/49/Egypt/Egypt-Elections-/Hire-a-thug-and-other-campaign-expenditures.aspx.

El Saadawi, Nawal. 1997. *The Nawal El Saadawi Reader.* London: Zed Books.

2007. *The Hidden Face of Eve: Women in the Arab World. 2nd edn.* London: Zed Books.

Elbaradei, Mohamed. 2011. "The Next Step for Egypt's Opposition: [Op-Ed]." *New York Times*, February 11, sec. A. www.nytimes.com/2011/02/11/opinion/11elbaradei.html.

Elsadda, Hoda. 1999. "al-Mar'a wa al-Zakira: Hoda Elsadda Muqabala" [Women and memory: an interview with Hoda Elsadda]. *Alif: Journal of Comparative Poetics.* Special issue: Gender and Knowledge: Contribution of Gender Perspectives to Intellectual Formations (JSTOR for Department of English and Comparative Literature, American University in Cairo) 19: 210–230. doi:10.2307/521935. JSTOR 521935.

2001. *Min Ra'idat al-Qarn al-'Ishrīn: Shakhṣyat wa Qaḍaya* [Women Pioneers of the Twentieth Century: Figures and Issues]. Cairo: The Women and Memory Forum.

2004. *A'isha Taymur: taḥadiyat al-thabit wa al-mutaghaīr fi al-qarn al-tasi' 'ashar* [Aisha Taymur: Challenges of Change and Continuity in the Nineteenth Century]. Cairo: The Women and Memory Forum.

2006. "Gendered Citizenship: Discourses on Domesticity in the Second Half of the Nineteenth Century." *Hawwa: Journal of Women of the Middle East and the Islamic World* (Brill) 4 (1): 1–28. doi:10.1163/156920806777504562

2011. "Women's Rights Activism in Post-Jan25 Egypt: Combating the Shadow of the First Lady Syndrome in the Arab World." *Middle East Law and Governance* 3 (1–2): 84–93.

Elsadda, Hoda, Summaya Ramadan, and Umayma Abu Bakr. 1998. *Zaman al-Nisa' wa al-zakira al-Badila* [Women's Time and Alternate Memory]. Cairo: The Women and Memory Forum.

Eltahawy, Mona. 2010. "Generation Mubarak/Generation Facebook." *The Huffington Post.* www.huffingtonpost.com/mona-eltahawy/generation-mubarakgenerat_b_625409.html.

Eman, Nahed, and Aliaa Nasef. 2011. "Salam Sabahy Toghani l-Thawrat Al-Ghaḍab" [Salmy Sabahy Sings for the Uprising]. *Al-Wafd,* January 26. Accessed February 4, 2013. https://goo.gl/NcYhEF.

Enloe, Cynthia H. 2000. *Bananas, Beaches and Bases: Making Feminist Sense of International Politics.* Berkeley; Los Angeles: University of California Press.

Entman, Robert M. 1993. "Framing: Toward Clarification of a Fractured Paradigm." *Journal of Communication* 43 (4): 51–58. doi:10.1111/j.1460-2466.1993.tb01304.x.

Esposito, John L. 1998. *Islam and Politics.* Syracuse, NY: Syracuse University Press.

Esposito, John L., and Dalia Mogahed. 2007. *Who Speaks for Islam?: What a Billion Muslims Really Think.* New York: Gallup Press.

Evans, Sara M. 1980. *Personal Politics: The Roots of Women's Liberation in the Civil Rights Movement and the New Left.* New York: Vintage Books. 1997. *Born for Liberty: A History of Women in America.* New York: Free Press.

Evans, Sara M., and Harry C. Boyte. 1986. *Free Spaces: The Sources of Democratic Change in America.* New York: Harper & Row. 1992. *Free Spaces: The Sources of Democratic Change in America: With a New Introduction.* University of Chicago Press.

Ez-Eldin, Mansoura. 2011. "Date With a Revolution: [Op-Ed]." *New York Times,* January 31, sec. A. Accessed November 21, 2013. www.nytimes.com/2011/01/31/opinion/31eldin.html.

Fadl, Belal. 2014. *Fatḥ Batn Al-Tarekh* [Opening the Body of History]. Cairo: Egypt: Dar al-Shorok.

Fahim, Kareem, and Mona El-Naggar. 2011. "Emotions of a Reluctant Hero Inject New Life Into the Protest Movement: [Foreign Desk]." *New York Times,* February 9, sec. A. Accessed November 21, 2013.

Falah, Ghazi-Walid. 2005. "The Visual Representation of Muslim/Arab Women in Daily Newspapers in the United States." In *Geographies Of Muslim Women: Gender, Religion, And Space,* ed. Ghazi-Walid Falah and Caroline Rose Nagel, 300–320. New York: Guilford Press.

Falah, Ghazi-Walid, and Caroline Rose Nagel, eds. 2005. *Geographies Of Muslim Women: Gender, Religion, and Space.* New York: Guilford Press.

Fallon, Kathleen, and Jocelyn Viterna. 2008. "Democratization, Women's Movements, and Gender-Equitable States: A Framework for Comparison." *American Sociological Review* 73 (August): 668–689.

Fanon, Frantz. [1961] 1963. *The Wretched of the Earth.* Trans. from the French by Constance Farrington. New York: Grove Press.

1965. "Algeria Unveiled." In *A Dying Colonialism*, trans. Haakon Chevalier, 35–64. New York: Grove Press.

Farhi, F. 1998. "The Contending Discourses on Women in Iran." *Third World Resurgence*, no. 94: 33–38. www.twnside.org.sg/title/iran-cn.htm.

"Fassad Aword" [Corruption Award]. 2011. *Shabakat Ramadan Al-Ikhbarya.* www.ramadan2.com/index.php/all-news/-25-/4016—6-q-2011-q.html.

Finifter, Ada W. 1967. "Dimensions of Political Alienation: A Multi-Variate Analysis." Ph.D. dissertation, University of Wisconsin.

Fisher, Josephine. 1993. *Out of the Shadows: Women, Resistance and Politics in South America.* London: Latin America Bureau.

Foran, John. 1993. "Theories of Revolution Revisited: Toward a Fourth Generation?" *Sociological Theory* 11 (1): 1–20.

Foucault, Michel. 1972. *The Archaeology of Knowledge & the Discourse on Language.* New York: Pantheon Books.

1980. *Power/Knowledge: Selected Interviews and Other Writings, 1972–1977.* New York: Pantheon Books.

1990. *The History of Sexuality: An Introduction.* New York: Vintage Books.

Franceschet, Susan. 2004. "Explaining Social Movement Outcomes: Collective Action Frames and Strategic Choices in First- and Second-Wave Feminism in Chile." *Comparative Political Studies* 37 (5): 499–530. doi:10.1177/0010414004263662.

Fraser, Nancy, and Linda Gordon. 1994. "'Dependency' Demystified: Inscriptions of Power in a Keyword of the Welfare State." *Social Politics: International Studies in Gender, State & Society* 1 (1): 4–31. doi:10.1093/sp/1.1.4.

Frederiksen, Maria. 2011. "The Key Role of Women in the Egyptian Revolution." *In Defence of Marxism*, March 8, sec. History and Theory. Accessed February 19, 2015. www.marxist.com/key-role-of-women-in-egyptian-revolution.htm.

Friedan, Betty. 1965. *The Feminine Mystique.* London: Gollancz.

Friedman, James W. 1977. *Oligopoly and the Theory of Games.* Amsterdam: North-Holland Pub. Co.

Friedman, Thomas L. 2011a. "Speakers' Corner on the Nile: [Op-Ed]." *New York Times*, February 8, sec. A. Accessed November 21, 2013. www.nytimes.com/2011/02/08/opinion/08friedman.html.

    2011b. "Out of Touch, Out of Time: [Op-Ed]." *New York Times*, February 11, sec. A. Accessed November 21, 2013. www.nytimes.com/2011/02/11/opinion/11friedman.html.

Gamson, William A. 1975. *The Strategy of Social Protest.* Homewood, Ill.: Dorsey Press.

    1988. "Political Discourse and Collective Action." In *From Structure to Action: Comparing Social Movement Research Across Cultures*, ed. Bert Klandermans and Hanspeter Kriesi, 219–244. London: JAI Press.

    1992. "The Social Psychology of Collective Action." In *Frontiers in Social Movement Theory*, ed. Aldon D. Morris and Carol McClurg Mueller, 53–76 New Haven, Conn.; London: Yale University Press.

    1995. "Constructing social protest." In *Social Movements and Culture*, ed. Hank Johnston and Bert Klandermans, 85–106. Minneapolis: University of Minnesota Press.

Gamson, William A., Bruce Fireman, and Steven Rytina. 1982. *Encounters with Unjust Authority*. Homewood, Ill.: Dorsey Press.

Gamson, William A., and Andre Modigliani. 1989. "Media Discourse and Public Opinion on Nuclear Power: A Constructionist Approach." *The American Journal of Sociology* 95 (1): 1–37.

Geertz, Clifford. 1973. *The Interpretation of Cultures: Selected Essays.* New York: Basic Books.

Gennep, Arnold van. 1960. *The Rites of Passage.* University of Chicago Press.

Gerecht, Reuel Marc. 2011. "How Democracy Became Halal: [Op-Ed]." *New York Times*, February 7, sec. A. Accessed November 21, 2013. www.nytimes.com/2011/02/07/opinion/07gerecht.html.

Ghonim, Wael. 2012. *Revolution 2.0: The Power of the People Is Greater Than the People in Power: A Memoir.* Boston: Houghton Mifflin Harcourt.

Giacaman, Rita, and Penny Johnson. 1989. "Palestinian Women: Building Barricades and Breaking Barriers." In *Intifada: The Palestinian Uprising Against Israeli Occupation*, ed. Zachary Lockman and Joel Beinin, 155–170. Boston: South End Press.

Gitlin, Todd. 1996. *The Twilight of Common Dreams: Why America Is Wracked by Culture Wars.* Reprint edn. New York: Holt Paperbacks.

Givan, Rebecca Kolins, Kenneth M. Roberts, and Sarah A. Soule. 2010. *The Diffusion of Social Movements: Actors, Mechanisms, and Political Effects.* Cambridge University Press.

Gladwell, Malcolm. 2010. "Small Change: Why the Revolution Will Not Be Tweeted." *The New Yorker*, October 4. www.newyorker.com/reporting/2010/10/04/101004fa_fact_gladwell.

Global Media Monitoring Project. 2010. "*Who Makes the News? International Media Support (IMS)*." London. www.i-m-s.dk/who-makes-the-news/.

Goffman, Erving. 1959. *The Presentation of Self in Everyday Life*. New York: Anchor Books.

1974. *Frame Analysis: An Essay on the Organization of Experience*. Cambridge, Mass.: Harvard University Press.

Goldstone, Jack A. 2001. "Toward a Fourth Generation of Revolutionary Theory." *Annual Review of Political Science* 4 (1): 139–187. doi:10.1146/annurev.polisci.4.1.139.

2011. "Cross-Class Coalitions and the Making of the Arab Revolts of 2011." *Swiss Political Science Review* 17 (4): 457–462. doi:10.1111/j.1662-6370.2011.02038.x.

Goldstone, Jack A., and Doug McAdam. 2001. "Contention in Demographic and Life-Course Context." In *Silence and Voice in the Study of Contentious Politics*, ed. Ronald Aminzade, Jack A. Goldstone, William Jr. Sewell, Sidney G. Tarrow, Charles Tilly, and Elisabeth Perry, 195–221. Cambridge University Press.

Goldstone, Jack A., and Charles Tilly. 2001. "Threat (and Opportunity): Popular Action and State Response in the Dynamics of Contentious Action." In *Silence and Voice in the Study of Contentious Politics*, ed. Ronald Aminzade, Jack A. Goldstone, William Jr. Sewell, Sidney G. Tarrow, Charles Tilly, and Elisabeth Perry, 179–194. Cambridge University Press.

Golley, Nawar Al-Hassan. 2003. *Reading Arab Women's Autobiographies: Shahrazad Tells Her Story*. Austin: University of Texas Press.

Goodwin, Jeff, and James M. Jasper. 2004. *Rethinking Social Movements: Structure, Meaning, and Emotion*. Lanham, Md.: Rowman & Littlefield.

Gordon, Hava Rachel. 2008. "Gendered Paths to Teenage Political Participation, Parental Power, Civic Mobility, and Youth Activism." *Gender & Society* 22 (1): 31–55. doi:10.1177/0891243207311046.

Gould, Deborah B. 2001. "Rock the Boat, Don't Rock the Boat, Baby: Ambivalence and the Emergence of Militant AIDS Activism." In *Passionate Politics: Emotions and Social Movements*, ed. Jeff Goodwin, James Jasper, and Francesca Polletta, 135–157. University of Chicago Press.

2009. *Moving Politics: Emotion and ACT UP's Fight against AIDS*. University of Chicago Press.

Graham-Brown, Sarah. 1988. *Images of Women: The Portrayal of Women in Photography of the Middle East, 1860–1950*. New York: Columbia University Press.

Grami, Amel. 2008. "Gender Equality in Tunisia." *British Journal of Middle Eastern Studies* 35 (3): 349–361.

Gramsci, Antonio. 1971. *Selections from the Prison Notebooks of Antonio Gramsci*. New York: International Publishers.

Greenberg, Jessica. 2014. *After the Revolution: Youth, Democracy, and the Politics of Disappointment in Serbia*. Stanford, Calif.: Stanford University Press.

Gruntz, Lucile, and Delphine Pagès-El Karoui. 2013. "Migration and Family Change in Egypt: A Comparative Approach to Social Remittances." *Migration Letters* 10 (1): 71–80.

Gurr, Ted Robert. 1970. *Why Men Rebel*. Princeton, NJ: Princeton University Press.

Habermas, Jurgen. 1989. *The Structural Transformation of the Public Sphere: An Inquiry into a Category of Bourgeois Society*. Cambridge, Mass.: MIT Press.

Haddad, Bassam, Rosie Bsheer, and Ziad Abu-Rish, eds. 2012. *The Dawn of the Arab Uprisings: End of an Old Order?* London: Pluto Press.

Haddara, Nadia, Baland Jalal, Gwendolyn Anderson, Mona M. Amer, and Joseph M. Simons-Rudolph. 2012. "Profile and Predictors of Voluntary Civic Engagement at a Private University in Egypt." *Global Journal of Community Psychology Practice* 4 (1): 1–11.

Hafez, Sherine. 2014. "The Revolution Shall Not Pass through Women's Bodies: Egypt, Uprising and Gender Politics." *The Journal of North African Studies* 19 (2): 172–185. doi:10.1080/13629387.2013 .879710.

Haist, Andrea. 2010. "This Reality Is Deplorable." In *Arabic Literature: Postmodern Perspectives*, ed. Angelika Neuwirth, Andreas Pflitsch, and Barbara Winckler, 158–170. London: Saqi Books.

Hall, Stuart. 1997. *Representation: Cultural Representations and Signifying Practices*. London: Sage Publications.

Hamdy, Naila, and Ehab H. Gomaa. 2012. "Framing the Egyptian Uprising in Arabic Language Newspapers and Social Media." *Journal of Communication* 62 (2): 195–211. doi:10.1111/j.1460-2466.2012.01637.x.

Hammami, Rema Eva. 1990. "Women, the Hijab and the Intifada." *Middle East Report*. Nos. 164–165: 24–78. http://independent.academia.edu/ MoizIsmail/Papers/1418928/Women_the_Hijab_and_the_Intifada.

Hampson, Fen Osler, and Bessma Momani. 2015. "Lessons for Policy." In *Arab Spring: Negotiating in the Shadow of the Intifadat*, ed. I. William Zartman, 439–463. Athens: University of Georgia Press.

Hamzawy, Amr, and Michele Dunn. 2010. "The Egyptian Parliamentary Elections: Facts and Figures." *Carnegie Endowment for International Peace*, November 28, sec. Monitoring. http://egyptelections.carnegieen dowment.org/2010/11/28/the-egyptian-parliamentaryelections-facts-and-figures.

Hassan, Hamdy A. 2010. "State versus Society in Egypt: Consolidating Democracy or Upgrading Autocracy." *African Journal of Political Science and International Relations* 4 (9): 319–329.

Hatem, Mervat F. 1992. "Economic and Political Liberation in Egypt and the Demise of State Feminism." *International Journal of Middle East Studies* 24 (2): 231–251. doi:10.2307/164296.

——— 1994. "The Paradoxes of State Feminism in Egypt (1970–1990)." In *Women and Politics Worldwide*, ed. Barbara Nelson and Najma Chowdhury, 226–242. New Haven, Conn.: Yale University Press.

——— 2000. "The Pitfalls of the Nationalist Discources on Citizenship in Egypt." In *Gender and Citizenship in the Middle East*, ed. Suad Joseph, 33–57. New York: Syracuse University Press.

——— 2005. "In the Shadow of the State: Changing Definitions of Arab Women's 'Developmental' Citizenship Rights." *Journal of Middle East Women's Studies* 1 (3): 20–45.

——— 2011. "Gender and Revolution in Egypt." *Middle East Report* 261 (Winter): 36–41.

Havel, Vaclav. 1990. "Upheaval in the East: Havel's Vision; Excerpts from Speech by the Czech President." *The New York Times*, January 2. www .nytimes.com/1990/01/02/world/upheaval-in-the-east-havel-s-vision-excerpts-from-speech-by-the-czech-president.html.

Havel, Vaclav, and John Keane. 1985. *The Power of the Powerless: Citizens Against the State in Central Eastern Europe*. London: Hutchinson.

Heikal, Azza. 2010. "Egyptian Women Revolution." *Al-Ahram Weekly*, August 29, sec. Opinion. http://weekly.ahram.org.eg/Archive/2010/1009/ op7.htm.

Heirich, Max. 1971. *The Spiral of Conflict Berkeley, 1964*. New York: Columbia University Press.

Hennebry, Jenna, and Bessma Momani. 2013. *Targeted Transnationals: The State, the Media, and Arab Canadians*. Vancouver: UBC Press.

Hesse-Biber, Sharlene Nagy, and Patricia Leavy. 2007. *Feminist Research Practice : A Primer*. Thousand Oaks, Calif.: Sage Publications.

Hijab, Nadia. 1988. *Womanpower: The Arab Debate on Women at Work*. Cambridge Middle East Library. Cambridge; New York: Cambridge University Press.

Hinnebusch, Raymond. 2015. "Change and Continuity after the Arab Uprising: The Consequences of State Formation in Arab North African

States." *British Journal of Middle Eastern Studies* 42 (1): 12–30. doi:10.1080/13530194.2015.973182.

Hirschman, Albert O. 2002. *Shifting Involvements: Private Interest and Public Action*. Twentieth-anniversary edn. Princeton, NJ: Princeton University Press.

Hoffmann, Michael and Amaney Jamal. 2012. "The Youth and the Arab Spring: Cohort Differences and Similarities." *Middle East Law and Governance* 4 (1): 168–188.

Hoodfar, Homa. 1997. *Between Marriage and the Market: Intimate Politics and Survival in Cairo*. Oakland: University of California Press.

Hunt, Scott A., Robert D. Benford, and David A. Snow. 1994. "Identity Fields: Framing Processes and the Social Construction of Movement Identities." In *New Social Movements: From Ideology to Identity*, ed. Enrique Larana, Hank Johnston, and Joseph Gusfield, 185-208. Philadelphia: Temple University Press.

Huntington, Samuel P. 1993. *The Third Wave: Democratization in the Late 20th Century*. Norman: University of Oklahoma Press.

2006. *Political Order in Changing Societies*. New Haven, Conn.: Yale University Press.

"Ibni fi Al-Midan" [My Son Is in the Square]. 2011. *Al-Ahram*, February 2012. Accessed February 4, 2013. www.ahram.org.eg/archive/441/2011/02/12/15/62374/219.aspx.

Ibrahim, Ahmed. 2011. "Ihdhar Kid Al-Nisa'" [Beware of Women's Slyness]. *Al-Wafd*,. January 26. Accessed February 4, 2013. https://goo.gl/auHcEa.

Ibrahim, Barbara L. and Dina Sherif, eds. 2008. *From Charity to Social Change: Trends in Arab Philanthropy*. American University in Cairo Press.

Ibrahim, Hafiz. 1996. *Hafiz Ibrahim: Al-A' mal Al-Sha'ryah Al-kamila* [Hafiz Ibrahim: His Poems]. Cairo: Dar Al-'oda.

Ibrahim, Omnia. 2011. "Female Protestors to Al-Wafd [Al-Tha'rat-l-Wafd]." *Al-Wafd*, February 4. Accessed February 4, 2013. https://goo.gl/9SbAmF.

Ibrahim, Sonallah. 1981. *Al-Lajna* [The Committee: A Novel]. Beirut: Dar El-Kutub.

1992. Zaat [Dhaat]. Cairo: Dar El-Kalima.

Ikhwanweb. 2013. "Muslim Brotherhood Statement Denouncing UN Women Declaration for Violating Sharia Principles: Ikhwanweb." *The Muslim Brotherhood's Official English Website*. March 14. www.ikhwanweb.com/article.php?id=30731.

Imig, Doug, and Sidney Tarrow. 2000. "Political Contention in a Europeanising Polity." *West European Politics* 23 (4): 73–93. doi:10.1080/01402380008425401.

International Labor Conference. 2008. Provisional Record, 97th Session, Geneva. No. 19, Part Two: Report of the Committee on the Application of Standards, P. 50. http://ina.bnu.edu.cn/docs/20140604145924775029.pdf.

Ismail, Salwa. 2009. "Youth, Gender and the State in Cairo: Marginalized Masculinities and Contested Spaces." In *Arab Society and Culture: An Essential Guide*, ed. Samir Khalaf and Roseanna Khalaf, 223–239. London: Saqi.

Jad, Islah. 1990. "From Salon to the Popular Committees: Palestinian Women. 1919–1989." In *Intifada: Palestine at the Crossroads*, ed. Roger Heacock and Jamal R. Nassar, 125–142. New York: Praeger Publishers.

Janus, Noreene Z. 1977. "Research On Sex-Roles in the Mass Media: Toward a Critical Approach." *Critical Sociology* 7 (3): 19–31. doi:10.1177/089692057700700302.

Jaquette, Jane S. 1973. "Women in Revolutionary Movements in Latin America." *Journal of Marriage & Family* 35 (2): 344–354.

Jaunzems, Tatiana Brooks. 2011. "Community Organizing in Egypt during and after the Revolution." *Social Policy* 41 (4): 58–61.

Jayawardena, Kumari. 1986. *Feminism and Nationalism in the Third World*. London: Zed Books.

Jenkins, J. Craig, and Charles Perrow. 1977. "Insurgency of the Powerless: Farm Worker Movements (1946–1972)." *American Sociological Review* 42 (2): 249–268. doi:10.2307/2094604.

Jiwani, Yasmin. 2005a. " 'War Talk' Engendering Terror: Race, Gender and Representation in Canadian Print Media." *International Journal of Media & Cultural Politics* 1 (1): 15–21. doi:10.1386/macp.1.1.15/3.

2005b. "The Great White North Encounters September 11: Race, Gender, and Nation in Canada's National Daily, The Globe and Mail." *Social Justice* 32 (4): 50–68.

2006. *Discourses of Denial: Mediations of Race, Gender, and Violence*. Vancouver: UBC Press.

Johansson-Nogués, Elisabeth. 2013. "Gendering the Arab Spring? Rights and (In)security of Tunisian, Egyptian and Libyan Women." *Security Dialogue* 44 (5–6): 393–409. doi:10.1177/0967010613499784.

Johnson-Davies, Denys. 2006. *The Anchor Book of Modern Arabic Fiction*. New York: Knopf Doubleday.

Johnston, Hank, and John A. Noakes. 2005. "Frames of Protest: A Road Map to a Perspective." In *Frames of Protest: Social Movements and the Framing Perspective*, ed. Hank Johnston and John A. Noakes, 1–29. Lanham, Md: Rowman & Littlefield Publishers.

Joseph, Suad. 2000. *Gender and Citizenship in the Middle East*. Syracuse, NY: Syracuse University Press.

Joseph, Suad, and Afsaneh Najmabadi. 2003. *Encyclopedia of Women & Islamic Cultures: Family, Law, and Politics*. Leiden: Brill.

Jumhuriyat Miṣr, Ministry of Justice. 1956. "Al Dustur" [The Constitution]. Al Matbaʿa al-Amirīa.

Kabbani, Rana. 1986. *Europe's Myths of Orient*. Bloomington: Indiana University Press.

Kandil, Hazem. 2012. *Soldiers, Spies, and Statesmen: Egypt's Road to Revolt*. London: Verso.

Kamalipour, Yahya R. 1995. *The US Media and the Middle East*. Westport, Conn.: Praeger.

Kaminski, Matthew. 2012. "The Return of Egypt's 'Deep State'." *Wall Street Journal*, June 15, sec. Opinion. http://online.wsj.com/article/SB100014 24052702303734204577468642662667770.html.

Kampwirth, Karen. 2002. *Women & Guerrilla Movements: Nicaragua, El Salvador, Chiapas, Cuba*. University Park: Pennsylvania State University Press.

Kandiyoti, Deniz. 2011. "Promise and Peril: Women and the 'Arab Spring.'" *openDemocracy*. Accessed September 28, 2015. www .opendemocracy.net/5050/deniz-kandiyoti/promise-and-peril-women-and-%E2%80%98arab-spring%E2%80%99.

——— 2012. "Disquiet and Despair: The Gender Sub-Texts of the 'Arab Spring.'" *openDemocracy*. Accessed September 28, 2015. www .opendemocracy.net/5050/deniz-kandiyoti/disquiet-and-despair-gender-sub-texts-of-arab-spring.

Karpat, Kemal H. 2004. *Studies on Turkish Politics and Society: Selected Articles and Essays*. Boston: Brill.

Kaufer, David, and Amal Mohammed Al-Malki. 2009. "A 'First' for Women in the Kingdom: Arab/West Representations of Female Trendsetters in Saudi Arabia." *Journal of Arab & Muslim Media Research* 2 (1–2): 113–133.

Keddie, Nikkie R., and Beth Baron, eds. 1991. *Women in Middle Eastern History: Shifting Boundaries in Sex and Gender*. New Haven, Conn.: Yale University Press.

Ketchley, Neil. 2014. "'The Army and the People Are One Hand!' Fraternization and the 25th January Egyptian Revolution." *Comparative Studies in Society and History* 56 (1): 155–186. doi:10.1017/S0010417513000650.

Khamis, Sahar. 2011. "The Arab 'Feminist' Spring?" *Feminist Studies* 37 (3): 692–695.

Khatib, Lina, and Ellen Lust. 2014. *Taking to the Streets: The Transformation of Arab Activism*. Baltimore, Md.: Johns Hopkins University Press.

King, Gary. 1994. *Designing Social Inquiry: Scientific Inference in Qualitative Research*. Princeton, NJ: Princeton University Press.

Kirkpatrick, David D. 2011a. "Mubarak Orders Crackdown, with Revolt Sweeping Egypt: [Foreign Desk]." *New York Times*, January 29,

sec. A. Accessed November 21, 2013. www.nytimes.com/2011/01/29/
world/middleeast/29unrest.html?pagewanted=all.

2011b. "Egyptians Defiant as Military Does Little to Quash
Protests: [Foreign Desk]." *New York Times*, January 30, sec. A. Accessed
November 21, 2013. www.nytimes.com/2011/01/30/world/middleeast/
30-egypt.html?pagewanted=all.

2011c. "Mubarak's Grip Is Shaken as Millions Are Called to Protest:
[Foreign Desk]." *New York Times*, February 1, sec. A. Accessed
November 21, 2013. www.nytimes.com/2011/02/01/world/middleeast/
01egypt.html.

2011d. "Extra-Legal Detentions, and a Mubarak Aide's Role in Them,
Anger Egyptians: [Foreign Desk]." *New York Times*, February 6, sec. A.
Accessed November 21, 2013. www.nytimes.com/2011/02/06/world/
middleeast/06detain.html.

2011e. "Wired, Educated and Shrewd, Young Egyptians Guide
Revolt: [Foreign Desk]." *New York Times*, February 10, sec. A. Accessed
November 21, 2013. www.nytimes.com/2011/02/10/world/middleeast/
10youth.html.

2012. "Mohamed ElBaradei Pulls Out of Egypt's Presidential Race,"
New York Times, January 14, sec. Accessed November 21, 2013. www
.nytimes.com/2012/01/15/world/middleeast/mohamed-elbaradei-pulls-
out-of-egypts-presidential-race.html.

Kirkpatrick, David D., and Mona El-Naggar. 2011. "Rich, Poor And a Rift
Exposed By Unrest: [Foreign Desk]." *New York Times*, January 31,
sec. A. Accessed November 21, 2013. www.nytimes.com/2011/01/31/
world/africa/31classwar.html.

Kirkpatrick, David D., and Jennifer Preston. 2011. "Google Executive Who
Was Jailed Said He Was Part of Online Campaign in Egypt: [Foreign
Desk]." *New York Times*, February 8, sec. A. Accessed November 21,
2013. https://ezpa.library.ualberta.ca/ezpAuthen.cgi?url=http://search
.proquest.com/docview/849605899?accountid=14474.

Kirkpatrick, David D., and David E. Sanger. 2011. "Egypt Officials Seek to
Nudge Mubarak Out: [Foreign Desk]." *New York Times*, February 5,
sec. A. Accessed November 21, 2013. www.nytimes.com/2011/02/05/
world/middleeast/05egypt.html.

Kitschelt, Herbert P. 1986. "Political Opportunity Structures and Political
Protest: Anti-Nuclear Movements in Four Democracies." *British Journal
of Political Science* 16 (1): 57–85. doi:10.1017/S000712340000380X.

Klandermans, Bert. 1992. "The Social Construction of Protests and
Multiorganizational Field." In *Frontiers in Social Movement Theory*,
ed. Aldon D. Morris, 77–103. New Haven, Conn.: Yale University Press.

Klandermans, Bert, and Suzan Staggenborg. 2002. *Methods of Social
Movement Research*. Minneapolis: University of Minnesota Press.

Koraa, Ibrahim, Samia Farouk, and Yasser Ibrahim. 2011. "Ḥikayat Shohada' Ma'rakat Al-Horīa" [The Story of the Liberation Battle Martyrs]. *Al-Wafd*, February 8. Accessed February 4, 2013. https://goo.gl/aK9AZW.

Korany, Bahgat. 2014. *Arab Human Development in the Twenty-First Century: The Primacy of Empowerment*. American University in Cairo Press.

Korany, Bahgat, and Rabab El-Mahdi. 2012. *Arab Spring in Egypt: Revolution and Beyond*. American University in Cairo Press.

Kries, Hanspeter. 1989. "The Political Opportunity Structure of the Dutch Peace Movement." *West European Politics* 12 (3): 295–312. doi:10.1080/01402388908424754.

——— 1995. *New Social Movements in Western Europe: A Comparative Analysis*. Mineapolis: University of Minnesota Press.

Kristof, Nicholas D. 2011a. "Exhilarated By the Hope In Cairo: [Op-Ed]." *New York Times*, February 1, sec. A. Accessed November 21, 2013. www.nytimes.com/2011/02/01/opinion/01kristof.html.

——— 2011b. "Watching Thugs With Razors and Clubs at Tahrir Sq.: [Op-Ed]." *New York Times*, February 3, sec. A. Accessed November 21, 2013. www.nytimes.com/2011/02/03/opinion/03kristof.html.

——— 2011c. "Militants, Women and Tahrir Sq.: [Op-Ed]." *New York Times*, February 6, sec. WK. Accessed November 21, 2013. www.nytimes.com/2011/02/06/opinion/06kristof.html.

Kulish, Nicholas. 2011. "An Economy Is Crumbling, Too: [Foreign Desk]." *New York Times*, February 1, sec. A. Accessed November 21, 2013.

Kulish, Nicholas, and Souad Mekhennet. 2011. "A Political Crisis Starts to Be Felt Economically as Commerce Slows to a Halt: [Foreign Desk]." *New York Times*, January 31, sec. A. Accessed November 21, 2013. www.nytimes.com/2011/01/31/world/middleeast/31alexandria.html.

Kuumba, M. Bahati. 2001. *Gender and Social Movements*. Walnut Creek, Calif.: AltaMira Press.

——— 2002. "'You've Struck a Rock' Comparing Gender, Social Movements, and Transformation in the United States and South Africa." *Gender & Society* 16 (4): 504–523. doi:10.1177/0891243202016004006.

Laba, Roman. 1990. *The Roots of Solidarity: A Political Sociology of Poland's Working-Class Democratization*. Princeton, NJ: Princeton University Press.

Lachover, Einat. 2009. "Women in the Six Day War through the Eyes of the Media." *The Journal of Israeli History* 28: 117–135. doi:10.1080/13531040903169685.

Lanfranchi, Sania Sharawi, and John Keith King. 2012. *Casting off the Veil: the Life of Huda Shaarawi, Egypt's First Feminist*. London: I. B. Tauris & Co. Ltd.

Letherby, Gayle. 2003. *Feminist Research in Theory and Practice.* Philadelphia: Open University Press.

Lewis, Reina. 1996. *Gendering Orientalism: Race, Femininity, and Representation.* New York: Routledge.

Libal, Kathryn. 2008. "Staging Turkish Women's Emancipation: Istanbul, 1935." *Journal of Middle East Women's Studies* 4 (1): 31–52. doi:10.2979/MEW.2008.4.1.31.

Lim, Merlyna. 2012. "Clicks, Cabs, and Coffee Houses: Social Media and Oppositional Movements in Egypt, 2004–2011." *Journal of Communication* 62 (2): 231–248. doi:10.1111/j.1460-2466.2012. 01628.x.

Louër, Laurence. 2011. "A Decline of Identity Politics." *International Journal of Middle East Studies* 43 (3): 389–390. doi:10.1017/S00207438 1100050X.

Lucas, Tim. 1998. "Youth Gangs and Moral Panics in Santa Cruz, California." In *Cool Places: Geographies of Youth Cultures*, ed. Tracey Skelton and Gill Valentine, 145–160. London: Routledge.

Lynch, Marc. 2012. *The Arab Uprising: The Unfinished Revolutions of the New Middle East.* New York: Public Affairs. Repr. 2013.

———. 2015. "How the Media Trashed the Transitions." *Journal of Democracy* 26 (4): 90–99.

Lynch, Marc, and Tobby Dodge. 2015. "The Arab Thermidor." *The Washington Post*, February 27. www.washingtonpost.com/blogs/monkey-cage/wp/2015/02/27/the-arab-thermidor/.

Mabro, Judy. 1991. *Veiled Half-Truths: Western Travellers' Perceptions of Middle Eastern Women.* London: I. B. Tauris & Co. Ltd.

Mada Masr. 2016. "Update: Egypt's Parliament Passes New NGO Law." *Mada Masr*, November 29. www.madamasr.com/en/2016/11/29/news/u/parliament-passes-new-ngo-law/.

———. 2017. "A-Z of Progress and Setbacks for Egyptian Women between Two International Women's Days." *Mada Masr*, March 8. www.madamasr.com/en/2017/03/08/feature/society/a-z-of-progress-and-setbacks-for-egyptian-women-between-two-international-womens-days/.

Mahdavi, Mojtaba. 2014. "Introduction: East Meets the West?" *Sociology of Islam* 2 (3–4): 103–110. doi:10.1163/22131418-00204001.

Mahmood, Saba. 2005. *Politics of Piety: The Islamic Revival and the Feminist Subject.* Alexander Street Anthropology. Princeton, NJ: Princeton University Press.

Maira, Sunaina. 2009. "'Good' and 'Bad' Muslim Citizens: Feminists, Terrorists, and U.S. Orientalisms." *Feminist Studies* 35 (3): 631–656.

Makara, Michael. 2016. "Rethinking Military Behavior during the Arab Spring." *Defense & Security Analysis* 32 (3): 209–223. doi:10.1080/14751798.2016.1199121.

Mannheim, Karl. [1923] 1952. "The Problem of Generations." In *Essays on the Sociology of Knowledge*, ed. P. Kecskemeti, 276–320. London: Routledge & Kegan Paul (First Published 1923).

Mariscotti, Cathlyn. 2008. *Gender and Class in the Egyptian Women's Movement, 1925–1939: Changing Perspectives*. Syracuse, NY: Syracuse University Press.

Martin, Justin D. 2011. "Palestinian Women, the Western Press and the First Intifada." *Journal of Arab & Muslim Media Research* 4 (1): 95–107. doi:10.1386/jammr.4.1.95_1.

Marvin, Carolyn, and David W. Ingle. 1999. *Blood Sacrifice and the Nation: Totem Rituals and the American Flag*. Cambridge University Press.

Masoud, Tarek. 2015. "Has the Door Closed on Arab Democracy?" *Journal of Democracy* 26 (1): 74–87. doi:10.1353/jod.2015.0013.

Matar, Dina. 2012. "Contextualising the Media and the Uprisings: A Return to History." *Middle East Journal of Culture and Communication* 5 (1): 75–79. doi:10.1163/187398612X624391.

Mayan, Maria J. 2009. *Essentials of Qualitative Inquiry*. Walnut Creek, Calif.: Left Coast Press.

McAdam, Doug. 1982. *Political Process and the Development of Black Insurgency, 1930–1970*. University of Chicago Press.

1990. *Freedom Summer*. New York: Oxford University Press.

1992. "Gender as a Mediator of the Activist Experience: The Case of Freedom Summer." *American Journal of Sociology* 97 (5): 1211–1240. doi:10.1086/229900.

1995. "'Initiator' and Spin-off" Movements: Diffusion Processes in Protests Cycles." In *Repertoires and Cycles of Collective Action*, ed. Mark Traugott, 217–240. Durham, NC: Duke University Press.

1999. *Political Process and the Development of Black Insurgency, 1930–1970*. 2nd edn. University of Chicago Press.

McAdam, Doug, and William H. H. Sewell. 2001. "It's About Time: Temporality in the Study of Social Movements and Revolutions." In *Silence and Voice in the Study of Contentious Politics*, ed. Ronald Aminzade, Jack A. Goldstone, William Jr. Sewell, Sidney G. Tarrow, Charles Tilly, and Elisabeth Perry, 89–125. Cambridge University Press.

McAdam, Doug, John D. McCarthy, and Mayer N. Zald. 1996. *Comparative Perspectives on Social Movements: Political Opportunities, Mobilizing Structures, and Cultural Framings*. Cambridge University Press.

McAdam, Doug, Sidney Tarrow, and Charles Tilly. 2001. *Dynamics of Contention*. Cambridge University Press.

2007. "Towards an Integerated Perspective on Social Movements and Revolution." In *Comparative Politics: Rationality, Culture, and Structure: Advancing Theory in Comparative Politics*, ed. Mark Irving

Lichbach and Ethan Zuckerman, 142–173. Cambridge University Press.

McCarthy, John D., and Mayer N. Zald. 1977. "Resource Mobilization and Social Movements: A Partial Theory." *American Journal of Sociology* 82 (6): 1212–1241.

McCauley, Lauren. 2012. "Egyptian Women Chop Their Locks in Protest of Fundamentalist Constitution." *Common Dreams*, December 26. www .commondreams.org/headline/2012/12/26-0.

McClintock, Anne. 1993. "Family Feuds: Gender, Nationalism and the Family." *Feminist Review*, no. 44: 61–80.

McGarth, Cam. 2012. "Radical Clerics Seek to Legalise Child Brides." *Inter Press Service*, November 14. www.ipsnews.net/2012/11/radical-clerics-seek-to-legalise-child-brides/.

McLarney, Ellen. 2013. "Women's Rights in the Egyptian Constitution: (Neo)Liberalism's Family Values." *Jadaliyya*, May 22. www.jadaliyya .com/pages/index/11852/womens-rights-in-the-egyptian-constitution_ (neo)li.

    2015. *Soft Force: Women in Egypt's Islamic Awakening*. Princeton, NJ: Princeton University Press.

Megahed, Nagwa, and Stephen Lack. 2011. "Colonial Legacy, Women's Rights and Gender-Educational Inequality in the Arab World with Particular Reference to Egypt and Tunisia." *International Review of Education / Internationale Zeitschrift Für Erziehungswissenschaft* 57 (3–4): 397–418.

Mekheimar, Marriam. 2013. "Naẓaryat Al-Jasd fi Al-Naẓaria Al-Sīasya: Dirasat fi Mafhoum Al-Nafs fi Al-Thawra Al-Maṣria" [The Concept of Body in Political Theory: A Case Study in the Conceptualization of the Self during the Egyptian Uprising]. Ph.D. dissertation, Cairo University.

Meriwether, Margaret Lee, and Judith E. Tucker. 1999. *A Social History Of Women And Gender In The Modern Middle East*. Boulder, Colo.: Westview Press.

Mernissi, Fátima. 1987. *Beyond the Veil: Male-Female Dynamics in Modern Muslim Society*. Bloomington: Indiana University Press.

    2001. *Scheherazade Goes West: Different Cultures, Different Harems*. New York: Washington Square Press.

Metawea, Mohamed. 2011. "Suhaj: Al-Ma'a Tusharik -l- Mara Al-'ula" [Women Participating in Protests for the First Time]. *Al-Ahram*, February 12. Accessed February 4, 2013. www.ahram.org.eg/archive/ 441/2011/02/12/29/62389/219.aspx.

Meyer, David S., and Suzanne Staggenborg. 1996. "Movements, Countermovements, and the Structure of Political Opportunity." *American Journal of Sociology* 101 (6): 1628–1660.

Michels, Robert. [1915] 1999. *Political Parties: A Sociological Study of the Oligarchical Tendencies of Modern Democracy*. New Brunswick, NJ: Transaction Publishers.

Miller, Jane. 1990. *Seduction: Studies in Reading and Culture*. London: Virago.

"Min Al-Haja Shams -l- Haja Zohra" [From Haja Shams to Haja Zohra]. 2011. *Al-Wafd*, February 9. Accessed February 4, 2013. http://goo.gl/Ohca4H.

Ministry of Communications and Information Technology, National Telecom Regulatory Authority – Telecom Egypt. 2011. "Household ICT Access and Use by Households and Individuals." *Egypt ICT Indicators*. October. www.new.egyptictindicators.gov.eg/en/Indicators/_layouts/viewer.aspx?id=528.

2012. "Household ICT Usage by Gender." *Egypt ICT Indicators*. July. www.new.egyptictindicators.gov.eg/en/Indicators/_layouts/viewer.aspx?id=594.

Mitchell, Timothy. 2000. *Questions of Modernity*. Minneapolis: University of Minnesota Press.

Moghadam, Valentine M. 1994. *Gender and National Identity: Women and Politics in Muslim Societies*. London: Palgrave Macmillan.

2011. "Engendering Democracy." *International Journal of Middle East Studies* 43 (3): 387.

2014. "Modernising Women and Democratisation after the Arab Spring." *The Journal of North African Studies* 19 (2): 137–142. doi:10.1080/13629387.2013.875755.

Mohamed, Eid, and Bessma Momani. 2014. "The Muslim Brotherhood: Between Democracy, Ideology and Distrust." *Sociology of Islam* 2 (3–4): 196–212. doi:10.1163/22131418-00204006.

Mohanty, Chandra Talpade. 1984. "Under Western Eyes: Feminist Scholarship and Colonial Discourses." *Boundary* 2 (12–13): 333–358.

Mohanty, Chandra Talpade, Robin L. Riley, and Pratt Minnie Bruce. 2008. *Feminism and War: Confronting US Imperialism*. London; New York: Zed Books.

Mohyeldin, Ayman. 2010. "Egypt Election Marred by Fraud." *Aljazeera*, November 29. www.aljazeera.com/news/middleeast/2010/11/2010112 9182221768843.html.

Momani, Bessma. 2015. *Arab Dawn: Arab Youth and the Demographic Dividend They Will Bring*. University of Toronto Press.

Molyneux, Maxine. 1985. "Mobilization without Emancipation? Women's Interests, the State, and Revolution in Nicaragua." *Feminist Studies* 11 (2): 227–254. doi:10.2307/3177922.

Morozov, Evgeny. 2011. *The Net Delusion: The Dark Side of Internet Freedom*. New York: Public Affairs.

Morris, Rosalind C. 2010. "Introduction." In *Can the Subaltern Speak?: Reflections on the History of an Idea*, ed. Rosalind C Morris, 1–3. New York: Columbia University Press.

Morse, Janice M., and Lyn Richards. 2002. *Read Me First for a User's Guide to Qualitative Methods*. Thousand Oaks, Calif.: Sage Publications.

Morsi, Eman S. 2008. "Strikes in Egypt: Female Workers on the Frontline." *Eng.babelmed.net*. http://eng.babelmed.net/cultura-e-societa/49-egypt/3143-strikes-in-egypt-female-workers-on-the-frontline.html.

Morsy, Maya. 2014. "Egyptian Women and the 25th of January Revolution: Presence and Absence." *The Journal of North African Studies* 19 (2): 211–229. doi:10.1080/13629387.2013.858035.

Mourad, Sara. 2013. "The Naked Bodies of Alia." *Jadaliyya*, January 1. Accessed September 22. www.jadaliyya.com/pages/index/9291/the-naked-bodies-of-alia.

Muhamed, Ahmed Taha. 1979. *Al-Mar'a Al-Miṣrīa bayn Al-Maḍy wa Al-ḥadr* [Egyptian Woman between the Past and the Present]. Cairo: al-Matba' al- Ta'lif.

Murakami, Haruki. [2002] 2006. *Kafka on the Shore*. New York: Vintage.

Musa, Salama. 1956. *Al-Mar'a Lyst Lu'bat Al-Rajul* [Woman Is Not the Plaything of Man]. Cairo: Salama Musa -l-nashr wa al-tawzi'.

Nachmias, David. 1974. "Modes and Types of Political Alienation." *British Journal of Sociology* 25 (4): 478–493.

Nassif, Hicham Bou. 2012. "Why the Egyptian Army Didn't Shoot." *Middle East Report*, no. 265: 18–21.

National Council for Women, and Noor Labib Dokhan. 2015. "Al-Mar'a Wa Al-Irhab" [Women and Terrorism Concept Note]." National Council for Women (NCW) in Cairo, Egypt. https://goo.gl/19NU2n.

Nazra for Feminist Studies. 2012. "Testimonies on the Recent Sexual Assaults in Tahrir Square Vicinity." http://nazra.org/node/115.

Nazra for Feminist Studies, El-Nadeem Centre for Rehabilitation of Victims of Violence and the New Women's Organization. 2013. "Tajmi' Shahadat ḥawl Al-I'tida'at Al-Jinsyah wa Al-Ightiṣab Al-Jama 'ī fī Midan Al-Tahrir wa Muḥituh Al-waqi'a Ma Byn 2011–2013 [A Collection of Testimonies of Sexual Harassment and Rape Incidents in Tahrir Square and its Vicinity 2011–2013]." Unpublished study by Cairo-based Nazra feminist group.

Nelson, Cynthia. 1991. "Biography and Women's History: On Interpreting Doria Shafik." In *Women in Middle Eastern History: Shifting Boundaries in Sex and Gender*, ed. Beth Baron and Nikkie R. Keddie, 310–334. New Haven, Conn.: Yale University Press.

——— 1996. *Doria Shafik, Egyptian Feminist: A Woman Apart*. American University in Cairo Press.

Newsom, Victoria A., and Lara Lengel. 2012. "Arab Women, Social Media, and the Arab Spring: Applying the Framework of Digital Reflexivity to Analyze Gender and Online Activism." *Journal of International Women's Studies* 13 (5): 31–45.

Newsom, Victoria A., Lara Lengel, and Catherine Cassara. 2011. "The Arab Spring: Local Knowledge and the Revolutions: A Framework for Social Media Information Flow." *International Journal of Communication* 5: 1303–1312.

Nobel Prize Org. n.d. "The Nobel Peace Prize for 2011." www.nobelprize .org/nobel_prizes/peace/laureates/2011/press.html.

Noonan, Rita K. 1995. "Women against the State: Political Opportunities and Collective Action Frames in Chile's Transition to Democracy." *Sociological Forum* 10 (1): 81–111. doi:10.1007/BF02098565.

Nouraie-Simone, Fereshteh. 2005. *On Shifting Ground: Muslim Women in the Global Era*. Feminist Press at the City University of New York.

Nowaira, Amira. 2013. "The Muslim Brotherhood Has Shown Its Contempt for Egypt's Women." *The Guardian*, March 18, sec. Opinion. www.theguardian.com/commentisfree/2013/mar/18/muslim-brotherhood-rejects-egyptian-womens-rights.

Nunns, Alex, and Nadia Idle. 2011. *Tweets from Tahrir: Egypt's Revolution as It Unfolded, in the Words of the People Who Made It*. New York: OR Books.

Okeke–Ihejirika, Philomina E., and Susan Franceschet. 2002. "Democratization and State Feminism: Gender Politics in Africa and Latin America." *Development and Change* 33 (3): 439–466. doi:10.1111/1467-7660.00262.

Oliver, Pamela E. 1989. "Bringing the Crowd Back in: The Nonorganizational Elements of Social Movements." *Research in Social Movements, Conflict and Change* 11 (1989): 1–30.

Oliver, Pamela E., and Hank Johnston. 2005. "Ideologies and Frames in Social Movement Research." In *Frames Of Protest: Social Movements And The Framing Perspective*, ed. Hank Johnston and John A. Noakes, 185–205. Lanham, Md.: Rowman & Littlefield.

Olson, Mancur. 1965. *The Logic of Collective Action: Public Goods and the Theory of Groups*. Boston: Harvard University Press.

Ortega, Mariana, and Linda Martín Alcoff. 2009. *Constructing the Nation: A Race and Nationalism Reader*. New York: SUNY Press.

Osman, Ahmed Zaki. 2012. "Women's Movement: A Look Back, and Forward." *Egypt Independent*, August 3. www.egyptindependent.com/womens-movement-look-back-and-forward/.

Ostrom, Elinor. 1990. *Governing the Commons: The Evolution of Institutions for Collective Action*. Cambridge University Press.

Ottaway, Marina. 2013. "After the Constitution, a New Battle in Egypt." *Insight Turkey; Ankara* 15 (1): 7–11.

Oxford Business Group. 2011. *The Report: Egypt 2011.* Oxford Business Group. https://books.google.ca/books/about/The_Report_Egypt_2011 .html?id=CAfaGlYX6gUC&redir_esc=y.

Pace, Michelle, and Francesco Cavatorta. 2012. "The Arab Uprisings in Theoretical Perspective: An Introduction." *Mediterranean Politics* 17 (2): 125–138. doi:10.1080/13629395.2012.694040.

Paige, Jeffery M. 1975. *Agrarian Revolution: Social Movements and Export Agriculture in the Underdeveloped World.* New York: Free Press.

Parashar, Swati. 2010. "The Sacred and the Sacrilegious: Exploring Women's 'Politics' and 'Agency' in Radical Religious Movements in South Asia." *Totalitarian Movements and Political Religions* 11 (3–4): 435–455. doi:10.1080/14690764.2010.546117.

Parker, Jane, and Janice Foley. 2010. "Progress on Women's Equality within UK and Canadian Trade Unions: Do Women's Structures Make a Difference?" *Relations Industrielles [Industrial Relations]* 65 (2): 281–303.

Pettman, Jan Jin. 1996. *Worlding Women: A Feminist International Politics.* London: Routledge.

Philip, Thomas. 1980. "Feminism and Nationalist Politics in Egypt." In *Women in the Muslim World,* ed. Lois Beck and Nikki Keddie. 277–295. Cambridge, Mass: Harvard University Press.

Piven, Frances Fox, and Richard Cloward. 1972. *Regulating the Poor: The Functions of Public Welfare.* New York: Vintage Books.

——— 1979. *Poor People's Movements: Why They Succeed, How They Fail.* New York: Vintage Books.

Plato. 1963. "Epistle VII (L. A. Post, Trans.)." In *The Collected Dialogues of Plato, Including the Letters,* ed. Edith Hamilton and Huntington Cairns, 1574–1603. Princeton, NJ: Princeton University Press.

Podeh, Elie, and Onn Winckler, eds. 2004. *Rethinking Nasserism: Revolution and Historical Memory in Modern Egypt.* Gainesville: University Press of Florida.

Pollard, Lisa. 2005. *Nurturing the Nation: The Family Politics of Modernizing, Colonizing and Liberating Egypt (1805–1923).* Berkeley: University of California Press.

Polletta, Francesca. 1997. "Culture and Its Discontents: Recent Theorizing on the Cultural Dimensions of Protest." *Sociological Inquiry* 67 (4): 431–450. doi:10.1111/j.1475-682X.1997.tb00446.x.

Porta, Donatella. 2005. "Making The Polis: Social Forums and Democracy in The Global Justice Movement." *Mobilization: An International Quarterly* 10 (1): 73–94. doi:10.17813/maiq.10.1.vg717358676hh1q6.

Porta, Donatella della, and Sidney Tarrow. 2012. "Interactive Diffusion: The Coevolution of Police and Protest Behavior with an Application to Transnational Contention." *Comparative Political Studies* 45 (1): 119–152. doi:10.1177/0010414011425665.

Posetti, Julie. 2007. "Unveiling News Coverage of Muslim Women: Reporting in the Age of Terror." *International Journal of Diversity in Organisations, Communities & Nations* 7 (5): 69–79.

Prakash, Gyan. 1995. "'Orientalism' Now." *History and Theory: Studies in the Philosophy of History* 34 (3): 199–212.

Pruzan-Jørgensen, Julie. 2012. *Islamic Women's Activism in the Arab World : Potentials and Challenges for External Actors*. København: Danish Institute for International Studies, (DIIS), Copenhagen.

Qasim, Amin. 1992. *The Liberation of Women: A Document in the History of Egyptian Feminism*. American University in Cairo Press.

Qāsim, Habbah, and Wahid Dasūqī. 2000. *Qadaya al-mar'a fi al-suhuf al-Miṣrīah: dirasa taḥlilīah li-suhuf al-Ahram, al-Wafd, al-Jumhuriīah al-Usbuʻiyah, wa-al-Shaʻb* [Women's Issues in Egyptian Print Press: An Analysis of al-Ahram, al-Wafd, al Jumhuriīah al-Usbuʻiyah, wa-al-Shaʻb]. Cairo: Markaz Qadaya al-Mar'a al-Miṣrya.

Ramdani, Nabila. 2013. "Women in the 1919 Egyptian Revolution: From Feminist Awakening to Nationalist Political Activism." *Journal of International Women's Studies* 14 (2): 39–52.

Ranchod-Nilsson, Sita, and Mary Ann Tétreault. 2000. *Women, States, and Nationalism: At Home in the Nation?* London: Routledge.

Ray, R., and A. C. Korteweg. 1999. "Women's Movements in the Third World: Identity, Mobilization, and Autonomy." *Annual Review of Sociology* 25 (1): 47–71. doi:10.1146/annurev.soc.25.1.47.

Razack, Sherene. 1998. *Looking White People in the Eye: Gender, Race, and Culture in Courtrooms and Classrooms*. University of Toronto Press.

Reichert, Christoph. 1993. "Labour Migration and Rural Development in Egypt: A Study of Return Migration in Six Villages." *Sociologia Ruralis* 33 (1): 42–60. doi:10.1111/j.1467–9523.1993.tb00946.x.

Reif, Linda L. 1986. "Women in Latin American Guerrilla Movements: A Comparative Perspective." *Comparative Politics* 18 (2): 147–169.

Reuters. 2011. "Attack on Egyptian Women Protesters Spark Uproar." *Reuters*, December 21. www.reuters.com/article/us-egypt-protests-women-idU STRE7BK1BX20111221.

Rich, Frank. 2011. "Wallflowers at the Revolution: [Op-Ed]." *New York Times*, February 6, sec. WK. Accessed November 21, 2013. www .nytimes.com/2011/02/06/opinion/06rich.html.

Richardson, John E. 2007. *Analysing Newspapers: An Approach from Critical Discourse Analysis*. Basingstoke: Palgrave Macmillan.

Ridd. 1987. "Power of the Powerless." In *Women and Political Conflict: Portraits of Struggle in Times of Crisis*, ed. Rosemary Ridd and Helen Callaway, 1–24. New York University Press.

Rizk, Yunan Labib. 2000. "Egyptian Women Make Their Mark." *Al-Ahram Weekly*, May 11. http://weekly.ahram.org.eg/2000/481/chrncls.htm.

Rizzo, Helen, Anne Price, and Katherine Meyer. 2012. "Anti-Sexual Harrassment Campaign in Egypt." *Mobilization* 17 (4): 457–479.

Robnett, Belinda. 1997. *How Long? How Long? African American Women in the Struggle for Civil Rights: African American Women in the Struggle for Civil Rights*. Oxford University Press.

Rofel, Lisa. 2007. *Desiring China: Experiments in Neoliberalism, Sexuality, and Public Culture*. Durham, NC: Duke University Press.

Rosenberg, Tina. 2011. "Revolution U." *Foreign Policy*, February 16. www.foreignpolicy.com/articles/2011/02/16/revolution_u?page=full.

Ross, Karen. 2011. *The Handbook of Gender, Sex and Media*. Malden, Mass.: Wiley-Blackwell.

Rudy, Sayres S. 2007. "Pros and Cons: Americanism against Islamism in the 'War on Terror.'" *The Muslim World* 97 (1): 33–78. doi:10.1111/j.1478-1913.2007.00158.x.

Russell, Mona L. 2004. *Creating the New Egyptian Woman: Consumerism, Education, and National Identity, 1863–1922*. New York: Palgrave Macmillan.

Sadiqi, Fatima. 2003. *Women, Gender, and Language in Morocco*. Leiden: Brill.

2016. *Women's Movements in Post-"Arab Spring" North Africa*. New York: Palgrave-Macmillan.

Sadiqi, Fatima, and Moha Ennaji. 2006. "The Feminization of Public Space: Women's Activism, the Family Law, and Social Change in Morocco." *Journal of Middle East Women's Studies* 2 (2): 86–114. doi:10.2979/MEW.2006.2.2.86.

Said, Atef. 2014. "We Ought to Be Here: Historicizing Space and Mobilization in Tahrir Square." *International Sociology* (December): 348–366. doi:10.1177/0268580914551306.

Said, Edward W. 1978. *Orientalism*. New York: Vintage Books.

1994. *Culture and Imperialism*. London: Vintage Books.

1997. *Covering Islam: How the Media and the Experts Determine How We See the Rest of the World*. Revised. New York: Pantheon Books.

Saiid, Aliaa. 2011. "Mutaṭw 'at City Stars fi Midan Al-Tahrir" [City Stars' Female Volunteers at Tahrir Square]. *Al-Wafd*, February 7. Accessed February 4, 2013. https://goo.gl/5pz4Bt.

Sakr, Naomi. 2004. *Women and Media in the Middle East: Power through Self-Expression*. Library of Modern Middle East Studies, 41. London: I. B. Tauris & Co. Ltd.

——— 2007. *Arab Television Today*. London: I. B. Tauris & Co. Ltd.

Saliba, Therese, Carolyn Allen, and Judith A. Howard, eds. 2002. *Gender, Politics, and Islam*. University of Chicago Press.

Sartori, Giovanni. 1970. "Concept Misformation in Comparative Politics." *The American Political Science Review* 64 (4): 1033–1053. doi:10.2307/1958356.

Sayigh, Rosemary. 2007. "Product and Producer of Palestinian History: Stereotypes of 'Self' in Camp Women's Life Stories." *Journal of Middle East Women's Studies* 3 (1): 86–105. doi:10.2979/mew.2007.3.issue-1.

Schochat, Ella. 1983. "Egypt: Cinema and Revolution." *Critical Arts: A South-North Journal of Cultural and Media Studies* 2 (4): 22–32.

Schwarzmantel, John. 2008. *Ideology and Politics*. Thousand Oaks, Calif.: Sage Publications.

Scott, James C. 1992. *Domination and the Arts of Resistance: Hidden Transcripts*. Rev. edn. New Haven, Conn.: Yale University Press.

Sedra, Paul. 2011. "Egyptian History without 'Egypt'? Privileging Pluralism in a Post-Revolution Pedagogy." *Jadaliyya*, May. www.jadaliyya.com/pages/TME1/1409/egyptian-history-without-egypt-privileging-plurali.

Seibt, Sébastian. 2011. "Egyptians Find Loophole to Government Web Blackout." *France 24*, February 1. www.france24.com/en/20110201-speak-to-tweet-egypt-twitter-google-join-protesters-internet-blackout-mubarak.

Seidman, Gay W. 1999. "Gendered Citizenship: South Africa's Democratic Transition and the Construction of a Gendered State." *Gender & Society* 13 (3): 287–307. doi:10.1177/089124399013003002.

Sewell, William Jr. 2001. "Space in Contention Politics." In *Silence and Voice in the Study of Contentious Politics*, ed. Ronald Aminzade, Jack A. Goldstone, William Jr. Sewell, Sidney G. Tarrow, Charles Tilly, and Elisabeth Perry, 51–89. Cambridge University Press.

Shaʿrawi, Huda. 1987. *Harem Years: The Memoirs of an Egyptian Feminist (1879–1924)*. Trans. Margot Badran. Feminist Press at the City University of New York.

Shaban, Abdel-Wahab. 2011. "Yum Al-Ghaḍab Yakshf Aṣalat Al-Shaʿb Al-Maṣry" [The Day of Rage Unleashes the True Ethics of Egyptians]." *Al-Wafd*, January 26. Accessed February 4, 2013. https://goo.gl/UHrfGE

Shadid, Anthony. 2011a. "Seizing Control of Their Lives and Wondering What's Next: [Foreign Desk]." *New York Times*, January 30, sec. A. Accessed November 21, 2013. www.nytimes.com/2011/01/30/world/middleeast/30voices.html.

2011b. "Street Battle Over the Arab Future: [Foreign Desk]." *New York Times*, February 3, sec. A. Accessed November 21, 2013. www.nytimes .com/2011/02/03/world/middleeast/03arab.html.

2011c. "Egypt Officials Widen Crackdown; US In Talks for Mubarak to Quit: [Foreign Desk]." *New York Times*, February 4, sec. A. Accessed November 21, 2013.

2011d. "Discontented within Egypt Face Power Of Old Elites: [Foreign Desk]." *New York Times*, February 5, sec. A. Accessed November 21, 2013. www.nytimes.com/2011/02/05/world/middleeast/05cairo.html.

Shadid, Anthony, and David D. Kirkpatrick. 2011. "Opposition in Egypt Begins to Unify around El Baradei: [Foreign Desk]." *New York Times*, January 31, sec. A. Accessed November 21, 2013. www.nytimes .com/2011/01/31/world/middleeast/31-egypt.html.

Shafik, Doria. 1956. "Egyptian Women" [Al- Mar'a Al-Miṣrīiyya]. *Bint Al-Nil Journal* 10 (Oct). http://dar.aucegypt.edu/bitstream/handle/10526/ 2235/oct%2056.pdf?sequence=1.

Shalakany, Amr. 2007. "On a Certain Queer Discomfort with Orientalism." *Proceedings of the ASIL Annual Meeting* 101 (January): 125–129. doi:10.1017/S0272503700025398.

Shams Al-Din, Mai. 2015a. "'mad Mubarak: 'la Al-Mogtam 'Al-Madany Al-Tafkir fi Aulayatoh Wa Mushkilatoh" [Emad Mubarak: The Civil Society Needs to Reconsider Its Priorities and Problems]. *Mada Masr*. Accessed September 29. www.madamasr.com/ar/sections/ politics.

2015b. "Al-Da'ra Al-Moghlaqa l-'unf Al-Dawla: Al-Matarīa Namozagan" [The Closed Circut of State Violence. The Case Study of Al-Mataraya]. *Mada Masr*. Accessed September 29. www.madamasr.com/ar/sections/ politics/.

Shayne, Julie D. 2004. *The Revolution Question: Feminisms in El Salvador, Chile, and Cuba*. New Brunswick, NJ: Rutgers University Press.

Shehata, Dina. 2014. "The Arab Uprisings and the Prospects for Building Shared Societies." *Development* 57 (1): 84–95. doi:10.1057/ dev.2014.29.

Shirazi, Faegheh. 2003. *The Veil Unveiled: The Hijab in Modern Culture*. Gainesville: University Press of Florida.

Shirky, Clay. 2008. *Here Comes Everybody: The Power of Organizing without Organizations*. New York: Penguin Press.

Sholkamy, Hania. 2012a. "Women Are Also Part of This Revolution." In *Arab Spring in Egypt: Revolution and beyond*, ed. Bahgat Korany and Rabab El-Mahdi, 153–174. American University in Cairo Press.

2012b. "The Jaded Gender and Development Paradigm of Egypt." *IDS Bulletin* 43 (1): 94–98. doi:10.1111/j.1759-5436.2012.00295.x.

Shorbagy, Manar. 2013. "Egyptian Women in Revolt: Ordinary Women, Extraordinary Roles." In *Egypt's Tahrir Revolution*, ed. Dan Tschirgi, Walid Kazziha, and Sean F. McMahon, 89–108. Boulder, Colo.: Lynne Rienner Publishers.

Shryock, Andrew. 2010. *Islamophobia/Islamophilia: Beyond the Politics of Enemy and Friend*. Indiana Series in Middle East Studies. Bloomington: Indiana University Press.

Sibley, David. 1995. *Geographies of Exclusion: Society and Difference in the West*. New York: Routledge.

Singerman, Diane. 1995. Avenues of Participation: Family, Politics, and Networks in Urban Quarters of Cairo. Princeton, NJ: Princeton University Press.

2013. "Youth, Gender, and Dignity in the Egyptian Uprising." *Journal of Middle East Women's Studies* 9 (3): 1–27.

Skalli, Loubna H. 2006. *Through a Local Prism: Gender, Globalization, and Identity in Moroccan Women's Magazines*. Lanham, Md.: Lexington Books.

2011. "Constructing Arab Female Leadership Lessons from the Moroccan Media." *Gender & Society* 25 (4): 473–495.

Skocpol, Theda. 1979. *States and Social Revolutions: A Comparative Analysis of France, Russia, and China*. Cambridge University Press.

Smeeta, Mishra. 2007. "'Saving' Muslim Women and Fighting Muslim Men: Analysis of Representations in The New York Times." *Global Media Journal* 6 (11): 2–20.

Smelser, Neil J. 1971. *Theory of Collective Behavior*. New York: Free Press.

Smith, Anthony D. 1996. "Opening Statement Nations and Their Pasts." *Nations and Nationalism* 2 (3): 358–365. doi:10.1111/j.1469-8219.1996.tb00002.x.

Snow, David A., and Robert D. Benford. 1988. "Ideology, Frame Resonance, and Participant Mobilization." *International Social Movement Research* 1 (1): 197–217.

1992. "Masters Frame and Cycles of Protest." In *Frontiers in Social Movement Theory*, ed. Aldon D. Morris and Carol McClurg Mueller, 133–155. New Haven, Conn.: Yale University Press.

2005. "Clarifying the Relationship between Framing and Ideology." In *Frames of Protest: Social Movements and the Framing Perspective*, ed. Hank Johnston and John A. Noakes, 205–212. Lanham, Md.: Rowman & Littlefield.

Snow, David A., and Dana M. Moss. 2014. "Protest on the Fly: Toward a Theory of Spontaneity in the Dynamics of Protest and Social Movements." *American Sociological Review* 79 (6): 1122–1143. 0003122414554081. doi:10.1177/0003122414554081.

Snow, David A., Sarah A. Soule, and Hanspeter Kriesi, eds. 2004. *The Blackwell Companion to Social Movements*. Oxford: Wiley-Blackwell.

Snow, David, and Danny Trom. 2002. "The Case Study and the Study of Social Movements." In *Methods of Social Movement Research*, ed. Bert Klandermans, 146–172. Minneapolis: University of Minnesota Press.

Snow, David A., E. Burke Rochford, Steven K. Worden, and Robert D. Benford. 1986. "Frame Alignment Processes, Micromobilization, and Movement Participation." *American Sociological Review* 51 (4): 464–481. doi:10.2307/2095581.

Soguk, Nevzat. 2011. "Uprisings in 'Arab Streets', Revolutions in 'Arab Minds'! A Provocation." *Globalizations* 8 (5): 595–599.

Sonbol, Amira El Azhary. 2005. *Beyond the Exotic: Women's Histories in Islamic Societies*. Syracuse, NY: Syracuse University Press.

Sorbera, Lucia. 2013. "Early Reflections of an Historian on Feminism in Egypt in Time of Revolution." *Anna Lindh Foundation*. www.annalindhfoundation.org/publications/early-reflections-historian-feminism-egypt-time-revolution.

Soule, Sarah A. 1997. "The Student Divestment Movement in the United States and Tactical Diffusion: The Shantytown Protest." *Social Forces* 75 (3): 855–882. doi:10.1093/sf/75.3.855.

Sperber, Jonathan. 1994. *The European Revolutions, 1848–1851*. Cambridge University Press.

Spivak, Gayatri Chakravorty. 1985. "The Rani of Simur: An Essay in Reading the Archives." *History and Theory* 24 (3): 247–272.

1988. "Can the Subaltern Speak?" In *Marxism and the Interpretation of Culture*, ed. Cary Nelson and Lawrence Grossberg, 271–313. Urbana: University of Illinois Press.

Sreberny, Annabelle. 2004. "Unsuitable Coverage: The Media, the Veil, and Regimes of Representation." In *Global Currents: Media and Technology Now*, ed. Tasha G. Oren and Patrice Petro, 171–185. New Brunswick, NJ: Rutgers University Press.

Sreberny-Mohammadi, Anabelle. 1993. "On Reading 'Islam and Communication.'" *Media, Culture & Society* 15 (4): 661–668.

Sreberny-Mohammadi, Annabelle, and Karèn Ross. 1996. "Women MPs and the Media: Representing the Body Politic." *Parliamentary Affairs* 49 (1): 103–115.

Stack, Liam, and Joseph Berger. 2011. "For Many Fleeing Egypt, a Long Wait: [Foreign Desk]." *New York Times*, January 31, sec. A. Accessed November 21, 2013. www.nytimes.com/2011/01/31/world/middleeast/31airport.html.

Staggenborg, Suzanne. 2001. "Beyond Culture Versus Politcs: A Case Study of a Local Women's Movement." *Gender and Society* 15 (4): 507–530. doi:10.1177/089124301015004002.

Steavenson, Wendell. 2011. "Who Owns the Revolution?" *New Yorker* 87 (22): 38–57.

Steinberg, Marc W. 1995. "The Roar of the Crowd: Repertoires of Discourse and Collective Actions among the Spitalfields Silk Weavers in Nineteenth-Century London." In *Repertoires and Cycles of Collective Action*, ed. Mark Traugott, 57–77. Durham, NC: Duke University Press.

1999a. *Fighting Words: Working-Class Formation, Collective Action, and Discourse in Early Nineteenth-Century England.* Ithaca, NY: Cornell University Press.

1999b. "The Talk and Back Talk of Collective Action: A Dialogic Analysis of Repertoires of Discourse among Nineteenth-Century English Cotton Spinners." *American Journal of Sociology* 105 (3): 736–780. doi:10.1086/210359.

Stephen, Lynn. 1997. *Women and Social Movements in Latin America: Power from Below.* Austin: University of Texas Press.

Suleiman, Elia. 2002. *Yadon Ilaheyya [Divine Intervention].* Arte France Cinéma. Produced by Humbert Balsan.

Suleiman, Michael W. 1965. "An Evaluation of Middle East News Coverage in Seven American Newspapers, July–December 1956." *Middle East Forum* 41 (2): 9–30.

Sutherlin, John W. 2012. "Middle East Turmoil and Human Rights: How Will the 'New' Regimes Expand Civil Liberties." *Perspectives on Global Development & Technology* 11 (1): 75–87.

Swedberg, Richard, and Ola Agevall. 2005. *The Max Weber Dictionary: Key Words and Central Concepts.* Stanford, Calif.: Stanford University Press.

Tabaar, Mohammad Ayatollahi. 2013. "Assessing (In)security after the Arab Spring: The Case of Egypt." *PS: Political Science & Politics* 46 (4): 727–735. doi:10.1017/S1049096513001261.

Tadros, Mariz. 2011. "The Muslim Brotherhood's Gender Agenda: Reformed or Reframed?" *IDS Bulletin* 42 (1): 88–98. doi:10.1111/j.1759-5436.2011.00204.x.

2012. "Mutilating Bodies: The Muslim Brotherhood's Gift to Egyptian Women." *openDemocracy*, May 24. www.opendemocracy.net/5050/mariz-tadros/mutilating-bodies-muslim-brotherhood%E2%80%99s-gift-to-egyptian-women.

2016. *Resistance, Revolt, and Gender Justice in Egypt.* Syracuse, NY: Syracuse University Press.

Taher, Nadia. 2012. "'We Are Not Women, We Are Egyptians': Spaces of Protest and Representation." *openDemocracy*. Accessed September 22. www.opendemocracy.net/5050/nadia-taher/we-are-not-women-we-are-egyptians-spaces-of-protest-and-representation.

Tarrow, Sidney G. 1983. *Struggling to Reform: Social Movements and Policy Change during Cycles of Protest*. Ithaca, NY: Center for International Studies, Cornell University.

    1992. "Mentalities, Political Cultures and Collective Action Frames: Constructing Meaning through Action." In *Frontiers in Social Movement Theory*, ed. Aldon D. Morris, 174–202. New Haven, Conn.: Yale University Press.

    1993. "Cycles of Collective Action: Between Moments of Madness and the Repertoire of Contention." *Social Science History* 17 (2): 281–307. doi:10.2307/1171283.

    1996. *Fishnets, Internets and Catnets: Globalization and Transnational Collective Action*. Madrid: Instituto Juan March de Estudios e Investigaciones.

    1998. *Power in Movement: Social Movements and Contentious Politics*. Cambridge University Press.

    2001. "Introduction." In *Silence and Voice in the Study of Contentious Politics*, ed. Ronald Aminzade, Jack A. Goldstone, William Seweller, Sidney G. Tarrow, Charles Tilly, and Elisabeth Perry, 1–14. Cambridge University Press.

    2012. *Strangers at the Gates: Movements and States in Contentious Politics*. Cambridge University Press.

Taylor, Verta. 1989. "Social Movement Continuity: The Women's Movement in Abeyance." *American Sociological Review* 54 (5): 761–775. doi:10.2307/2117752.

    1995. "Watching for Vibes: Bringing Emotions into the Study of Feminist Organizations." In *Feminist Organizations: Harvest of the New Women's Movement*, ed. Myra Ferree, 223–233. Philadelphia: Temple University Press.

Telhami, Shibley. 1990. *Power and Leadership in International Bargaining: The Path to the Camp David Accords*. New York: Columbia University Press.

Terman, Rochelle. 2010. "The Piety of Public Participation: The Revolutionary Muslim Woman in the Islamic Republic of Iran." *Totalitarian Movements and Political Religions* 11 (3–4): 289–310. doi:10.1080/14690764.2010.546086.

Tétreault, Mary Ann. 1993. "Civil Society in Kuwait: Protected Spaces and Women's Rights." *Middle East Journal* 47 (2): 275–291.

1994. *Women and Revolution in Africa, Asia, and the New World*. Columbia: University of South Carolina Press.

"The Battle of the Camel: Understanding the 'Counter-Revolutionaries.'" 2013. *Daily News Egypt*, February 2. www.dailynewsegypt.com/ 2013/02/02/the-battle-of-the-camel-understanding-the-counter-revolutionaries/.

"The Camp David Accords 1978" n.d. *Jimmy Carter Presidential Library and Museum*. www.jimmycarterlibrary.gov/documents/campdavid/. Accessed May 19, 2015.

The National. 2012. "Women of the Arab Spring Give Voice to Their Hopes and Aspirations." *The National*, January 14. www .thenational.ae/lifestyle/women-of-the-arab-spring-give-voice-to-their-hopes-and-aspirations.

The Social Research Centre. 2008. "Economic Participation of Women in Egypt." *The American University in Cairo*. www1.aucegypt.edu/src/ wsite1/research/research_economicparticipation.htm.

Thomas, Landon. 2011. "In Turkey's Example, Some See a Map for Egypt: [News Analysis]." *New York Times*, February 6, sec. A. Accessed November 21, 2013. www.nytimes.com/2011/02/06/world/middleeast/ 06turkey.html.

Thompson, Wayne E., and John E. Horton. 1960. "Political Alienation as a Force in Social Action." *Social Forces* 38 (3): 190–195.

Tilly, Charles. 1975. *The Formation of National States in Western Europe*. Princeton, NJ: Princeton University Press.

1978. *From Mobilization to Revolution*. Boston: Addison-Wesley.

1995. *Popular Contention in Great Britain, 1758–1834*. Cambridge, Mass.: Harvard University Press.

1997. "Parliamentarization of Popular Contention in Great Britain, 1758–1834." *Theory and Society* 26 (2–3): 245–273. doi:10.1023/ A:1006836012345.

2008. *Contentious Performances*. Cambridge University Press.

Tilly, Charles, and Sidney G. Tarrow. 2007. *Contentious Politics*. Boulder, Colo.: Paradigm Publishers.

Todorov, Tzvetan. 1984. *Mikhail Bakhtin: The Dialogical Principle*. Minneapolis: University of Minnesota Press.

Tripp, Charles. 2014. "The Politics of Resistance and the Arab Uprisings." In *The New Middle East: Protest and Revolution in the Arab World*, ed. Fawaz A. Gerges, 135–154. New York: Cambridge University Press. http://eprints.soas.ac.uk/18484/.

Tuchman, Gaye. 1978. "Introduction: The Symbolic Annihilation of Women." In *Hearth and Home: Images of Women in the Mass Media*, ed. Arlene Kaplan Daniels, James Benét, and Gaye Tuchman, 3–38. New York: Oxford University Press.

Tuchman, Gaye, Arlene Kaplan Daniels, and James Walker Benét. 1978. *Hearth and Home: Images of Women in the Mass Media.* New York: Oxford University Press.

Tucker, Judith E., ed. 1993. *Arab Women: Old Boundaries, New Frontiers.* Bloomington: Indiana University Press.

1998. *In the House of the Law: Gender and Islamic Law in Ottoman Syria and Palestine.* Berkeley: The University of California Press.

Turner, Edith. 2012. *Communitas: The Anthropology of Collective Joy.* New York: Palgrave Macmillan.

Turner, Victor W. 1967. *The Forest of Symbols: Aspects of Ndembu Ritual.* Ithaca, NY: Cornell University Press.

1969. *The Ritual Process: Structure and Anti-Structure.* New York: Aldine de Gruyter.

1974. *Dramas, Fields, and Metaphors: Symbolic Action in Human Society.* Ithaca, NY: Cornell University Press.

1977. "Variations on a Theme of Liminality." In *Secular Ritual,* ed. Sally Falk Moore and Barbara G. Myerhoff, 36–52. Assen: Van Gorcum.

1979. *Process, Performance, and Pilgrimage: A Study in Comparative Symbology.* Delhi: Concept Publishing Company.

1983. "*Liminal to Liminoid, in Play, Flow, and Ritual: An Essay in Comparative Symbology.*" In *Play Games and Sports in Cultural Contexts,* ed. J. C. Harris and R. J. Park, 123–164. Champaign, Ill.: Human Kinetics Publishers.

UNDP. 2010. "The Arab Human Development Report." United Nations Development Programme – Regional Bureau for Arab States (RBAS).

UN Women. 2013. "Study on Ways and Methods to Eliminate Sexual Harassment in Egypt." www.unwomen.org/wp-content/uploads/2013/02/Sexual-Harassment-Study-Egypt-Final-EN.pdf.

US Department of State. 2009–2017. "Foreign Military Financing Account Summary." January 20, 2009–January 20, 2017. https://2009-2017.state.gov/t/pm/ppa/sat/c14560.htm.

Vasilaki, Rosa. 2011. "'Victimization' Versus 'Resistance': Feminism and the Dilemmatics of Islamic Agency." Paper presented at conference, Reconstructing Gender, Race and Sexuality after 9/11. British International Studies Association, Manchester, April 27–29, 2011, 1–20.

Vickers, Jill. 2006. "Bringing Nations in: Some Methodological and Conceptual Issues in Connecting Feminisms with Nationhood and Nationalisms." *International Feminist Journal of Politics* 8 (1): 84–109. doi:10.1080/14616740500415490.

2008. "Gendering the Hyphen: Gender Dimensions of Modern Nation-State Formation in Euro-American and Anti- and Post-Colonial Contexts." In *Gendering The Nation-State: Canadian and Comparative Perspectives*, edited by Yasmeen Abu-Laban, 21–45. Vancouver: UBC Press.

Viterna, Jocelyn S. 2006. "Pulled, Pushed, and Persuaded: Explaining Women's Mobilization into the Salvadoran Guerrilla Army." *American Journal of Sociology* 112 (1): 1–45. doi:10.1086/502690.

Vivian, Bradford. 1999. "The Veil and the Visible." *Western Journal of Communication* 63 (2): 115–139. doi:10.1080/10570319909374633.

Volo, Lorraine Bayard de. 2004. "Mobilizing Mothers for War Cross-National Framing Strategies in Nicaragua's Contra War." *Gender and Society* 18 (6): 715–734. doi:10.1177/0891243204268328.

Wael, Gayle. 2014. "Betrayal or Realistic Expectations? Egyptian Women Revolting." *Interfaith* 6 (1): 478–491.

Wall, Melissa, and Sahar El Zahed. 2011. "The Arab Spring: 'I'll Be Waiting for You Guys': A YouTube Call to Action in the Egyptian Revolution." *International Journal of Communication* 5: 1333–1343.

Walker, Cherryl. 1991. *Women and Resistance in South Africa*. Cape Town: D. Philip; New York: Monthly Review Press.

Walsh, Denise M. 2012. "Does the Quality of Democracy Matter for Women's Rights? Just Debate and Democratic Transition in Chile and South Africa." *Comparative Political Studies* 45 (11): 1323–1350. doi:10.1177/0010414012437165.

Warskett, Rosemary. 2001. "Feminism's Challenge to Unions in the North: Possibilities and Contradictions." *Socialist Register* 37: 329–342. http://socialistregister.com/index.php/srv/article/view/5770/2666#.WXGa64jyvIU.

"Was the Arab Spring Worth It?" 2015. *Foreign Policy*. Accessed September 10. https://foreignpolicy.com/2012/06/18/was-the-arab-spring-worth-it/.

Watts, Charlotte, and Cathy Zimmerman. 2002. "Violence against Women: Global Scope and Magnitude." *Lancet (London, England)* 359 (9313): 1232–1237. doi:10.1016/S0140-6736(02)08221-1.

Waylen, Georgina. 1994. "Women and Democratization Conceptualizing Gender Relations in Transition Politics." *World Politics* 46 (3): 327–354. doi:10.2307/2950685.

West, Guida, and Rhoda Lois Blumberg. 1988. "Reconstructing Social Protest from a Feminist Perscpective." In *Women and Social Protest*, ed. Guida West and Rhoda Lois Blumberg, 3–35. New York: Oxford University Press.

Westerveld, Judith. 2010. "Liminality in Contemporary Art: Gerrit Rietveld Academie." *Yumpu.com*. www.yumpu.com/en/document/view/21521866/liminality-i-n-contemporary-art-gerrit-rietveld-academie.

Westman, Jack C. 1991. "Juvenile Ageism: Unrecognized Prejudice and Discrimination against the Young." *Child Psychiatry and Human Development* 21 (4): 237–256. doi:10.1007/BF00705929.

Weyland, Kurt. 2016. "Crafting Counterrevolution: How Reactionaries Learned to Combat Change in 1848." *American Political Science Review* 110 (2): 215–231. doi:10.1017/S0003055416000174.

Wilkins, Karen. 1995. "Middle Eastern Women in Western Eyes: A Study of U.S. Press Photographs of Middle Eastern Women." In *The US Media and the Middle East*, ed. Yahya R. Kamalipour, 51–61. Westport CT: Praeger.

Williams, Paul, and Colleen Popken. 2012. "US Foreign Policy and the Arab Spring: Ten Short-Term Lessons Learned." *Denver Journal of International Law & Policy* 41 (1): 47–61.

Winegar, Jessica. 2012. "The Privilege of Revolution: Gender, Class, Space, and Affect in Egypt." *American Ethnologist* 39 (1): 67–70. doi:10.1111/j.1548-1425.2011.01349.x.

Wood, Gordon S. 1993. *The Radicalism of the American Revolution*. New York: Vintage.

Woolf, Virginia. 1938. *Three Guineas*. London: Hogarth Press.

Wyer, Robert S., and D. E. Carlston. 1979. *Social Cognition, Inference, and Attribution*. Hillsdale, NJ: Lawrence Erlbaum.

Wyer, Robert S., and Thomas K. Srull. 1994. *Handbook of Social Cognition: Applications*. Hillsdale, NJ: Lawrence Erlbaum.

Yates, Miranda, and James Youniss, eds. 1999. *Roots of Civic Identity: International Perspectives on Community Service and Activism in Youth*. Cambridge University Press.

Yeganeh, Nahid. 1993. "Women, Nationalism and Islam in Contemporary Political Discourse in Iran." *Feminist Review* (44): 3–18. doi:10.2307/1395192.

Yegenoglu, Meyda. 1998. *Colonial Fantasies: Towards a Feminist Reading of Orientalism*. Cambridge University Press.

Young, Robert. 2004. *White Mythologies : Writing History and the West*. 2nd edn. London; New York: Routledge.

Youniss, James, Susan Bales, Verona Christmas-Best, Marcelo Diversi, Milbrey McLaughlin, and Rainer Silbereisen. 2002. "Youth Civic Engagement in the Twenty-First Century." *Journal of Research on Adolescence* 12 (1): 121–148.

Yuval-Davis, Nira. 1993. "Gender and Nation." *Ethnic and Racial Studies* 16 (4): 621–632. doi:10.1080/01419870.1993.9993800.

1997. *Gender and Nation*. Thousand Oaks, Calif.: Sage Publications.

Zaatari, Zeina. 2006. "The Culture of Motherhood: An Avenue for Women's Civil Participation in South Lebanon." *Journal of Middle East Women's Studies* 2 (1): 33–64.

Zahedi, Ashraf. 2007. "Contested Meaning of the Veil and Political Ideologies of Iranian Regimes." *Journal of Middle East Women's Studies* 3 (3): 75–98. doi:10.2979/mew.2007.3.issue-3.

"Zawaj Jadid fi Al-Midan" [New Wedding Ceremonies at Al-Tahrir Square]. 2011. *Al-Wafd*, February 8. Accessed February 4, 2013. https://goo.gl/3IFhDM.

Zemlinskaya, Yulia. 2009. "Cultural Context and Social Movement Outcomes: Conscientious Objection and Draft Resistance Movement Organizations in Israel." *Mobilization* 14 (4): 449–466.

Zoch, Lynn M., and Judy VanSlyke Turk. 1998. "Women Making News: Gender as a Variable in Source Selection and Use." *Journalism and Mass Communication Quarterly* 75 (4): 762–775.

Zolberg, Aristide R. 1972. "Moments of Madness." *Politics and Society* 2 (2): 183–208.

Zubaida, Sami. 1989. *Islam, the People and the State: Essays on Political Ideas and Movements in the Middle East*. London; New York: Routledge.

Zuhur, Sherifa. 1992. *Revealing Reveiling: Islamist Gender Ideology in Contemporary Egypt*. SUNY Series in Middle Eastern Studies. Albany: State University of New York Press.

Index